Ships OF Mercy

THE TRUE STORY OF THE
RESCUE OF THE GREEKS
SMYRNA, SEPTEMBER 1922

▣ ▣ ▣

BY CHRISTOS PAPOUTSY

▣ ▣ ▣

PETER E. RANDALL PUBLISHER LLC
Portsmouth, New Hampshire
2008

ISBN10: 1-931807-66-3
ISBN13: 978-1-931807-66-1

Library of Congress Control Number: 2008921511

Peter E. Randall Publisher LLC
PO Box 4726
Portsmouth, NH 03802

www.perpublisher.com

Book design: Grace Peirce

Additional copies available from:
www.helleniccomserve.com/shipsofmercyc.html

Contents

Acknowledgments

I OFFER MY HEARTFELT THANKS TO MY WIFE MARY WHO advised, guided, and commented on this work. She challenged me to push deeper into this project along the way. The book would be very different and much worse but for the acute insights provided by my wife, friends, and colleagues who took time to read drafts, brainstorm ideas, and discuss everything from the central thesis to the minutest detail. A book so long in the making inevitably benefits from many helping hands, but those people I would particularly like to acknowledge are as follows: Crystal Ward Kent, for her diligent assistance with the organizing and preparation of materials; Sarah Robinson, consultant at the Library of Congress; Alexander Baron, British research consultant; Etienne Cavalie, French research consultant; Roger L. Jennings, grandson of Asa K. Jennings; George Katramopoulos, Athenian author and Smyrna catastrophe survivor; the late Mrs. Filio Haïdemenou who was also an author and eyewitness; Dr. Richard Clairmont, classics professor and translator at the University of New Hampshire; Stavros Anestidis, director of the Center for Asia Minor Studies in Athens; Stellios A. Capsomenos, researcher at the Centre of Asia Minor Studies in Athens; James Valsamides, formerly of Estia of Nea Smyrnis in Athens; Gen. Avgoustinos G. Kambas, president of Estia of Nea Smyrnis in Athens; Meni Atsigbasi, president of Enosis Mikrasiaton Kallonis in Lesvos; Bill Ameredes, former president of the Asia Minor Hellenic American Society based in Ohio; Bill Theodasakis, director of the Memorial Committee of Asia Minor 1922; our good friend, poet, and scholar Dino Siotis; our good friends Bill and Nina Gatzoulis, President of Hellenic Society Paideia of New Hampshire and professor at the University of New Hampshire, respectively; George Makredes; Alex Panos; Marjorie Housepian Dobkin; Prof. Stavros T. Stavrides of LaTrobe University of Australia; staff at the Kutz family YMCA Archives in Minnesota; our good friend and scholar Christos Stavrakoglou, retired headmaster of the Kalloni public high school in Lesvos; Commodore Nikolaos Lahanos, H. N. Rtd., Secretary General of the Hellenic Maritime Museum in Piraeus; Vice Admiral Constantin Paizis-Paradelis, H. N. Rtd., Chairman of the Hellenic Maritime Museum in Piraeus; Captain Michael Anderson, Swedish Naval Archives; John Psaropoulos, Editor-in-chief of the *Athens News* in Greece; Marina Papakostidou, archivist for *To Vima* and *Athens News*; Agnes Masson, director of the Historic Maritime Archives in Vincennes, France; Iain MacKenzie, Curatorial E Ministry of Defense, Admiralty Library at Great Scotland Yard in London; Luc Devolder, Belgian minister; Colonel M. Fahir Altan, Turkish General Staff in Ankara; Lieutenant Taner Duvenci, Military Attaché at the Embassy of Turkey in Washington, D.C.; Terry Tucker, Esq.

Finally, my deepest gratitude to the many people around the world who participated by completing the general survey and offering support, assistance, and encouragement on my ten-year odyssey for the truth.

Preface

MORE THAN A DECADE AGO, we began a journey to uncover the truth about what happened to the Greek citizens in Smyrna, Turkey, from September 1 to September 30, 1922. It was a time of both tragedy and heroism, but as the years passed, events were lost to history. Few modern books even discuss Smyrna, but the aftermath has left its mark on hundreds of thousands of families, and the misunderstandings surrounding the events resonate today in Greece's relationship with other nations.

During that period, September 1922, hundreds of thousands of Greek women, children, and elderly men stood on the Smyrna quay with their backs to the sea. They had been driven there after Smyrna fell to the Turkish army. The Greek army had been routed, and immediate help was not forthcoming. For a time, it looked as though these desperate people would die either in the sea or in one of the violent outbreaks that were becoming increasingly common. While they awaited their fate, they suffered from hunger and thirst, and baked under the hot sun.

For more than eighty years, Greek history has claimed that American warships were in the Smyrna harbor, yet provided no help. In fact, many Greeks have said that when the city's citizens swam out to these ships, they were forced away. Stories were told of American sailors throwing scalding water on them, smashing their hands with tools, and pushing them away with poles. The Smyrna citizens who were rescued from the quay were supposedly saved by Japanese ships. America, many Greeks say, turned a blind eye. Furthermore, many Greeks hold America largely to blame for this nightmare occurring in the first place. They believe that the United States and her World War I Allies double-crossed the Greeks, by first ordering them to march into Turkey, then abandoning them when the Turks pushed the Greek army back to the coast.

Yet, the facts about Smyrna have always been sketchy. Did events really unfold as many Greeks and others believe? We decided to find out the truth, as we believe that all sides need to know, without doubt, what occurred in Smyrna during September 1922. We also wanted to recognize the loss of Smyrna and the suffering of the refugees, and acknowledge one of the most painful and infamous exoduses in history—that of the Ionian Greeks from the land of their heritage.

Our research took us all over the world. We spent more than a decade visiting museums, libraries, government archives, media archives, the war departments of numerous nations, and historical departments. We hired translators and conducted interviews. We pored through microfilm and read scores of books and magazine articles. We searched worldwide via the Internet. Gradually, our search began to yield answers—surprising answers, yet answers that were corroborated again and again through multiple sources.

This book is unique in that it reveals several key pieces of history that were lost for more than eight decades. Relations among several nations have been strained due to these misunderstandings. Equally tragic, deeds of heroism and sacrifice have gone unnoticed by recent generations. This book helps right a wrong, and brings to light what we hope will be healing information.

Our research has uncovered indisputable facts that have told the truth. The story is powerful and surprising, and one the world should hear.

Introduction

*T*ODAY SMYRNA IS CALLED IZMIR. Izmir is a fully Turkish city, but this was not always so. Once the streets of Smyrna rang with many dialects; once her vitality and her soul were Greek. As late at the 1920s, Smyrna was a place of many cultures, blending as they had for centuries in this vital seaport.

To fully understand how the events at Smyrna unfolded, it is important to take a step back in time. Some of the events had their roots in wars and political actions from decades earlier. Others went back even further, to ancient land claims and lost empires. Religion played a role, too, as the centuries-old historic conflict between Christians and Muslims reared its ugly head. The Smyrna catastrophe was in part a result of the unrest that had been brewing for some time between Turks and Greeks within the Ottoman Empire; it was also brought about by the continuing desire for the vibrant lands of Asia Minor.

The Ottoman Empire

Today, we think of Turkey as one relatively small country, as it is depicted on a map. But for centuries, Turkey, as head of the Ottoman Empire, ruled a large portion of the world. At its height, the Ottoman Empire stretched from parts of Europe to Asia Minor and northern Africa. It existed from roughly the sixteenth century until 1923, when the empire was divided among other nations and Turkey became a republic.

The interior of Turkey is rugged, broken by jagged mountains and high plateaus. More than once it has played a key role in Turkey's survival, as many an army has come to ruin in the treacherous mountain passes. Such a harsh land has begotten a tough, sturdy race, known for fierce passions and great skills as warriors. Along the coast the land is different, and so are the people. Here, numerous cultures have blended for centuries, and the blending shows in the art and architecture, in the bazaars, in the customs and dress of the citizens. Smyrna, on Turkey's coast[1], was a city like this—educated, cultured, a beautiful urban center full of vitality.

One of the strongest cultural influences throughout the coastal Ottoman Empire was that of Greece. Greeks had claimed this part of Asia Minor since the eighth century BC. Alexander the Great expanded this claim with his conquests, and for the thousands of years since, Greek descendants kept their culture alive in this part of the world. Even suffering under rule by the Turks did not diminish the Greek influence, and the two cultures were interwoven in a myriad of ways.

The Greeks were primarily Christian, as were a number of other significant minorities within the Ottoman Empire. The Turks were mainly Muslim. This major philosophical difference did cause clashes, but they passed, and Greeks and Turks, Armenians and Kurds, continued to meld in the rich lands of Asia Minor.

Turkey has always had international significance, due particularly to her location. She sits at the gateway to two continents, occupying the tip of Europe and the westernmost part of Asia Minor. She also controls one of the world's most strategic waterways: the Straits of the Dardanelles.

Istanbul, Turkey's former capital, has been a vital port for more than twenty-six hundred years. Ancient Greeks founded the settlement as a trading port, called Byzantium. The Roman emperor Constantine captured Byzantium and renamed it Constantinople, making it the capital of the Roman Empire. The Turks overtook the port in 1453, and it served as their capital until 1923. In 1929, it was renamed Istanbul, and after the Turkish revolution of the early twentieth century, Ankara became the new capital.

Turkey was founded during the eleventh century, when bands of Turkish horsemen invaded Asia from Turkestan, a high, dry land situated between China, Russia, and Afghanistan and once part of the vast Mongol Empire. Over time, these fierce warriors conquered the Arabs in Syria and Palestine and the Christians of the Byzantine Empire in Asia Minor. In 1071, they even took over Jerusalem and the Holy Land. For two centuries, the Christians of Europe fought the Turks in seven crusades. When it was over, the Turks still held their lands, but were faced with a different danger—attack from new invaders from Turkestan.

These invaders were led by Othman I (also called Osman I). He founded the dynasty of Turkish rulers called Osmanli, or sons of Osman. In time, the English transformed the name to Ottoman. Othman's sons pushed his conquests to the Aegean coast. The Turks then, through barter, gained a foothold on the eastern side of the Dardanelles in Gallipoli. Later, Thrace was conquered, then Serbia, then Macedonia, and then part of Greece. Constantinople fell next, in 1453, along with Bosnia, Albania, and more of Greece. Mesopotamia, Egypt, and Arabia followed. By now, Selim, the current Turkish ruler, was calling himself "caliph"—ruler of all Muslims. The Turkish sultan was now head of the Muslim world.

The empire continued its expansion through the next several centuries, obtaining Hungary, Algiers, Oman, Tripoli, and the island of Rhodes. But by the 1700s, a series of weak sultans began to cost Turkey some of her lands. Austria drove the Turks out of Hungary in 1718; Russia annexed the Crimea in 1783; and in 1821, Greece began her long fight for independence.[2] Russia again struck the Turks, in 1806 and 1828, winning back the Caucasus and the northeast coast of the Black Sea. By 1852, the Ottoman Empire was failing and the nations of Europe were circling like wolves. The prize was control of the straits and vast territories.

Over the coming decades, one battle after another ensued as nations jockeyed for possession of the straits. Russia pursued them most vigorously, as they were vital to her economic survival. They are the only outlet from her Black Sea ports to the Mediterranean and the world's oceans. Russia would initiate conflict in 1854 and 1877 as she vied for the straits, but these attempts failed. By this time, the Ottoman Empire was clearly in a decline, but European nations continued to prop up the sultan, and control of the straits remained with Turkey into the twentieth century.

The Balkan wars of 1912 and 1913 would subtract more lands from the empire, and by the start of World War I, its days were numbered. During the Great War, Turkey would side with Germany, and, as a result, was faced with severe loss of territory. When Germany was defeated, the victorious Allied nations each made claims to her diverse lands, and even though the empire had shrunk in recent decades, the spoils were still significant. And, as always, there was the prize of the straits.

The Riches of Asia Minor

Many a nation has coveted the rich lands of Asia Minor, but for centuries much of the region fell under the sprawling dominion of the Turks. When World War I ended, the Ottoman Empire, and its treasure trove of territory, was ripe for the picking. The Allied nations were eager to divide up these spoils, and spent several years after the Armistice debating who would get what. In a fateful turn of events, that decision-making process was never completed, and the lack of a binding treaty would have dire consequences.

Equally tempting to world powers, and equally difficult to decide, was who would control the Straits of the Dardanelles. This vital, narrow waterway connects the Aegean Sea with the inland Sea of Marmara. The Sea of Marmara in turn connects to the Black Sea and mighty Russia through the Straits of the Bosporus. At the time of Smyrna (1922), the Dardanelles were bound by Turkish lands, as they had been for centuries. In fact, desire for control of the straits can be traced back to the Trojan War, which many historians believe was fought not over Helen's capture, but rather for ownership of this critical passageway. Since that time, numerous nations have made their bid to rule the Dardanelles, but the Ottoman Empire has held that right for the longest period. After World War I, with the Ottoman Empire in disarray, the Allies once again contemplated the tantalizing prize of the straits. Its strategic importance undoubtedly influenced the decisions that were made, not only during the treaty-making process, but also in the fateful days of the Greco-Turkish conflict.[3]

The Ottoman Empire also encompassed the oil-rich lands of Mesopotamia (now Iraq), and the industrialized Western world was eager to control these fields. Thus, dividing the empire was fraught with economic and political incentives, all of which played a role in the treaty-making process.

After World War I, there were numerous individual peace settlements among the nations involved. One of these was the Treaty of Sèvres, which was intended to be the peace agreement between the Allied and associated powers and Turkey (the Ottoman Empire). Under the Treaty of Sèvres, various Allied nations received different segments of the empire. Among the Allied countries gaining territory was Greece, which sought to have her ancestral lands of eastern Thrace, Smyrna, and other sections of Asia Minor restored. The Italians, miffed at not receiving certain lands that they desired, decided to seize them by force. They landed soldiers on the Adalia coast and began heading north toward Smyrna. Because the Greeks had the closest Allied garrison (in Macedonia), the Allied powers asked them to head off the Italian maneuver. The Greeks complied, and quickly occupied Smyrna.

Meanwhile, the Turks, outraged at the loss of so much territory, deposed the sultan (who was cooperating with the Allies) and launched a revolution. They installed Mustapha Kemal, a former general, as leader, and in a bold move refused to lay down their arms, regrouped their army, and stood ready to battle the Greeks. For the next two years, from 1920 to 1922, the Greco-Turkish conflict raged over these lands where both countries had made historic claims.

The Allies, after initiating the conflict, remained neutral. They became avid observers of a squabble that soon spiraled out of control. The Treaty of Sèvres, which might have altered the course of events, was still not ratified, and for the entire conflict was debated in Paris.

War is always horrible, but the Greco-Turkish conflict created one of the largest human exoduses in history, as more than one million people sought escape from the Turkish horde.

The spark that ignited the Smyrna catastrophe was the fierce, all-consuming nationalism that swept over Turkey. Enraged at the empire being chopped up, Turkish rebels called for a "Turkey for the Turks" and pledged to fight to retain their lands. Their battle cry also brooked no tolerance for non-Turks or Christians, and turned a fight over territory into a far bloodier conflict over race and religion. The Ottoman Empire had been enriched for centuries by diverse cultures and religions, and though relations among the various groups were at times uneasy, on the whole they lived in peace. Many ethnicities worked as colleagues, lived as neighbors, and enjoyed trade and prosperity. This cooperative existence was shattered by the Turkish rebellion, and whole populations of Greeks, Armenians, Kurds, and other minorities were swept away in a whirlwind of violence.

While the armies clashed and the Allies debated in Paris, much of the civilian population of Asia Minor fled for their lives, congregating at Smyrna on the Turkish coast in hopes of escape. The onrushing Turkish army was hell-bent on driving them from their homes, and no one could withstand its onslaught. If the Greeks and others stayed, they would die or be taken as prisoners into the Turkish interior. Flight was their only hope, but their headlong rush ended at Smyrna. Here, with their backs to the sea, these thousands upon thousands of men, women, and children stood huddled on the Smyrna quay. For nearly thirty days, they baked under the hot sun and suffered perishing thirst, hunger, and brutality. For nearly thirty days they prayed for rescue. It came in a way that no one could have predicted. This is the story of that rescue.

End Notes

1. As noted, Turkey was part of the extensive Ottoman Empire. The geographic region in which Turkey is located is called Asia Minor. Asia Minor is a large peninsula in western Asia lying between the Black Sea (near Russia) and the Mediterranean; it includes most of Asiatic Turkey. For the sake of this story, "Turkey" and "Ottoman Empire" are used interchangeably. At the time of the Smyrna catastrophe, Turkey was the head of the Ottoman Empire, which was in its final days.

2. The war between the Greeks and Turks of 1920 is sometimes mistaken for the Greek War of Independence. The Greek War of Independence began on March 25, 1821, when Bishop Germanos of Patra raised the Greek flag at the Monastery of Agia Lavra in the Peloponnesus. The revolution against the Turks of the Ottoman Empire ended in 1832 with the Treaty of Constantinople, which ensured Greece's independence. However, after this war, Macedonia, Thrace, the Aegean islands, Asia Minor, and Constantinople still remained under Ottoman rule. (For a more complete history, see chapter 8.)

3. Though frequently called the Greco-Turkish war, war between Greece and Turkey was never officially declared. Technically, this event was the Greco-Turkish conflict.

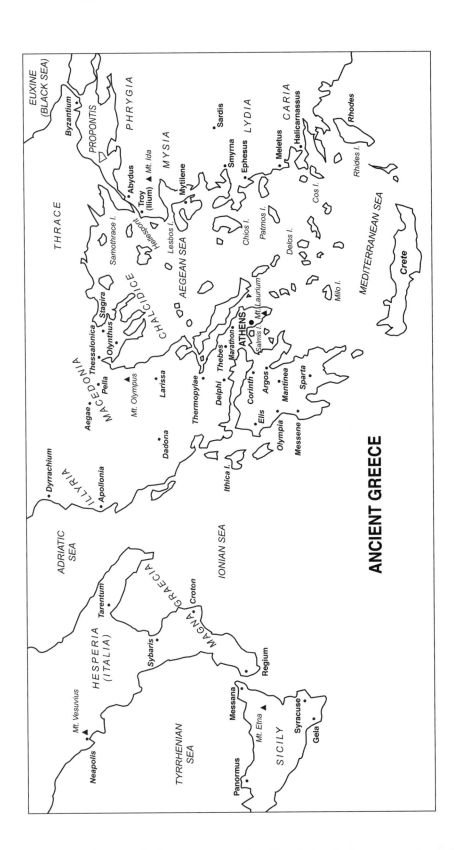

ANCIENT GREECE

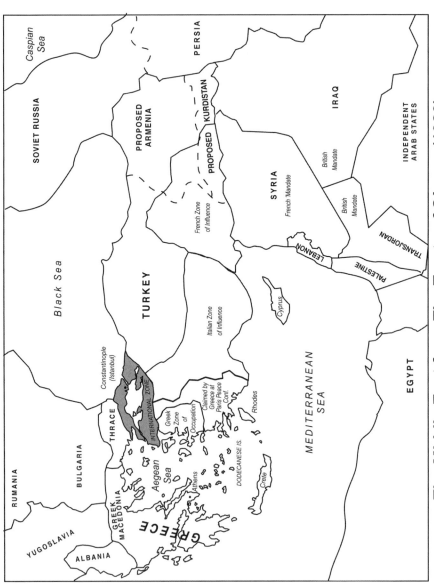

The Middle East from The Treaty of Sèvres (1920) to The Treaty of Lausanne (1923)

Author's Notes

*I*N THE QUOTED MATERIAL, the spelling and grammar may seem inaccurate. In many cases, it reflects the spelling and grammar of the time. In other cases, translated material is quoted, so differences and inconsistencies reflect the switch from another language to English. Because these are direct quotes, the material has been reprinted exactly as originally written or stated.

Also, the quoted material may at times show different spellings for place-names. For example, Mudania is seen as Moudania; Broussa is seen as Brusa. These differences reflect how the spelling of the names have changed over time, and also illustrate how various cultures spell the names. Again, within the quotes, we have left the spelling intact, as originally written.

George Horton, American consul general at the time of Smyrna.

CHAPTER 1

Smyrna: The Martyred City

The Martyred City

Glory and Queen of the Island Sea
Was Smyrna, the beautiful city,
And fairest pearl of the Orient she—
O Smyrna, the beautiful city!
Heiress of countless storied ages,
Mother of poets, saints and sages
Was Smyrna, the beautiful city!

One of the ancient, glorious Seven
Was Smyrna, the sacred city,
Whose candles all were alight in Heaven—
O Smyrna, the sacred city!
One of the Seven hopes and desires
One of the Seven Holy Fires
Was Smyrna, the Sacred City.

And six flared out in the long ago—
O Smyrna, the Christian city!
But hers shone on with constant glow—
O Smyrna, the Christian city!
The others died down and passed away,
But hers gleamed on until yesterday—
O Smyrna, the Christian city!

Silent and dead are the church bell ringers
Of Smyrna, the Christian city,
The music silent and dead the singers
Of Smyrna, the happy city;
And her maidens, pearls of the Island seas
Are gone from the marble palaces
Of Smyrna, enchanting city!

She is dead and rots by Orient's gate,
Does Smyrna, the murdered city,
Her artisans gone, her streets desolate—
O Smyrna, the murdered city!
Her children made orphans, widows her wives
While under her stones the foul rat thrives—
O Smyrna, the murdered city!

They crowned with a halo her bishop there,
In Smyrna, the martyred city,
Though dabbled with blood was his long
white hair—
O Smyrna, the martyred city!
So she kept the faith in Christendom
From Polycarp to St. Chrysostom,
Did Smyrna, the glorified city!

—George Horton[1]

*I*N 1922, SMYRNA WAS ONE OF THE MOST BEAUTIFUL AND cultured cities on the Aegean Sea. The city embraces a deep-water harbor, and upon entering the bay travelers were struck by the sight of the Two Brothers, twin mountain peaks that mark the entrance. On the right-hand side of the harbor, atop Mount Pagus, the remains of an ancient fortress lingered. The ruins of this old castle of the Acropolis were largely Byzantine, but the basements of the great walls, and part of the southwest tower, striking with its overlay of red trachyte, were of the Greek epoch. Stretching below the fortress lay Smyrna, nestled in the curve of the bay and climbing the slopes of Mount Pagus.

The beauty of Smyrna's harbor rivaled that of Naples, wrote George Horton, the American consul stationed there during the time of the Greco-Turkish conflict. The glistening azure of the Aegean, dotted with islands, spread before the city, providing breathtaking waterfront views. Rugged mountains rose behind. The city itself was a stunning mixture. Elegant homes, country clubs, and modern office buildings somehow blended with ancient monuments. In the ethnic neighborhoods, narrow, twisting streets ran between tightly packed red-roofed homes, where neighbors' balconies nearly touched. In the Turkish quarter, along the slopes of Mount Pagus, minarets and cypress trees rose above the landscape, and the primitive domiciles made visitors feel transported back in time.

In "History's Greatest Trek," Melville Chater, a writer for *National Geographic*, describes his last visit to Smyrna, just weeks before her destruction:

"When in the late summer of 1922, I steamed in between two far-flung promontories, while the sun spilled over Mount Pagos to illumine the sweep of red-roofed houses clothing its flanks, I little realized that I was watching one of the last dawns to rise over ancient Smyrna.

"Once ashore, on the shipping-camel crammed quay, my companion and I threaded among camel trains and through narrow streets from whose overhanging balconies two neighbors might shake hands.

"A climb to the topmost arch of Mount Pagos' crumbling fortifications afforded a view of the outspread checkerboard of Smyrna's sedulously separated quarters—the Turkish marked by minarets and cypresses; the Frankish, outstanding with fine residences, and the Greek and Armenian, crammed with an amazing density of small shops—the whole red-roofed panorama girdled by an illimitable sweep of blue waters which stretched horizonward within the gulf's embracing shores.

"'Let's make a last snapshot of Smyrna,' we say before descending from Mount Pagos."

Indeed, Chater's photo was among the very last of Smyrna as she was.

◙ ◙ ◙

Smyrna's deep-water harbor made her a successful commercial port. The largest sea-going vessels of the day could safely anchor in her waters, and the city bustled with trade. Foreigners were drawn to Smyrna by its gorgeous location, mild climate, business opportunities, and vibrant way of life. Smyrna was an exotic blend of cultures; Greeks, Armenians, Turks and what the locals called, Levantines, citizens of mixed blood[2], comprised the majority of her residents. Horton notes in his book, *Blight of Asia*:

"At the time of [Smyrna's] destruction it is probable that the inhabitants exceeded five hundred thousand in numbers. The latest official statistics give the figure as four hundred thousand, of whom one hundred and sixty-five thousand were Turks, one hundred and fifty thousand Greeks, twenty-five thousand Jews, twenty thousand foreigners: ten thousand Italians, three thousand French, two thousand British and three hundred Americans."

In 1922, the city was divided along cultural lines, although, as Horton notes, this was not by plan. In *Blight of Asia*, he describes the general delineations:

"The city was divided largely into quarters, though this was not a rigid arrangement. The Turkish lay to the east and to the south, and, as is usual in all mixed Ottoman towns, occupied the highest part, extending up the sides of Mount Pagus (and does still for that matter, as it was not burned). Architecturally, it is a typical jumble of ramshackle huts, with very few, if any, buildings of superior order. To the east are grouped most of the Jews, while the Armenian quarter lay to the north of the Turkish and contiguous with it. The Greek area was north again of the Armenian."

Smyrna's climate was mild, resembling that of Southern California. Winter rarely brought snow, and in summer, refreshing breezes from the sea, called the *embates*, or in Smyrna dialect, the *imbat*, helped keep the heat from becoming oppressive. Such congenial weather fostered a vital, dynamic city, with people actively engaged in trade and cultural pursuits. The principal promenade was on the quay, which was one of the city's cultural and economic centers. Luxurious hotels, clubs, cafés, theaters, agencies, and modern office buildings all spread along the waterfront. Located nearby was the American theater, called by Horton "the prettiest building of its kind in the Ottoman Empire," plus the homes of Smyrna's most prominent merchants, most of whom were Greek, Armenian, and Dutch. The waterfront was also the site of several foreign consulates, which enhanced the city's multicultural flavor. Horton describes these residences as "elegant in appearance and contain[ing] treasures of rugs, expensive furniture, works of art and Oriental curios."

The main business thoroughfare of Smyrna was the rue Francque. Here were the great department and wholesale stores of the Greeks, Armenians, and Levantines. This was the shopping mecca of the city, drawing

Smyrna's lovely deep-water harbor, circa 1922.

scores of residents and tourists. Ladies in the latest European fashion thronged the streets, enjoying the bounty of merchandise. During the afternoon—the prime shopping hours—the crowds were so great that moving along the street was difficult.

In summer, the greengrocers were out in full force, selling an abundance of fruits, vegetables, and grains. Among the most popular were the region's famous "sultanieh raisins," from little grapes that have no seeds. These sweet treats were sold in bunches sometimes weighing as much as four pounds.

Residents were bustling, energetic, and lived life fully. There was always an activity under way. Teas, dances, and musical concerts were regularly scheduled, and salons were held in the homes of wealthy Armenians and Greeks. Four large clubs provided entertainment and relaxation: the Cercle de Smyrne was frequented mostly by British, French, and Americans; the Sporting boasted a prime location on the quay and a lovely garden; the Greek Club and the Country Club, near the American college, had excellent golf links and a race course.

For all its culture and urbanization, however, Smyrna was also a city of the East, a destination for nomadic traders, a place of bazaars and exotic wares. Visiting the Turkish quarter was like stepping into another time. Horton notes that it was much like being transported into the pages of the *Arabian Nights*. Women were rarely seen; when they were visible they were veiled from head to toe, creating an air of mystery. Along the narrow streets sat the *hodjas*, kindly old men who offered letter-writing services for those who needed assistance. Mussulmen in their fezzes smoked their water pipes beside antique fountains or in the shade of a sprawling grapevine. These scenes could have been from centuries ago. Here in the Turkish quarter, time stood still and strict Muslim ways prevailed.

In 1922, Smyrna was not only a mix of East and West; she was also a city blending the modern ways of the twentieth century—motor cars, movie theaters, telephones—with ancient ways of life. Writes Horton:

"In no city in the world did East and West mingle physically in so spectacular a manner as at Smyrna, while spiritually they always maintained the characteristics of oil and water. One of the common sights of the streets was the long camel caravans, the beasts passing in single file, attached to ropes, and led by a driver on a donkey in a red fez and rough white-woolen cloak. These caravans came in from the interior (of Turkey) laden with sacks of figs, licorice root, raisins, wood, tobacco and rugs. While the foreigner is apt to be afraid of these ungainly beasts, one often saw a Greek or Armenian woman in high-heeled boots and elegant costume, stoop and lift the rope between two camels and pass under. At the north end of the city is a railroad station called 'Caravan Bridge,' because nearby is an ancient stone bridge of that name, over which the camel caravans arriving from as far away as Bagdad and Damascus, used to pass."

The camels trod the same route they had for centuries, and bearing much the same goods.　It would take them five or six days to trek in from Ouchak, many of them carrying carpets of long wool, for which the region is famous. These carpets were called *sofrali* because they are decorated in the center with a rose, which indicates the placement of the table, or *sofra*. It was this taste of the exotic, this connection with an ancient past, that gave Smyrna her mystique. She was a city at once timeless and modern, and the combination was fascinating.

The sounds of Smyrna reflected her heritage. One would hear the cries of camel drivers, the calls of merchants, conversations in a dozen languages, laughter and music from her restaurants and cafés. In contrast to the refined entertainments of the salons, her streets and cafés resonated with the infectious songs of the *politakia*, orchestras of stringed instruments, such as guitars, mandolins, and zithers. The performers played with gusto, singing songs of their native lands and often improvising on the spot. The politakia were loved by visitors and residents alike and were often invited into private houses to entertain.

Smyrna was a lighthearted, carefree city. Even World War I had not gotten the best of her residents. Horton tells a story that captures the essence of Smyrna's character:

"During the Great War, the British bombed the fortress [at harbor's entrance]. At first, the sound of the big guns terrified the inhabitants, but when it was discovered that there was no intention of throwing shells into the city itself the whole population gathered on the housetops and at the cafes to witness the flashing and the bursting of the projectiles. The cannonading was plainly visible from the quay and became a regular theatrical performance, chairs on sidewalks being sold at high prices."

Hundreds of foreigners had business interests in Smyrna, drawn by the oil and by abundant crops of tobacco, licorice, figs, raisins, and other commodities. Along the broad quays, paved with large, flat stones, would be stacked an abundance of trade goods, including the region's famous figs, cotton, Phocaean salts, wheat, and, of course, Oriental rugs and carpets. Smyrna's residents, with their broad range of tastes and their interest in modern ways, were also ripe for goods. At the start of the Greco-Turkish conflict, during the early days of the Greek occupation, sales of agricultural tools and automobiles skyrocketed.

American companies were among those with interests in Smyrna. Standard Oil Company was present, as was the MacAndrews and Forbes Licorice Company. MacAndrews and Forbes employed thousands and owned a spacious office complex. All the major tobacco companies of the day were also represented. Sales were very good, as they did millions of dollars in annual business. Also successful were the American exporters of figs, raisins, and carpets. The Americans and other nationals recognized Smyrna's possibilities.

The soul of Smyrna, the essence, was tied to her ancient past. The roots of Smyrna were very old and they were not Turkish; they were Greek. In fact, Smyrna is one of the oldest cities in the world. The Greek poet Pindar wrote of Smyrna in 500 BC, and Homer called the city home. Greek mythology tells that an Amazon named Smyrna placed in its cradle the gifts of grace, strength, and beauty. Ionian Greeks had settled along these shores well before the time of Alexander the Great. When he conquered much of Asia Minor, in 323 BC, Smyrna had fallen on hard times. It is said that Alexander was inspired by the goddess Nemesis, who came to him in a dream, to rebuild the city. After praying to Apollo, Alexander vowed to do just that, and put two of his generals, including his half brother, Antigonus, in charge of its reconstruction. The city blossomed and eventually rivaled Rome in terms of culture and education. In 133 BC, Smyrna became a Roman territory, and was visited by several emperors. Both Tiberius and Marcus Aurelius created great works in Smyrna, so taken were they by the city's charms. While Tiberius ruled Rome, Smyrna was destroyed by an earthquake, but Marcus Aurelius rebuilt its walls. Soon Smyrna, with its "Scroll of Philosophy," its great speakers, and its library, rivaled Ephesus. It was equally well known for its theaters, its school of medicine, and its religious ceremonies. It was called both the Crown of Ionia and the Jewel of Asia, so broad was its fame.

Horton writes:

"The 'Mother Civilization,' spread to old Greece, to Sicily, to Italy, and along the shores of the Black Sea, and finally to Europe and America. It is more than probable that Homer was a Smyrniote, or an inhabitant of Asia Minor, and for countless years, his writings were a sort of Bible or sacred book, molding the character of millions. Perhaps the earliest conception of monogamy, certainly the most beautiful, comes from Homer's poems. Our conception of the family is Greek; we get it from the *Odyssey*, very probably written in Smyrna, thousands of years ago."

In the 1870s, the renowned archaeologist Heinrich Schliemann found remnants of the fabled city of Troy in Asia Minor. Soon after, other key discoveries were made in the region. Scholars began to realize that Greek and Asian civilizations had been blending for far longer than they initially thought. The civilization of Crete was contemporary with that of Egypt, and Smyrna was older still. American scholars and archaeologists flocked to Smyrna and other sites throughout Asia Minor. Major excavations were held at Sardis and Colophon, and during the last excavation at Sardis, thirty gold coins of Croesus were discovered[3]. Horton took charge of these invaluable artifacts during the Smyrna disaster. He brought them to the United States, along with the first consignment of original marbles, and arranged for them to be sent to the Metropolitan Museum of New York[4].

Smyrna's ancient history lived on in a variety of sites. There was the Tomb of Tantalus, dedicated to the mythical founder of the town, who oversaw Smyrna from 580 to 520 BC. This striking beehive-type monument stood atop Mount Yemanla[5]. Even the city's water supply came from an ancient source known as the Baths of Diana. The Baths of Diana were a series of verdant pools lined with cypress. They had been a recreational spot stretching back to the days of antiquity[6].

The road from Smyrna to Boudja goes past the beautiful Valley of St. Anne, so named because she is supposed to be buried there. Through this valley flows the river Meles (also called Oued-Meles); some scholars believe that Homer may have composed his great epics along its banks. The Meles supplied three Roman aqueducts that were still standing in 1922, their classic stone arches dramatic against the sky. Among them was the Great Aqueduct of Alexander, a marvel of ancient architecture.

Thus, with her roots firmly entrenched in Greek culture, the modern civilization and economy of Smyrna were also essentially Greek. The powerful mills of Nazli, which before the Greco-Turkish conflict supplied

Smyrna's quay, circa 1922, was the center of the city's activities, and also home to many fine hotels.

excellent flour not only to Smyrna, but also to Turkey at large and even Europe, were founded by Greeks. Of the 391 factories in Smyrna, 341 were Greek and 14 were Turkish. Two of the principal native schools were Greek. The Homerion, was an institute for girls and the Evangelical School was for boys, the latter under British protection. In the Greek quarter alone there were seventy-nine schools, attended by both boys and girls. The library of the Evangelical School was recognized by scholars as having an invaluable collection of books, manuscripts and inscriptions. These would be irrevocably lost in the coming tragedy.

Smyrna was also one of the earliest Christian cities. Ancient Ionia is the land of the Seven Cities of the Revelation and the Seven Churches with their seven torches of fire[7]. The torches of the other six went out long ago, but Smyrna's had burned until 1922. Great assemblies of early Christians had been held in Asia Minor at Nicaea, Ephesus, and Chalcedon; the legendary church founders St. Paul, and the two St. Gregorys, were born here. Polycarp established a Christian church at Smyrna and was consecrated a bishop of Smyrna by St. John. He was later martyred here in AD 156. When the fire of 1922 struck, two ancient copies of the Bible, one kept in a church at Smyrna, the other in a small Christian village, were lost. According to Horton, the Christians of this village had brought the Bible with them from Ephesus when that town was sacked by Turks centuries ago. Once again, their home would be destroyed, and this time the Bible would be lost as well.

The destruction of the American consulate during the Smyrna catastrophe included the loss of invaluable pieces of US history, as Smyrna is one of America's oldest foreign offices. Among the items ruined were dispatches signed by Daniel Webster and other noted Americans; documents describing raids by the infamous Barbary pirates; an account of the saving of a famous Polish patriot by an American cruiser; and a dozen magnificent old wood prints depicting the Battle of Navarro.

In the zealous rage of the Turks to drive out all other ethnic groups, no consideration was made to preserve artifacts of a historical or a cultural nature. The benefit to future generations or the world at large was superseded by nationalistic fervor. All that mattered was driving the Greeks out— no thought was given to the fact that without the Greeks, Smyrna would not have existed. Greek culture, Greek history, Greek economic initiative—these shaped Smyrna. When fire swept over the city, centuries of history, art, and

TOP LEFT: *The Great Aqueduct of Alexander, named for the town's founder, Alexander the Great. Shown here around 1922, the aqueduct was built in Roman times.*

TOP RIGHT: *East met West in Smyrna. Camels were not an uncommon sight. The caravans journeyed to Smyrna from Damascus as they had for thousands of years.*

LEFT: *Smyrna's Greek quarter, around 1922. Note the narrow streets.*

glorious architecture were destroyed. A vibrant city rich in diversity and blooming with potential was reduced to ashes. In the end, Smyrna's tragedy was the world's tragedy.

Horton wrote, "The question is often asked: 'When will the Turks rebuild Smyrna?'" He replies, "Turkish Smyrna was not burned." Only the Smyrna of Greece and Armenia died that day. Without their influence, the Smyrna that was cannot return.

End Notes

1. "Smyrna: The Martyred City," from *Blight of Asia*, by George Horton, former American consul general of Smyrna.

2. Levantines were foreign residents of Smyrna whose forefathers had settled in the Near East a century or two before. They were Asian in custom and culture, yet not by birth. Many had also intermarried with local Greeks and Armenians.

3. Croesus lived about 6 BC. He was the last king of Lydia and noted for his great wealth.

4. After the Greco-Turkish conflict, according to Horton in *Blight of Asia*, both the coins and the marble were returned to Turkey, the result of political pressure.

5. In Greek mythology, Tantalus was a son of Zeus. He was doomed to stand in water that always receded when he tried to drink it, and to stand under a tree whose fruit he could not reach.

6. In the years following the fall of Smyrna, many of the ancient sites fell into disrepair. Some have since been restored. Today, archaeological researchers have found that human civilization existed in Smyrna since 6000 BC.

7. According to Revelation, St. John had a vision that focused on seven churches in Asia. The churches were in the cities of Ephesus, Philadelphia, Sardis, Pergamum, Thyatira, Laodicea, and Smyrna. The seven torches represented the seven spirits of God.

Moustapha Kemal, or Ataturk, as he liked to be called, was the leader of the Turkish revolution. Calling for a "Turkey for the Turks," he pushed for the expulsion of all minorities from Turkey.

CHAPTER 2

The Nightmare Begins

And I saw, and behold, a pale horse, and its rider's name was
Death, and Hades followed him.
—Revelation 6:7

*E*VEN TODAY, GREEKS CALL IT "THE CATASTROPHE,"
referring to the eradication of the Greek presence in Asia Minor at the hands
of the Turks. This wholesale "cleansing, which also removed Armenians,
took place in the fall of 1922 as Turkish forces swept across the land, driving
mass numbers of Greek Christians and the remaining Armenians before
them."[1] The horde wound up with their backs to the sea at Smyrna.

For thousands of years, Greek settlements had thrived along the coast
of Asia Minor, but this heritage was wiped out in a period of roughly one
month—September 1922. During these last days of the Greco-Turkish
conflict, hundreds of thousands of people were killed, imprisoned, or driven
out as part of a nationalistic fanaticism that proclaimed "Turkey for the
Turks." Moustapha Kemal, leader of the Turkish army and father of the
Nationalist movement, trained his troops well. They would leave no Greek,
Armenian, or Christian behind.

The Turkish army Arrives

August 1922—Smyrna is thrown into chaos as the Greek army makes its
frantic retreat to the sea. They are a battered, disheveled group, utterly

drained of fight. Many have been at war for a long time, having recently fought in World War I and the Balkan wars. Now they face defeat. They are desperate to escape. The soldiers know that if the Turks catch them, they will be shot or suffer a fate worse than death—to be taken prisoner and vanish into the Turkish interior. Those who are captured will never be heard from again.

The citizens watch the army pass. A few soldiers drop by the wayside. Some residents take a huge risk and hide these wounded or exhausted men, outfitting them in farmer's clothes and sheltering them until they can escape. Everyone knows what is coming.

As the army flees, terror grips the citizens of Smyrna with an almost palpable force. The majority of the citizens are Greek Christians, and they are aware of Moustapha Kemal's mandate of Turkey for the Turks. Their continued existence in Smyrna will not be tolerated. The Armenians, the other significant minority in the city, feels the same sense of dread. Many remember the pogroms inflicted by the Young Turks movement a few years earlier. Now, once again, death is sweeping down on them. Many citizens try to leave the city, but transportation is limited. What boats exist are quickly filled and gone. Adding to the chaos, hundreds of refugees from other towns have swarmed into Smyrna ahead of the marching Turks, creating a bottleneck of impossible proportions. In the wake of the Greek army's departure, the city officials also exit Smyrna. For several days, there is no government, no law at all in Smyrna, just this breathless waiting for what will soon come down the road.

When the Turkish army rode into town about eleven o'clock on the morning of September 9, all was quiet. Shops and cafés were closed. Windows were shuttered. For the most part, the townsfolk stayed inside. Then a group of refugees stampeded up the street. One threw a bomb into the midst of the cavalry. The Turks fired back, and a few civilians were killed. Order was quickly restored and at first it seemed that the day might be spent in an uneasy peace. This was not to be the case, however.

Anna Birge, wife of an American missionary stationed in Smyrna, writes in *American Accounts Documenting the Destruction of Smyrna by the Kemalist Turkish Forces, September 1922*:

"The first [Turkish troops] that entered were dressed in black, with black fezzes with their red crescent and red star, riding magnificent horses, carrying long curved swords, proudly they rode into the city. With one hand raised, they called out to the terrified inhabitants, 'Fear Not! Fear Not!,' but the inhabitants of Smyrna, knowing the reputation of the Turk were filled with terror. All morning long the Turkish army marched into the city, and about three o'clock that afternoon they started the most terrible looting, raping and killing that it is possible to describe in words. Whole companies of soldiers broke into the stores on the business streets and swept them clean of their goods.

"The city was systematically looted, and things were carried in carts down to the Turkish quarters. The American teachers in our American Girls School watched the soldiers kill civilians in the street in front of the school, enter homes and kill families and throw them out onto the street, and then take cart loads of goods along with them. When the sun set that evening dead bodies were lying all over the streets of the doomed city."

The Turkish army quickly targeted the city's Christian leader, the archbishop. The Greek archbishop Chrysostomos[2] was well known and respected. George Horton, American consul general in Smyrna, characterized Chrysostomos as eloquent and charismatic. He noted that Chrysostomos reached out to all the diverse minorities of Smyrna in the spirit of unity and good fellowship. He was good friends with the Armenian archbishop and the American clergy, and supportive of the work of American charities within the city. Chrysostomos believed in the union of Christian churches, and hoped they might work together in a concerted effort for the cause of Christ. He was a frequent speaker at the local college, and supported better education for Eastern clergy.

According to Horton's *Report from Turkey*, a U.S. consular document,[3] Chrysostomos knew he was going to die if he remained in Smyrna when the Turks arrived. He came to the consulate just before the army's arrival, causing Horton to pen these words, "As he sat there in the consular office, the shadow of his approaching death lay upon his features. Some who read these lines—some few, perhaps—will understand what is meant. At least twice in my life I have seen that shadow upon a human visage and have known that person was going to die."

Horton reports that Chrysostomos was offered refuge in the French consulate and an escort by French marines but refused, saying, "I am a shepherd and must stay with my flock." He remained at his church as the army arrived. Some time later, a Turkish officer and two soldiers seized him and brought him before Nureddin Pasha, the commanding officer. Pasha

LEFT: *The Greek archbishop Chrysostomos was killed by a mob during the Smyrna catastrophe.*

BELOW: *This wax figurine of the archbishop Chrysostomos is on display at the Estia Nea Smyrnis Museum (an Onassis Foundation) in Athens.*

ordered the archbishop turned over to the Turkish mob that had gathered in front of Turkish military headquarters. He was spat upon, his beard was torn out by the roots, then he was beaten and stabbed. His body was dragged through the streets. Polycarp, the patron saint of Smyrna, was burned to death in the stadium overlooking the town in AD 156. Centuries later, with the death of Chrysostomos, the last Christian bishop of Smyrna was martyred.

Chrysostomos' death set off an orgy of destruction. The *New York Times* of October 21, 1922, published this account by the Reverend S. Ralph Harlow, professor of history and sociology at the International College at Smyrna:

"The Eastern Church, to which most of the Christians of Smyrna belong . . . is in close affiliation with the Church of England. The present Archbishop Crysostum, who is reported as massacred, was a very liberal man and exceedingly friendly with the Americans. Shortly before [my] leaving Smyrna he asked me to preach at one of his large services and urged his clergy and Greek teachers of the city to be present.

"Of the more than 100 beautiful Greek churches in the city, probably all have been looted or burned. Just before I left Smyrna, I visited a number of villages and towns which the Turks had occupied. Every Christian church had been desecrated.

"Not content with wreaking their hatred on sacred pictures and places, the Turks had turned to the tombs of the dead. In one churchyard, where some of the holiest of their priests and leaders were buried, near Smyrna, I found not a single grave untouched. Every tomb had been broken open and bodies of the dead were still lying strewen about.

"The massacre at Smyrna was expected. In the 500 years of Turkish reign over the Christian population of Asia Minor there has not been a single period of twenty-five years free from some awful massacre. During the days of the terrible deportations and massacres of World War I, I traveled up and down the Bagdad Railway and I saw whole cities driven out to starvation and death and women cruelly beaten.

"Smyrna was the first place in the Near East where American missionary work was undertaken. For more than 100 years now, American missionaries have been in Smyrna. During most of this time they have had schools, and for the last twenty-five years have had two colleges, the International for young men[4], and the American Collegiate Institute, for girls, sending forth a steady stream of young men and women, and many of the women have become teachers, doctors, nurses and social welfare leaders throughout the Near East."

▣ ▣ ▣

When darkness fell on Smyrna, the violence escalated and screams rent the night. Now Turkish citizens were turning on their neighbors, caught up in the barbaric frenzy that had seized the city. The Armenian quarter was targeted; by daybreak, more than thirty bodies would be strewn about the streets of that section, and nearly every home and business was vandalized.

According to George Horton, in *Report on Turkey*, on September 9, the Turks set up armed guards outside the Armenian quarter, thus keeping those within from escaping and also preventing outside aid. Other soldiers then entered the neighborhood, killing, looting and destroying property. Women and female children were raped; the men and older boys were slaughtered. Some Armenians escaped or managed to go into hiding.

Horton writes that the Turks made a "systematic and thorough job" of killing Armenian men:

"The squads of soldiers which had given the inhabitants a certain amount of comfort, inspiring the belief that the regular [Turkish] army was beginning to function and would protect the citizens, were chiefly engaged in hunting down and killing Armenians. Some were dispatched on the spot while others were led out into the country in squads and shot, the bodies being left in piles where they fell. The Americans belonging to the various charitable institutions whose duties took them into the interior of the town, reported an increasing number of dead and dying in the streets.

"A native-born American reporter [noted] that he had seen a man beaten to death with clubs by the Turks, 'till there was not a whole bone left in his body.'"

Horton also recorded that a representative of a U.S. tobacco firm entered the consulate "white and trembling," having just seen an old man dismembered by Turkish swords outside on the street.

Loot was carried by the cartload from the Armenian bazaars, along with cargoes of bodies. From Horton's official memoranda of September 12: "A party of Americans saw nine cartloads of dead bodies being carried off in the neighborhood of the Konak [Turkish government house] and another party saw three such cartloads in the neighborhood of Point Station."

The minorities and Christians of Smyrna were right to be afraid, as reports of massacres occurring in the interior had been trickling in for days. In the *New York Times* of September 7, 1922, the Reverend S. Ralph Harlow, wrote, "'The Turks are so pleased with their slaughter that they even have official pictures taken of the tortures and massacres. I had a lot of these official pictures which I gave to an American Consul to send to Washington. They show the Turkish governor of a province, a Turkish General, and the high priests and other officials, dressed in their best, smiling and looking on at the executioner performing his tortures below them."

An American missionary wrote this letter, dated September 21, 1922, and reprinted in *Report from Turkey*:

"Our Murray house across the street was locked up and protected only by an American flag hung from an upper window, but we had several Marines from the American destroyers with us who behaved splendidly all the way through and were a great comfort to us. Of course we had many trying things during the time we were there together, from Saturday, September ninth, until Wednesday, thirteenth, when we left, because the place was on fire. Most of the people who had fled to us for refuge behaved wonderfully patiently under the lack of bread and many difficulties. We had eighty small babies, and one born there. We organized a hospital etc., and had gotten the commissariat running with the difficulty overcome, as we supposed, of lack of bread.

"All ovens in the Christian quarters, where we were, at least, and probably everywhere, had been ordered closed, from Sunday until Wednesday, when the city burned. It looks now to me like a definite attempt to starve the population out.

"The Red Cross insisted on the ovens being opened for them and the people were then burned out.

"The looting and murder went on steadily under our eyes—a murdered man lay before our Murray house door for days, under the American flag, his blood spattered all over our steps, etc. There were dead and dying everywhere. The silence of death finally reigned over us and was broken during the last three days only by the fierce Chetahs[5] breaking in doors of houses, shooting the poor cowering inhabitants, looting, etc., and at night, the howling of homeless dogs and the feet of wandering horses clanging over the rough stones of the street. After the third day of the occupation of Khemal's army, fires began to break out in the Christian quarter of the city. Miss Mills and some of our teachers saw soldiers starting fires. I myself saw a Cheta carrying a load of firewood on his back up an alley, from which later on the fire which caught our building came."

Otis Swift, correspondent for the *Chicago Tribune*, visited the Greek islands on which refugees had been deposited following the Smyrna catastrophe. In one of his reports he writes: "Hospitals of the Greek islands are crowded by people who had been beaten and attacked by the Turks. In a hospital at Chios I saw a child who still lived, though shot through the face by a soldier who had killed its father and violated its mother. In the same hospital, there was a family of six orphan Armenians. A four-year-old baby of this family had been beaten with rifle butts because no money had been found sewn in its clothes."

The *New York Times* ran the following account on October 15, 1922, of a young stowaway who escaped the horrors of Smyrna:

"Constantine Skatziris, a Greek, 27, a refugee from Smyrna, saved by sailors from the United States destroyer Litchfield, arrived here yesterday from Naples aboard a steamship Guglielmo Peirce. He told immigration inspectors that his parents had been slain before his eyes, but that his sister, whose whereabouts he does not know, had been saved. His story was told through the assistance of Archer J. Covo of 420 West Twenty-third Street, who acted as interpreter.

"Skatziris said that he had kept a small grocery store in the Greek section of Smyrna near the plague hospital. On October 16, three days after the town had been fired[6], a Turkish bandit, a giant in stature, who had been a hamel, or porter, on the customs quay before the war and who had acquired fame as a wrestler, had entered Smyrna at the head of a band of cutthroats and had set fire to any buildings that were not burning. Then they had started to kill the inhabitants and loot houses.

"'They rushed into my store in the forenoon,' said the stowaway, 'brandishing long, broad-bladed knives, and attacked my father and mother and my brother, Thomas, who were trying to keep the Turkish robbers from taking goods. My parents were killed. One bandit seized my sister, Katherina, and bore her away on his shoulders. I pursued him while my brother fought desperately in a corner of the store.

"'I searched everywhere for her. At last I was told she had been carried off by the brigands to their caves in the mountains back of Smyrna, where they had been hiding and preying on the country people since the Greek army had entered in the Spring of 1921.

"'After hiding all day, I went to the American Consulate, where I found some naval officers and sailors from the destroyer in the harbor which were taking off the refugees to the steamships bound for Greece.

"'I got to the waterfront with great difficulty, as the heat from the burning ruins was intense and the smoke from the tobacco warehouses was suffocating. Because the streets are very narrow in Smyrna, it was impossible to pass down them. The flames had spread across from side to side and the roadway was piled with debris.

"'At the Custom House steps I met a boatman who knew my family. He told me that Katherina had been saved by sailors from the American destroyer, but could not inform me of which steamships she had been taken to. There were fully 2,000 refugees, men, women and children, on the quay when I was there, five days after the fire started. The last news I heard was that the American Consulate had been fired by the Turkish bandits, or irregulars, as they were styled.

"The stowaway said the Turks had not attempted to interfere with the Armenians, Greeks, Jews and other refugees when they had come under the protection of the American sailors, but that many had been killed in the streets before they could reach the waterfront. Their bodies had been thrown into the flames in order to hide all traces of the crimes committed by the invaders.

"He said an Italian steamship had taken him to Brindisi. At Naples he had hidden away on the *Guglielmo Peirce* to get to America, where he says he has friends, although he does not know where they live . . .'"

The Fire

As the days passed, Armenians disappeared from the streets; they had either been killed or gone into hiding. Soon thereafter, a fire broke out in the Armenian quarters. Some sources, mostly Turkish, have claimed that the Armenians and Greeks set these fires themselves, to keep the Turks from having Smyrna, but most eyewitness accounts (and only a relative few are relayed here) attribute this fire to the Turks. They say the Turks started the

TOP: *Strong winds fanned the flames that destroyed Smyrna, shown here in the conflagration of September 1922. Refugees packed the quay, seeking escape from the Turkish army.*

MIDDLE: *The Turkish cavalry patrolled the quay, keeping the refugees pinned to the shore; there were also incidents of robbery, rape, and assault.*

BOTTOM: *The flames have increased in short order.*

flames in an effort to drive Armenians and others out of hiding. This seems closer to fact as the greatest loss of life was clearly suffered by the Armenians and Greeks; it was their homes and possessions that were lost in the blaze, and the Turkish section of the city was not touched.

"[T]hey set fire to it [the Armenian quarter] in various places by carrying tins of petroleum or other combustibles into the houses or by saturating bundles of rags in petroleum and throwing these bundles in through the windows," writes Horton in *Report from Turkey.* "They planted small bombs under the paving stones in various places in the European parts of the city to explode and act as a supplementary agent in the work of destruction caused by the burning petroleum which Turkish soldiers sprinkled about the streets. The petroleum spread the fire and led it through the European quarter and the bombs shook down the tottering walls. One such bomb was planted near the American Girls' School and another near the American consulate."

Horton cites C. Claflin Davis, chairman of the Disaster Relief Committee of the Red Cross, Constantinople Chapter, as another eyewitness to the start of the fire. Davis was standing in front of the American Consulate when soldiers poured petroleum in front of the building.

Horton describes the buildings of Smyrna as much more flammable than might have been expected. The city had a history of earthquakes, and he points out that many structures were built on a skeleton of wood and timber to prevent them from being easily shaken down. When a wall became very hot, the wooden timbers inside the plaster and masonry caught fire and everything crumbled. The proximity of the buildings added to the rapid spread of the fire.

Miss Minnie Mills was dean of the Intercollegiate Institute, one of the oldest American-run schools in Turkey. Known for being both brave and competent, she sheltered many refugees during the Smyrna crisis. In *Blight of Asia*, she says, "I could plainly see the Turks carrying tins of petroleum into the houses, from which, in each instance, fire burst forth immediately afterward. There was not a single Armenian in sight, the only persons visible being Turkish soldiers of the regular army in smart uniforms."

The fires came perilously close to Mills and her students. "Soon after lunch, fire broke out very near the school, and spread rapidly," she recalls. "I saw with my own eyes a Turkish officer enter a house with small tins of petroleum or benzine, and in a few minutes the house was in flames. Our

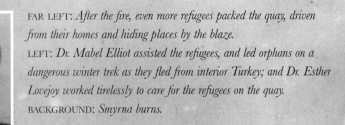

FAR LEFT: *After the fire, even more refugees packed the quay, driven from their homes and hiding places by the blaze.*

LEFT: *Dr. Mabel Elliot assisted the refugees, and led orphans on a dangerous winter trek as they fled from interior Turkey; and Dr. Esther Lovejoy worked tirelessly to care for the refugees on the quay.*

BACKGROUND: *Smyrna burns.*

teachers and girls saw Turks in regular soldier's uniforms, and in several cases, officer's uniforms, using long sticks with rags at the end which were dipped in a can of liquid, and carried into houses which were soon burning. There was no one in the streets at that time, but bands of Turkish soldiers. While the fire started just across the street from our school, throughout the quarter [the Armenian quarter] every third or fifth house was set on fire. . . . The wind, though not very strong, was away from the Turkish quarter and blowing toward the Christian quarters, and it looked as though they waited for a favorable wind."[7]

Miss Mills recounted another horrifying tale, whereby a great throng of Christians was crowded into the narrow street, their escape blocked by Turkish soldiers. The flames were approaching and the soldiers were forcing the people into those houses in the path of the fire. The people were screaming and crying, "Save us! The Turks are going to burn us alive!" But there was nothing anyone could do.

Mrs. King Birge, wife of an American missionary, related the following account in *Report from Turkey:* "I went up to the tower of the American College," she wrote, "and with a pair of field glasses, could plainly see Turkish soldiers setting fire to houses. I could see Turks lurking in the fields, shooting at Christians. When I drove down to Smyrna from Paradise to Athens, there were dead bodies all along the road."

When the fire was set, a strong wind was blowing toward the Christian section and away from the Turkish section; thus, the Turkish quarter was spared while the rest of the city was engulfed. Desperate refugees became trapped on the quay, with the sea at their backs and fire all around them.

Dr. Oran Raber, an assistant professor of botany on a trip through Europe, happened to be in Smyrna at the time of the Catastrophe. He talked with civilians who told him to stay away from the Armenian quarter and warned of the massacres. As quoted in *American Accounts Documenting the Destruction of Smyrna by Kemalist Turkish Forces September 1922*, when the fire broke out, Dr. Raber said, "Instead of attempting to extinguish the fire, the Turks, thoroughly enraged, aided and directed it by petrol. Kemal no longer had control of his forces, and from that time till Friday morning the city was the property of the strongest and the least principled. . . . From what I saw and from evidence collected from both Turks and Greeks, there is only one conclusion: The burning of Smyrna was the work of the Turks."

The *New York Times* of September 16, 1922, reported this cable from Near East Relief: "Smyrna is afire. The fire started in the Armenian quarter during the looting of the bazaars and spread quickly to the European section, destroying the American Consulate, the Y.M.C.A. and the most important buildings. Ten naturalized American citizens are unaccounted for."

Perhaps the most eloquent description of the conflagration comes from the American journalist Melville Chater, who wrote of the tragedy in *History's Greatest Trek*, which covers both the changing situation in the Near East and his travels there. Chater was familiar with the issues and ideologies of Asia Minor, having written a number of articles for *National Geographic* and other publications on Armenia, the Kurds, and Turkey. Here he describes the fire:

"A few days after the triumphal entry of the Turks, the army of quay squatters saw flames dancing in the old wood-constructed Armenian quarter, a mile and a half away. The dance became a fiery hurdle race, as the wind-fanned flames leaped from balcony across the narrow streets; then the race became a hungry conflagration whose roaring mouth ate through and gulped down that mile-and-a-half breadth of city down to where the refugee multitude huddled between a waste of fire and a waste of sea.

"And now fresh multitudes were disgorged upon them—fleeing Smyrniotes laden, refugeelike, with snatched-up babies and bedding. The city became a Titanic blast furnace, whose wind-driven flames fanned the quay with so dreadful a heat that the multitudes dipped their blankets in the sea and swaddled themselves. Maddened horses, their harnesses afire, ran amuck through the press, leaving a wake of crushed bodies, which roasted where they lay.

"All afternoon, until the sun died in rayless eclipse behind the cindery pall, and all night long, by the glare, the flood of men and beasts debouched from the doomed city upon delirious quay. Afrighted faces mingled with wide-eyed animals, and human cries with neigh of horses, the scream of camels, and last, the squeaking of rats, as they scuttled by in droves from the underworld of a lost Smyrna . . .

"When with the dawn the Disaster Relief Committee's workers headed their motorcars towards the quay, at times dismounting to clear corpses from the streets leading hither, two-thirds of Smyrna lay blackened and smoldering, an outstretched chaos. From the announcement board of

767.68/321[34]

Telegram Received

Constantinople
Dated September 15, 1922
Rec'd 3 p.m.
Secretary of State,
Washington D.C.
185. September 15, noon.
Following from Smyrna: "Fourteenth. Am convinced Turks burned Smyrna except Turkish section conforming with definite plan to solve Christian minority problem by forcing allies evacuate Christian minorities. Believe that they will now prepare for an attack on Constantinople Merrill."

BRISTOL

WSB
[Stamped: Department of State, September 16, 1922, Division of Near Eastern Affairs]
[Stamped: Department of State, Filed September 20, 1922, Division of Political and Economic Information]
767.68/333a[35]

Telegram Sent
Department of State Washington

Government
Secstate
U.S.S. *Maryland*
No. 50 for Hughes

My/44, September/15,/3/p.m.

Situation/in/Near/East/extremely/acute,/with/possibility of/ complications/which will/involve/Great Britain/and/Allies/in/war with/Turkey./....

[from page 3 of document]

Confidential/reports/received from/our many officials at Smyrna, /and British Foreign Office,/indicate/that Turks burned/the city/in conformity with/definite/plan to/ solve the Christian/minority/problem/by/forcing/the evacuation of/the minorities./The return of/several/hundred thousand Christians/to their/homes/is apparently/ made/impossible/by the/wholesale/destruction/of villages/ by/ retreating/ Greeks/as well/as by/advancing

[continues on page 4 of document]

advancing Turks.

Reports/indicate/heavy loss/of/American property in Smyrna. Native Americans are all safe. No further/details/received/regarding/missing/naturalized citizens./Three/ American destroyers/are still/in Smyrna/assisting/relief/workers/and protecting/the American/property which escaped/the fire....

[last page is page 5 of document]

[signed]
Phillips
Acting
NE/AWD/LVD

[Stamped, Received September 18, 1922 9:59 PM INDEX BUREAU TELEGRAPH SECTION]

AT LEFT: *Admiral Mark Bristol, commander of U.S. Naval forces in Smyrna waters during the catastrophe.*

FAR LEFT: *Reprint of telegram from Admiral Bristol to the U.S. Secretary of State.*

BELOW LEFT: *Reprint of telegram from "Phillips" to U.S. Secretary of State.*

BACKGROUND: *Smyrna in flames.*

a charred cinema theater, standing stark amid desolated acres, glared like a red-letter epitaph 'The Dance of Death!'[8] High on Pagos' crests rose the unscathed Turkish quarters' minarets like symbols of victory."

The Rapes

The night brought even more terrors to women, who came to fear the darkness most of all. The rape of Christian and Armenian women and girls was widespread. Dr. Mabel C. Elliott, of the American Women's Hospitals, Near East Branch, Greek Unit, sent a letter to George Horton, which is excerpted here. Dr. Elliott cared for the refugees at the height of the Smyrna crisis while they were stranded on the quay:

"My position as a woman physician makes me peculiarly well placed to know about the treatment of young girls by the Turks. In my four-year experience in Turkey I think it rather remarkable that I have yet to see the Turkish girl or woman who has been ravished. As a marked contrast to this, I have seen hundreds of Christian girls who have been in the hands of Turkish men. The late Smyrna disaster was no exception to this and I can justly come to the conclusion from what I have seen with my own eyes that the ravishing of Christian girls by Turks in Smyrna was wholesale. I have actually examined dozens of such girls and have had the story from them of the experiences of other girls with them. By actual examination I have proved that their story in regard to this was not exaggeration, so I have no reason to believe that any statement they made in regard to their companions was not true.

"The treatment of girls in Smyrna during the late disaster of 1922 is unspeakable and I am willing to go on record as an American physician and as director of an organization doing a very large medical work in Greece following the Smyrna disaster, as having made this statement.

In *American Accounts Documenting the Destruction of Smyrna by Kemalist Turkish Forces September 1922*, the representative of an American tobacco house says, "I watched in Cordelio, a suburb of Smyrna, [as an] Armenian family, husband, wife and children, walk out of their beautiful home down to the sea and drown themselves. The Turkish officers requisitioned the homes of the Greeks and Armenians and English in Cordelio, and filled them with the most beautiful of the Greek and Armenian girls, whom they had captured. A Turkish officer said to me, 'We have those houses filled with those girls, and they dance for us naked every night. If you want to see a fine show come over and see it.'"

Wholesale drowning was not unusual. Countless eyewitnesses reported families drowning themselves rather than face death, enslavement, or imprisonment at the hands of the Turks. Other drownings occurred because of overcrowding when the mass of refugees shifted this way and that on the quay. The waters of Smyrna Harbor were awash with corpses at various times during the tragedy.

The Quay

By now, hundreds of thousands of refugees are jammed on the Smyrna quay. It is a scene from Hell. Women are crying over the loss of husbands, brothers, and sons to the Turks, who are seizing all men aged eighteen to forty-five for deportation to the interior. Children are separated from their mothers in the crush of the mob. Their wails pierce the heart. Some are trampled to death. Turkish soldiers push through the masses, ripping away what few valuables the refugees have left in their possession. There are random beatings and killings. The people have no means of keeping clean, no sanitation; soon the quay is a reeking sewer, breeding disease. By day, the sun beats down, and the people suffer from the heat, thirst, and hunger. At night, the rapes begin, women defiled in front of their families or dragged away. There is no escape. With the start of the fire, terror grips the refugees anew, and indeed some are so close to the blaze that their possessions catch fire. The mass shifts as far from the flames as possible but the heat is still unbearable. The sea beckons. With ships, there would be escape, but no ships have yet come.

Dr. Esther Lovejoy[9] of the American Relief Association, was one of the first Americans to minister to the refugees on that Godforsaken quay. She described the situation in Smyrna to the *New York Times* in several articles, the first on Monday, October 19, 1922:

"I was the first American Red Cross woman in France," she wrote, "but what I saw there during the great war seems a love feast beside the horrors of Smyrna. When I arrived in Smyrna there were massed on the quays 250,000 people—wretched, suffering and screaming with women beaten and with their clothes torn off them, families separated and everybody robbed.

"Knowing their lives depended on escape before Sept. 30[10], the crowds remained packed along the water front—so massed that there was no room to lie down. The sanitary conditions were unspeakable.

"Three-quarters of the crowd were women and children, and never have I seen so many women carrying children. It seemed that every other woman was an expectant mother. The flight [and] the conditions brought on many premature births, and on the quay with scarcely room to lie down and without aid most of the children were born. In the five days I was there more than 200 such confinements occurred.

"Even more heart-rendering were the cries of the children who had lost their mothers or mothers who had lost their children. They were herded along through the great guarded enclosure[11], and there was no turning back for lost ones. Mothers in the strength of madness climbed the steel fences fifteen feet high and in the face of blows from the butts of guns sought the children who ran about screaming like animals.

"The condition in which these people reached the ships cause[s] one to wonder if escape were better than Turkish deportation. Never has there been such systematic robbery. The Turkish soldiers searched and robbed every refugee. Even clothing and shoes of any value were stripped from their bodies.

"On September 28, the Turks drove the crowds from the quays, where the searchlights of the allied warships[12] played on them, into the side streets. All that night the screams of women and girls were heard and it was declared next day that many were taken for slaves.

"It is a crime for which the whole world is responsible in not having through the civilized ages built up some means to prevent such orders as the evacuation of a city and the means with which it was carried out. It is a crime for the world to stand by through a sense of neutrality and permit this outrage against 200,000 women."

The second *Times* article appeared on October 21, 1922. Dr. Lovejoy remembers the experience as follows:

"The shrieks of the hundred and fifty thousand or more women and children during the night when the Turkish robbers came to get their little remaining money from them were worse than anyone can imagine [what] the inferno was like.

"It was like the wild continuous moan of the angry ocean and I could not shut it out from my ears. Turkish officers as well as soldiers, joined in robbing these unfortunate people, and the screams of the women and children when the men were torn away from their sides would have pierced the heart of a savage. All men from 18 to 45 were taken prisoner and sent to the interior, although they were civilians and had not taken part in the fighting in Asia Minor. The mothers [often] were separated from their children in the chaos which reigned on the quay during the evacuation of Smyrna and [sometimes they] went away on different ships.

"There were nearly one hundred thousand people on the shore when I left there on September 20, and I heard they were taken away later. Nothing the Germans ever perpetrated in Belgium approached the atrocities committed by the Turks in Asia Minor. There were fully 350,000 refugees crowded together in Smyrna on September 23 when the Turks sent an airplane over the city to drop papers stating that they all had to be out of the city before September 30 or they would be sent into the interior.

"The women living day and night on the cobblestones without blankets and most of them without shoes, their hair hanging down in matted coils and their disheveled dress were indescribable. In their wild appearance they were more like animals than human beings. Many of the poor unfortunates went insane and fought at the gates like demons with the Turkish soldiers to prevent their husbands from being taken from them. The American soldiers did all they could but were prevented from any official acts because the United States was neutral."

The American journalist Chater vividly describes the horrors of the quay in his article "History's Greatest Trek." "For another week," he wrote, "the remaining 200,000 continued to live and die, and bring other beings to birth on that unforgettable quay. With Smyrna's bakeries burned, or idle because of water shortage, they gorged on raw flesh, torn from animals' carcasses, or on the sea biscuit that the American sailors brought ashore in tins.

"Burned, too, were all hospitals and their occupants; so within that multitude—so densely packed that one could not lie down without being crushed to death—women gave birth to stillborn babies and sheltered them against their dried-up breasts, for lack of burial place, until a fresh stampede—perhaps over the arrival of a bucket of water—opened a momentary pathway for them to lay their burdens in the all-receiving sea.

"By now the emerald-clear waters showed a bottom strewn with the drowned, and gangs of body fishers were coolly plying hooked lengths of telegraph wire for the loot of finger-rings and turned-out pockets."

Other nationals did not escape the bloodlust that gripped Smyrna. At nearby Boudja, the DeJongs, a wealthy Dutch family, were murdered by the Turks, their bodies left in the streets. Doctor Murphy, a retired British army surgeon, was attacked in his home at Bournabat. His daughters hid and were later rescued, but Murphy was beaten to death while trying to prevent the rape of a servant girl. On September 11, an American doctor, Alexander MacLachlan, president of the American College at Paradise, and Sergeant Louis Crocker, chief in charge of sailor guard, were stripped and beaten by Turkish soldiers. The two had tried to prevent Turkish soldiers from looting the American settlement house. A Turkish student intervened but was ignored and the two men were lined up against a wall to be shot. Two U.S. Marines witnessed the attack from a nearby rooftop but were ordered by the sergeant not to fire, less they too be attacked and the situation escalate. Finally, a Turkish officer appeared on the scene and stopped the shooting.

The Debate

There are numerous reports as to why the Turkish army embarked on the massacres. Chief among them is the charge that Moustapha Kemal and his officers ordered them as part of Kemal's plan to rid Turkey of "undesirable" cultural and religious elements. Kemal was committed to having a purely Turkish, Muslim state. This commitment is cited again and again by both American military and civilian sources in Smyrna. Some have claimed that the Turkish officers lost control of their soldiers, but this seems unlikely. Turkish soldiers were known and even admired for being well disciplined in battle and showing absolute obedience to their commanders. It seems unlikely that this would change. Kemal himself was recognized as an extremely able-bodied officer, capable of inspiring great loyalty, and obviously charismatic in that he successfully won over a nation to become his followers. It is unfathomable that he would suddenly lose power in Smyrna. The third reason often cited is that the Turkish army included *chetahs*, irregular troops who aided in the fighting and were paid in loot. Turkish officials claimed that most of the barbaric acts were committed by the chetahs, over whom they said they had little control.

However, the looting, killing, and debauchery were so widespread that the numbers of victims alone make it plain that regular troops were involved. The fact that the victims were clearly targeted as Armenians and Greek Christians also illustrates that more was at work than a few soldiers running amok. There were instances of Turkish officers intervening to stop bloodshed, and even providing aid, and these are noted later in this book, but sadly, these were few and far between.

In fact, it is widely believed by American military, reporters and civilians stationed at Smyrna that the great fire that destroyed the city was set by the Turks to cover up much of the murder and looting that had taken place. The fire was set in the Armenian quarter and spread through the Christian quarter. The Turkish quarter was never touched. Following are two telegrams sent by U.S. Naval officers in Smyrna:

On September 15, 1922, Admiral Mark Bristol, commander of the U.S. fleet in Smyrna, cabled the following to the U.S. Secretary of State:

"Following from Smyrna: Fourteenth. Am convinced Turks burned Smyrna except Turkish section conforming with definite plan to solve Christian minority problem by forcing allies evacuate Christian minorities. Believe they will now prepare for an attack on Constantinople Merrill."

The next telegram was sent on September 15 to the Department of State:

"Telegram Sent
    Department of State Washington
Government
Secstate
USS Maryland
No. 50 for Hughes
My/44, September/15/ 3/p.m.

"Situation in Near East extremely acute, with possibility of complications which will involve Great Britain and Allies in war with Turkey. Confidential reports received from our many officials at Smyrna, and British Foreign Office, indicate that Turks burned the city in conformity with definite plan to solve the Christian minority problem by forcing evacuation of the minorities. The return of several hundred thousand Christians to their homes is apparently made impossible by the wholesale destruction of villages by retreating Greeks as well as by advancing Turks.

"Confidential reports indicate heavy loss of American property in Smyrna. Native Americans are all safe. No further details received regarding missing naturalized citizens. Three American destroyers still in Smyrna assisting relief workers and protecting American property which escaped the fire."—Phillips, Acting NE/AWD/LVD (Stamped, Received September 18, 1922, 9:59 PM INDEX BUREAU TELEGRAPH SECTION)"

Further dispatches from Bristol relay the following:

"Tuesday, September 14, 1922, The fire continued to burn through the night though considerably diminished. Several separate fires were observed to start in locations different from the general conflagration, plainly indicating incendiarism. The Passport Office, located upon the north pier of the inner harbor, burned after midnight with many heavy explosions, probably caused by gasoline, as a number of drums had been observed in and near this building a day or two previously. This building was only a few hundred yards from the LITCHFIELD's anchorage, and the actions of the person that fired it were plainly observed by Vice Consul Barnes from the forecastle, although the distance was too great to allow for any sort of identification. A number of Turkish troops were stationed at the inshore end of the building at the time.

"Several of the relief workers as well as Vice Consul Barnes reported to me that there was a noticeable change on shore in the temper of the Turkish troops and civilians towards the Armenians. The impression they received was that every able-bodied Armenian man was being hunted down and killed wherever found, even small boys of between 12 to 15 years armed with clubs (were) taking part in the hunt. I myself witnessed from the ship through binoculars a case of a man in civilian clothes being held up by a squad of Turkish soldiers; after considerable brutal handling and what appeared to be a search of his person, he was bound and thrown over the seawall and shot."

▣ ▣ ▣

George Horton, the American consul general, also made it clear that the Turkish massacres were planned. Horton had a good grasp of the situation. He had spent thirty years in diplomatic service and was fluent in six languages, including Greek and Turkish. He writes in one of his dispatches:

"I have the honor to also point out that all massacres on a large scale perpetrated by the Turks, and the history of the Turkish empire is largely a history of massacres, are always ordered by higher authorities. Anyone who is believes that the forces of Mustapha Kemal got out of hand at Smyrna and that he controlled them as soon as he could, knows nothing about the history of Turkey or the events in the Near East. I believe also that if the Allied Fleets in Smyrna harbor, the French, Italians, British and Americans had emphatically told Mustapha Kemal that there must be no massacring, none would have taken place. If they had told him today that he must cease carrying off men between eighteen and forty-five into the interior, he would stop, but when he sees the great powers of the world sitting by in security on their battleships watching his fearful procedures, he is emboldened to greater and still greater excesses. The sight of a massacre going on under the eyes of the great powers of Europe and with their seemingly tacit consent is one that I hope never to see again."

Horton also outlined these certain basic principles behind the massacre in *Report on Turkey*.

Fundamental Principles

1) Turkish massacres are always carried out by order of superior authorities. This is a well-known principal and the way in which various historic massacres have been conducted abundantly proves it. Such was the case at Smyrna, and Moustapha Khemal's statement that he could not control his troops is false. It is a curious fact that the Turk is still able to deceive Europeans, despite long observation of his tactics. It is probable that one emphatic word to the Turkish commander by the French Admiral would have stopped the massacre and the horrors that followed.

2) It should be borne in mind that it has been for some time the policy of the Turkish nationalists to exterminate and eliminate the native Christian element in Turkey. Any one forming plans for future business or diplomatic relations with Turkey should bear this in mind and be fully (aware) of the changed conditions in the country.

3) Khemalism has been built up by the Allies by their weakness and dissension. The conduct of France has been one of faithlessness to the Allies, with the purpose of obtaining concessions, and undermining British influence in the Near East. Great Britain, on account of labor opposition and Mussulman unrest in India, is obliged to swallow this bitter pill, with the hope that concessions to Khemal will quiet the Mussulmans of India. This is a mistake and has been a mistaken policy from the beginning. The entry of Khemalists into Constantinople will arouse the Mussulmans of India beyond control.

▣ ▣ ▣

Many besides Horton believed that the Turks deliberately covered up evidence of the massacres. Mark O. Prentiss, writing in *The New York Times* of September 24, 1922, noted, "Major Claflin Davis of the American Red Cross secured official permission to investigate the ruins of the Armenian churches. When he was approaching them with an escort a terrific explosion caused complete collapse of the structures, destroying all evidence of the rumored massacres . . . "

The cause for the debate seems to have its roots in the Turkish camp. In *American Accounts Documenting the Destruction of Smyrna by the Turkish Khemalist Forces, September 1922*, it is noted that "the groundwork for this theory [that no massacres by Turks occurred and that the Armenians started the fire] was laid even as the tragic events were unfolding in Smyrna, since we know from contemporary Turkish sources such as the reminiscences of Halide Edib, Kemal's American trained English translator, that this story along with the theory that Armenian nationalists set fires and bombs was systematically disseminated to the western press."

Despite this maneuver, most American media consistently reported on the atrocities. This is telling because the United States had significant economic interests within Turkey, yet the media continually relayed damaging stories of the massacres, fires, and general treatment of the refugees. American military officers, relief workers and private citizens, many of whom were employed by corporations with economic interests in Turkey, also spoke out. To hear the same story from such diverse groups cannot help but indicate validity.

The Deaths

How many were massacred? Accurate estimates seem impossible to find, but George Horton provides this information in *The Blight of Asia*:

"Official statistics give the Armenian inhabitants of Smyrna as twenty-five thousand and it is certain that the larger part of the men of this community were killed, besides many women and girls, also numerous Greeks. A despatch to the *London Daily Chronicle* of September 18, 1922, says, 'The lowest estimate of lives lost given by the refugees places the total at one hundred and twenty thousand.'

"Reuter's Agency, in a dispatch of the same date, makes the following statement: 'From none of the accounts is it possible to give the exact figures of the victims, but it is feared that in any case they will be over one hundred thousand.'

"Mr. Roy Treloar, newspaper correspondent, wired as follows (on September 20, 1922): 'Nureddin Pasha commenced a systematic hunting down of Armenians, who were gathered in batches of one hundred, taken to the Konak and murdered.'

"The *London Times* correspondent telegraphed: 'The killing was carried out systematically.' Turkish regulars and irregulars are described as rounding up likely wealthy people in the streets and, after stripping them, killing them in batches. Many Christians who had taken refuge in the churches were burned to death in buildings which had been set on fire."

Officials of Near East Relief back up Horton's statements regarding the large numbers of deaths. These missionaries worked closely with the Greeks, Armenians, and Turks, and lived among their charges. In *The Story of Near East Relief*, witnesses to the catastrophe relayed this fact: "The whole non-Turkish population of the city was rendered homeless and destitute by the burning and complete destruction of non-Moslem Smyrna. The entire Christian population of the hinterland, composed of hundreds of thousands of Greeks and Armenians, had fled before the advancing Turkish army into the city seeking safety and protection. Some escaped in boats to the friendly Greek islands but most of them were helpless, terror-stricken refugees, surrounded by an implacable enemy that seemed committed to their expulsion from the city and the country."

If rescue had not come for the refugees, the death toll would have reached staggering proportions. An entire culture would have vanished from the earth, murdered on the Smyrna quay, or vanished into the interior of Turkey to who knows what fate. But rescue did come, from a most unlikely quarter.

End Notes

1. The Armenians had already been driven out of other parts of Turkey, particularly near the Black Sea and eastern/northeastern section, during the pogroms conducted by the Young Turks during 1918 and 1919.

2. In the Greek Orthodox Church, Chrysostomos would be called the "metropolitan" which is roughly equivalent to the archbishop. At Smyrna, he was commonly referred to by both titles. He is also called by his Greek name, Chrysostomos.

3. George Horton's, *Report from Turkey*, includes text from his previous book, *The Blight of Asia*.

4. The International College also had a branch for women, and many Armenian girls studied there. The American Collegiate Institute was also called the American College.

5. Chetahs were irregular Turkish troops, hired to help fight and paid in loot.

6. Most likely, the date in the paper is wrong—probably a confusion in translation. The town was fired upon on September 16, not October 16. There were also hundreds of thousands of refugees on the quay.

7. Initially, the wind was not very strong, but that quickly changed. By all accounts, it became incredibly strong and drove the fire into a blaze of unstoppable proportions.

8. Ironically, *The Dance of Death* was the name of the last movie playing at the Smyrna theater, and that name was emblazoned on the marquee at the time of the great fire.

9. Esther Pohl Lovejoy, a physician and member of the American Relief Association and American Women's Hospitals, a service organization organized in 1917 to work with the sick in countries ravaged by war. Dr. Lovejoy also served with the Red Cross on the battlefield in World War I.

10. Kemal had ordered that all refugees must exit Smyrna by September 30 or be transported as prisoners (a death sentence) to the interior. This arbitrary deadline was a mockery, as at the time it was issued, there was no transport and no means of escape for the hundreds of thousands of refugees on the quay. Rescue would eventually come, and American officers did successfully get the deadline extended.

11. As refugees headed toward the ships, they had to pass through a series of gates. It was impossible to go back through the gates, so if a refugee was separated from his possessions, family members, or children, there was no recourse. As they were processed through these gates, there was further occasion for looting, although once American and British officers became involved, this was stopped for the most part.

12. Because they were under the directives of government-ordered neutrality, the ships' crews could not intervene directly. By shining their ships' powerful searchlights on the quay, they could provide some measure of protection, thereby limiting the nighttime rapes, robberies, and attacks. However, as noted by personal accounts, such as that of the stowaway Constantinas Skatziros, many sailors ashore did intervene in a more direct way in preventing rapes, seizures, and attacks, and were not reprimanded by their superiors for doing so.

CHAPTER 3

The Rescue:
"Greek Flags Down!"

There are thousands to tell you it cannot be done,
There are thousands to prophecy failure;
There are thousands to point out to you, one by one,
The dangers that wait to assail you.
　　　　　—Edgar A. Guest, "It Couldn't Be Done"

BY MID-SEPTEMBER OF 1922, THE TOWN OF SMYRNA WAS in flames. Even at a distance of sixty miles, the cloud of pungent smoke could be seen. Within the smoke, chaos reigned, as desperate people sought a way out.

On the Smyrna quay, hundreds of thousands of Greek refugees stood trapped. Hope had long since died. They were roasting under the blazing sun, dying of thirst and starvation, and victims of every kind of brutality. Adding to the misery, the Turkish commander had decreed that all refugees must leave the city by September 30 or be deported to the interior of Asia Minor—a death sentence for all Christians. Time was running out. It seemed as if no one would come.

Asa Jennings was an unlikely hero. He was not a big, strapping American but rather a small man of barely five foot two. Born in Ontario, New York, Jennings had suffered an attack of tuberculosis in both his lungs and his spine, but it had never weakened his spirit. He joined the YMCA at the age of twenty-four. After holding numerous stateside YMCA posts, he served as a Methodist pastor for ten years. When World War I broke out, he eagerly accepted a YMCA position overseas. He was stationed in Le Mans, France, at the height of the war, and after the Armistice went on to Czechoslovakia. In 1922 he came to Turkey, where he served as secretary for boys work at the YMCA in Smyrna. As a leader in local relief efforts, Jennings had succeeded in establishing a hospital for women and children and in providing housing for others.

Papers supplied by his grandson contain a paragraph from the minutes of the International Committee of the YMCA, that notes, "Mr. Jennings' entire career was characterized by an ardent love for his fellow man, by untiring and deep devotion to the cause to which he had given his life, by vision where frequently others could not see, by optimism in the face of hindrances, which made him great and which will continue with us through the years to come."

William T. Ellis, a reporter for the *Saturday Evening Post* in 1923, describes him as an "everyman," an average person risen to extraordinary heights by circumstance. "Nobody would ever have picked him for the hero's part; he properly belonged among the 'supes.' Jennings was no 'old hand' in Smyrna or the Near East, and no leading citizen. In fact, he was only a rather recent assistant Young Men's Christian Association secretary, an ex-Methodist preacher, who would never get an appointment on account of his size, his good looks, his 'air,' or his oratory. He was only the common or garden variety Y.M.C.A. worker. Withal, though, he was Kipling's sort of American who, 'Turns a keen, untroubled face, Home to the instant need of things.'"

As Ellis wrote, Jennings was not experienced in Middle East politics, nor was he a "smooth talker," but he had the courage of his convictions. This resolve to take action when others would not commanded both attention and respect during the dark days of Smyrna.

Jennings's role in Smyrna's history came about by chance. Excerpts in his own words speak of what transpired as the city fell. They come thanks to an interview with R. W. Abernethy, which took place in March 1923 on board the S.S. *Fezera*, eighteen months after Smyrna's fall. Abernethy, a secretary of the International Committee of the YMCA of New York City, featured this interview in his book, *Spirit of the Game,* in a story called "The Great Rescue." Jennings's story opens in August of 1922.

"All along the line, Greek forces were withdrawing," Jennings recalls. "Villages both inside and outside the zone handed over to Greece were either totally or partially destroyed . . . so that every road to the sea was chocked with troops and refugees running from the Turks.[1]

"This was all a complete surprise to us in Smyrna. The first news we had of this final battle was that the Greeks were successful. The next word came in that they had suddenly begun to retreat, then that they were retreating in disorder, driving their nationals before them. We did not wait long to have this confirmed, for soon refugees began to drift into the city. Naturally, the Greeks and Armenians in Smyrna were thrown into a panic, and made frantic efforts to leave before the disaster occurred that they could plainly foresee. But everybody had to get a Greek visa before leaving, and with a normal population that included 175,000 Greeks, and 40,000 Armenians, you can see what a hopeless task that was . . .

"About the 20th of August, the first of 60,000 or more Greek troops began to arrive, and immediately embarked on transports which were awaiting them. Thousands of refugees flooded the city looking to the Greek army to protect them in this last possible stand. But their supposed protectors had no intention of doing this, their sole concern being to get away as soon as possible. As a result, the military forces left in safety, abandoning thousands of their fellow Christians, who choked the quay, pleading for protection."

◧ ◧ ◧

The American consul general, Dr. George Horton, called together the men of the American colony and discussed means of protecting American lives and property. He also warned the group that much might be required of them. When Jennings asked about help for the refugees, Horton suggested Jennings think of options.[2] As it turned out, the refugees soon would indeed become Jennings's sole focus.

Over the next few days, Jennings rounded up supplies for the hapless refugees and began to secure a way for his family to leave. Smyrna was becoming more violent each day, and Jennings knew their lives were in danger.

"On the ninth of September, the vanguard of the Turkish army appeared, their advance being delayed somewhat by the desultory resistance of the last of the Greek forces," writes Jennings. "Just outside Smyrna, on the heights that are known as Paradise, occurred the last engagement between the two armies. Now our home was on those slopes, and though I was in the city at the time, my family witnessed the whole affair. When I got home that night, my two boys rushed up to me shouting, 'Gee, Dad, you ought to have been here. You could see them shooting and falling down everywhere!' They had, you see, the typical enthusiasm of youth for war and its glamour. About 10,000 Greeks were captured in this affair before the army gave way and made for the ships."

Although the victorious Turkish army entered Smyrna without incident, it wasn't long before tension flared among the Turks, Greeks, and Armenians. Skirmishes broke out, and it became risky to be on the streets.

"I remember the exciting time I had on the morning of September 13, when I was on my way to the office," says Jennings. "I was coming through the Armenian quarter, and as ill luck would have it, fell in with a mob. There was firing on both sides, for of course, Turkish soldiers were everywhere. I had long since taken the precautionary measure of arming myself with an American flag, for that little bit of bunting was of more potential defense than any Colt automatic. Finding myself in this pleasant little party, I pulled out my flag, pinned it on, and made for the nearest wall. I finally reached it and then walked sideways for quite a distance, for I had always been told that if you must be shot by all means avoid being shot in the back."

That morning Jennings was told that the Navy had issued orders that all Americans must leave within the hour. The family fled so hastily that their dinner was left on the stove. One of his Armenian employees at the YMCA was terrified of what might befall him at the hands of the Turks and approached Jennings for help. Because families were allowed to claim one household servant, Jennings named the boy his "servant" for the day, thereby ensuring his rescue.

With his family accounted for, Jennings returned to the city, now focusing on the thousands of refugees who needed his help. Fire was raging in the Armenian quarter and looting, rape, and killing were rampant. The situation of the refugees stranded on the quay was becoming ever more desperate. People were being robbed and murdered outright; an all-out massacre seemed horrifyingly probable. Jennings knew he was facing the greatest challenge of his life. Could he, one man, work a miracle and save hundreds of thousands of innocent people?

Jennings saw anchored in the harbor the French ship, the *Pierre Loti*. He resolved to ask them for assistance in removing some of the refugees. Thanks to Captain Halsey Powell, who was in charge of the American destroyer flotilla, also anchored in the harbor, Jennings was given a motor launch to go out to the French ship. He made his request but the French captain refused; Jennings then turned his attention to the Italian ship *Constantinople*, begging the captain for assistance. The Italian captain said he could not take on any refugees unless his sailing orders were changed; he did allow, however, that the Italian consul in Smyrna could do that.

Upon hearing this, Jennings agreed to pay the captain 5,000 lire to take two thousand refugees and land them on Mytilene, and an additional 1,000 for the extra trouble this would cause him. The captain agreed, and Jennings's role as coordinator of the rescue was under way. He was careful to notify the Turks that he had a ship and was planning to evacuate some refugees. The Turks agreed to the rescue measures as long as none of the evacuees was a man of military age. Transport to the *Constantinople* went according to plan but was closely supervised by the Turks. In a few cases, young men tried to go aboard the ship in disguise, but these ruses were discovered by the Turks and the men remained behind.

By four o'clock that afternoon, the *Constantinople* was loaded. The captain requested that Jennings accompany the refugees to make sure they could land at Mytilene. As Jennings boarded, he was met with throngs of grateful Greeks.

"I could scarcely get through the mass of people that crowded around me," he recalls. "They fell at my feet in gratitude. They kissed me. Old men got on their knees, kissing my hands and feet, tears streaming down their faces. They did everything they could to show their thanks. It was one of the hardest experiences I ever went through. When I finally reached the cabin assigned me, I dropped on the berth and burst out crying. It was nerve-wracking and yet I think my tears were tears of joy as well, that God had enabled me to bring safety to those 2,000 unfortunates."

En route to at Mytilene, Jennings organized two relief committees, one of Greeks and one of Armenians, to take charge of the landing of the refugees. He then wired the Constantinople chapter of the Red Cross, telling them that his ship loaded with refugees was about to land, and asking that this landing be placed under the aegis of the Red Cross. He also requested that he, Jennings, be given official authorization to act as he saw fit. Both authorizations were quickly forthcoming. The governor general of Mytilene agreed to take not only the two thousand refugees en route, but also as many more as they could feed. As Mytilene was already burdened by evacuated Greek troops and those civilians who had been able to flee Smyrna before the Turkish occupation, Jennings knew resources

Asa Jennings and his family.

were getting tight. However, he was able to arrange for food from the Near East warehouses,[3] thereby solving that immediate problem.

Jennings knew time was running out for evacuating the rest of the refugees from the Smyrna quay. The Turks had given a deadline of September 30, and though Jennings had secured a place for the refugees to go, he needed the means to transport them. He required ships, lots of ships. The twenty transports that had evacuated the Greek army were still anchored in the outer harbor of Mytilene, under the command of General Frankos of the south army. Could they be used? They were his only hope.

Jennings rushed to get permission, but Frankos said he could spare only six, and only with a guarantee of their protection. Jennings knew that Commander Powell had secured permission from the Turkish authorities for Greek ships to enter the Smyrna harbor provided they did not fly the Greek flag or tie up at any wharf, but Frankos insisted on written assurance. Jennings boarded the *Litchfield*, an American destroyer, and wired Powell that he was coming to Smyrna to get a written guarantee. When he arrived, Powell met him with the appropriate papers and immediately ordered the *Litchfield* to return Jennings to Mytilene. Powell had not only provided assurance that the Turks would not harm the Greek ships as long as required conditions were followed, but he had also said in the papers that American destroyers would accompany the ships in and out of the harbor, if desired.

Jennings raced to Mytilene, and arrived at 1 in the morning. He woke General Frankos, showed the guarantee, and asked for all twenty of the Greek transports. Frankos hesitated, fearing a hitch somewhere. The Turks had no navy, but if they were able to seize the Greek ships, they could then capture Chios, Mytilene, and other islands in the Aegean. He demanded further proof of the Turks' sincerity. Jennings replied that he personally would accompany the Greek ships in and out of the harbor.

Jennings's narrative includes the following exchange. "'Does that mean you will protect the ships?'" Frankos asked.

"I couldn't help but smile to myself at the thought that my presence on a ship meant more to him than the protection of two or three American destroyers, but I replied, 'It means that we believe the Turks to be sincere and we will not break confidence with them. We Americans have assumed full responsibility for the evacuation of that quay, provided we can get the ships. Will you, or won't you, give us these ships?' "

Still Frankos hesitated and with a sinking heart Jennings realized that a quick decision was not forthcoming. He prayed for guidance, feeling sure it would come, and it did, in the vision of a ship.

". . . I saw through the grey, early morning mist a familiar looking warship in the harbour. It looked like an American battleship, and yet I knew that there were no American battleships around these waters.[4] I asked [someone] what is was, and was told that it was the Greek ship KILKIS. Then I remembered. Somewhere, sometime before the war, I had read a dispatch to the effect that the United States Government had sold the Greek Government the old battleship MISSISSIPPI. And there she was, with a different flag and a different name, lying at anchor right out there in the harbor. I could have cried for sheer joy, for somehow I had a strange confidence that through her I could get help."

Jennings borrowed a rowboat and set out for the *Kilkis*. He had decided to go over General Frankos' head and speak directly to the authorities in Athens. Jennings relayed the situation to the captain of the *Kilkis*, and the captain helped Jennings encode a message to Athens. In it, Jennings

explained the situation and urgently requested that all Greek ships in the
waters around Smyrna be put at his disposal.

"This was about four o'clock in the morning, so I didn't expect a reply
for a little time," remembers Jennings, "but soon one came back demanding
to know who I was. Now that was a very natural query. I had been in that
part of the world only about a month, and no one had ever heard of me.
So I cabled back that I was in charge of the American Relief at [Mytilene].
And I was. I didn't explain, however, that I held the position solely by virtue
of the fact that I was the only American there!"

To Jennings's dismay, the Athens authorities replied that such a
request would require cabinet action, and the cabinet was not in session.
The request, therefore, would go to the prime minister, who would call
a meeting of the cabinet. There then proceeded a flurry of telegrams as
the Greek cabinet asked for detailed assurances of protection and Jennings
attempted to provide them. By four o'clock that afternoon there was still no
sign of the ships being released. By now, Jennings was desperate; he knew
the plight of the refugees was in his hands, and valuable time was slipping
away.

"I . . . threw convention to the winds. I resolved to serve an ultimatum
to the Greek Government and I did," he writes. "It was a rash thing to do,
I'll admit, but heroic measures were necessary and so I staked it all on this
one. I told them that if I did not receive a favorable reply by six o'clock
that evening, I would wire openly, without code, so that the message would
be picked up by any wireless station near, that the Turkish authorities had
given permission for Greek ships to evacuate refugees from Smyrna, that
the American navy had guaranteed protection to these ships, that I had
assumed responsibility for directing them to Greek soil in safety, that all
we lacked was ships, and that the Greek Government would not permit
Greek ships to save Greek and Armenian refugees awaiting certain death
or worse!

"I had thrown all my cards on the table. It was their throw next, and it
came immediately in the form of a request that under no condition should
I send any message save in code. I saw then and there that those Cabinet
officials were giving this matter pretty serious attention.

"There was nothing to do but wait until six o'clock. It wasn't long,
however, before another wire was handed me asking if I would go with the
first ship. I answered, 'Yes, by all means.' I didn't realize all that lay back of

that question, but found out later that they wanted this assurance because if the first ship were captured or sunk they could say that an American was on it, that the Americans had led them into the trap, and that, therefore, America was responsible.

"Six o'clock was drawing near, and I began to fear that I would have to make good my threat, when a wire was received stating that the Greek Government had placed all ships in the Aegean Sea at my disposal!" he continues. "That wire meant that I had been promoted to the rank of Admiral of the Greek navy! It meant much more, however. It meant safety and life to thousands who saw no hope; thousands who were crowding that quay looking wistfully to the open sea for some help, doubting whether any would come. Again, I sent up a prayer of thanks."

Upon receiving notice of his "admiralty," Jennings joked that all he knew about ships "was to be sick on them," and now he was in charge of them. Thankfully, he had a good ally in Captain Theophonitis, of the *Kilkis*. The captain informed the twenty ships in the Mytilene Harbor of the day's events and of Jennings's new role as admiral. He then impressed upon them that they must be ready to leave at midnight. When some officers balked at this timetable and began to make excuses as to the readiness of their craft, Theophonitis threatened court-martial. Soon the ships were ready.

In the meantime, Jennings selected the *Propondis* for his flagship, as her captain spoke some English. "He was tickled to death to think his ship had been selected," remembers Jennings. "Whether he realized that this meant that he was to head the procession and be the first one, therefore, to enter the Turkish harbor, I don't know. I didn't stop to press details upon him!

"At twelve o'clock I was ready, and ordering the Greek flag run down, an American flag flown in its stead, and a signal flag that meant 'Follow Me' to be run up aft," he continues. "I mounted the bridge and ordered full steam ahead! I have had quite a few thrills in my life, but I believe none equaled that one."

About halfway to Smyrna, the American destroyer *Lawrence* drew alongside. Commander Wolleson, knew Jennings and offered him a ride. But Jennings, seeing that things were under control, and remembering his promise to the Greek cabinet to go with the first ship, declined. He would stay with "his" fleet, although the *Lawrence* did sail along as escort.

"I wish you could have been with me as we sailed into Smyrna harbor!" says Jennings. "I shall never forget that moment as long as I live.

From quite a way out I could see from my station on the bridge the smoking ruins of what had once been the business part of town. Directly in front, gaunt bricks and stone skeletons of once-fine buildings pushed themselves up dizzily from the charred debris that covered the ground. It was the most desolate, fearsome sight I ever saw. And at the water's edge stretching for miles was what looked like a lifeless black border." He recalls: "Yet I knew it was a border not of life, but of living sufferers waiting, hoping, praying, as they had been doing every moment for days—waiting, hoping, praying for ships, ships, ships. As we approached, and the shore spreading [spread] out before us, it seemed as if every face on that quay was turned toward us, and every arm outstretched to bring us in. Indeed I thought the whole shore moved out to grasp us. The air was filled with the cries of thousands, cries of such transcendent joy that the sound pierced to the very marrow of my bones. No need for us to tell them what these ships were for! They who had scanned that watery horizon for days looking wistfully for ships, did not have to be told that here was help, here indeed was life and safety! Never had I been so thankful, so truly happy, as I was that early morning as I realized that at last, but thank God in time, I had been able to bring to these despairing legions a new hope, yes, a new life."

Captain Powell had not been idle while Jennings was securing ships. He had notified Turkish officials of Jennings's doings, and all parties worked in concert to load the refugees as expeditiously as possible. All the Greek ships in the Aegean did take part in the rescue, and by the deadline of September 30, all Smyrna refugees had been removed. The Turks kept their part of the bargain, although they continued to stand firm on their ruling that no men of military age could be evacuated.

Jennings then got an extension of eight days from Turkish officials in order to evacuate refugees from the neighboring towns of Aivali, Chesme and others. Hundreds of thousands of refugees[5] flooded Mytilene, Chios, Salonica, Piraeus, Patras, Crete, and other locales. By one estimate, the Greek population increased by 25 percent from this influx of refugees. Despite the burden this placed on services, however, the Greeks met the need, giving food and shelter to all who arrived.

. . . continued on page 58

ΝΑΥΤΙΚΟΝ ΣΗΜΑ

Ans to telegram Sent Sept 22

General Frankou

After communication with the general staff I acknowledge you all the ships now in Piræus harbor have been seized by the Government and those ordered to Mitylene for the transport of the Refugees from the Asia Minor Coast. Stop
I acknowledge you also that the commander of the Navy has been ordered to be in communication with the American Admiral with reference regulation of the transportation.

Frankou Brig. Genl.

(handwriting of Asa K. Jennings)
Answer to telegram sent Sept. 22
(written at top of page)

General Frankou

After communication with the
General Staff I acknowledge you
all the ships now in Piraeus
harbor have been seized by the
Government and have been
ordered to Mitylene for the
transport of the Refugees from
the Asia Minor coast. Stop.
I acknowledge you also that the
Commander of the Navy has
been ordered to be in communication
with the American Admiral with
reference regulation of the transportation.
Frankou Brigadier General

ΝΑΥΤΙΚΟΝ ΣΗΜΑ

NUPM
Capt Powell
12 ships and sufficient coal Mit
with total carrying capacity of 180
persons each trip await favorable
reply Athens to your generous
before being released stop other
also available stop Expecting rep
every moment stop If favorable
will send some of ships today
and others tonight stop
Call me
Jennings

File 169-22
JBR:WOG.

U. S. S. LITCHFIELD. (#336),
Smyrna, Asia Minor,
22nd September 1922.

Mr. A. K. Jennings,
American Relief Committee,
Mityleni, Greece.

Sir:-

In accordance with orders received at Smyrna from Captain H. Powell, U.S. Navy, (U.S.S. EDSALL), the ships at Mityleni are ordered to proceed to Smyrna for the purpose of transporting refugees to Mityleni.

Ships will not be molested in anyway providing they do not fly the Greek Flag (No flag is necessary), and do not tie up to Quay or Pier.

If desirable, ships can be escorted into and out of the harbor.

If possible send USS EDSALL radio call when ships leave Mityleni for Smyrna. Flour is on the way for Mityleni from Smyrna is a ship.

U.S.S. EDSALL Call "NUPM".

J. B. Rhodes,
Lieutenant-Commander, U.S. Navy,
Commanding U.S.S. LITCHFIELD.

ΝΑΥΤΙΚΟΝ ΣΗΜΑ

Mr Jennings on behalf of American Re
Committee gratefully appreciates the Hell
Governments prompt cooperation in connec
with the transport of the Smyrna Refugees

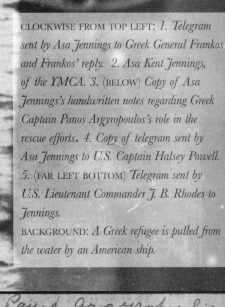

CLOCKWISE FROM TOP LEFT: *1. Telegram sent by Asa Jennings to Greek General Frankos and Frankos' reply. 2. Asa Kent Jennings, of the YMCA. 3.* (BELOW) *Copy of Asa Jennings's handwritten notes regarding Greek Captain Panos Argyropoulos's role in the rescue efforts. 4. Copy of telegram sent by Asa Jennings to U.S. Captain Halsey Powell. 5.* (FAR LEFT BOTTOM) *Telegram sent by U.S. Lieutenant Commander J. B. Rhodes to Jennings.*

BACKGROUND: *A Greek refugee is pulled from the water by an American ship.*

(handwriting of Asa K. Jennings)

Capt Panos Argyropoulos
is hereby appointed to be
in charge of transportation
and direction of ships assigned
to the American Relief Committee
Mitylene during the emergency connected
with the evacuation of Smyrna
and elsewhere due to the advance
of the Kemal army -

    A.K. Jennings
    Chairman Emergency Committee
    Mitylene

BACKGROUND: *Refugees on the quay with American small craft arriving.*
BELOW: *American sailors assist with rescue of the refugees.*

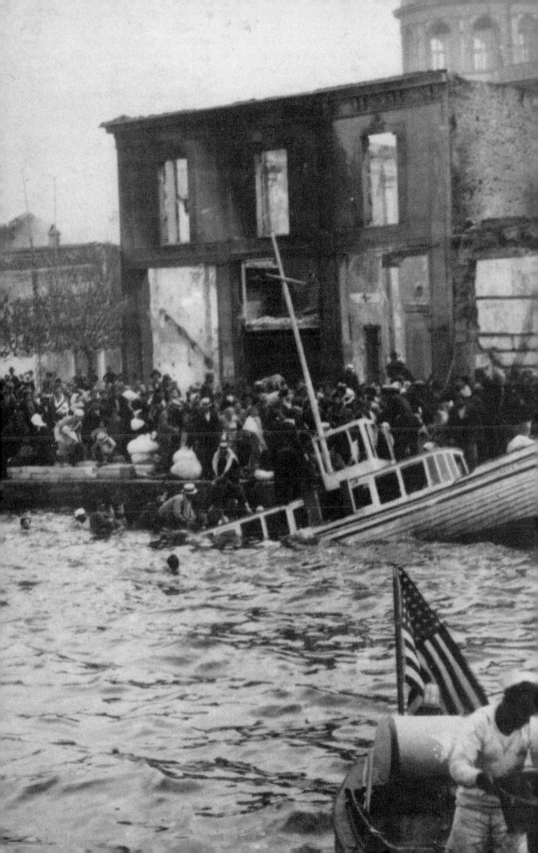

While Jennings was involved in the Smyrna rescue, a political revolution occurred in Greece, and the islands of Mytilene, Chios, and others in
the Aegean came under the control of the revolutionaries. Four days later,
Athens and the rest of Greece followed suit. Jennings feared that the new
government would void the agreements for use of the ships and placement
of the refugees, but this government continued the authorization and the
rescue went as planned.

The sights of Smyrna remained with Jennings for the rest of his life.
"You have no idea what it was like," he recalled. "What would we not
have given for the peace and calm and safety of this night [the night of
the interview]! Those poor creatures had nowhere to go. On three sides
of them were Turkish soldiers, barring the way. Ahead was the harbor and
the open sea, with Turkish soldiers picketed to shoot anyone attempting to
swim away. All they owned was the little they had with them on the quay, for
houses and possessions were in ashes. And to see husbands snatched from
the side of wives, and fathers from little children, was almost too terrible to
endure. I have wondered since many, many times how I lived through those
days. I guess it was because God knew I so much needed strength that He
gave it to me. I can account for it in no other way."

Asa Jennings, an ordinary man, had just saved hundreds of thousands
of Greek citizens from certain death. His conviction that something had to
be done allowed him to overcome obstacles that others might have found
insurmountable.

End Notes

1. Accounts vary about the behavior of the retreating Greek soldiers during the Smyrna rout. This book does not attempt to determine which accounts are true. Some say the Greek soldiers terrorized the citizens and forced all nationals, as well as the Armenians, to abandon their homes and flee; others tell a different story. They note that the Greek army was in tatters. Most soldiers had been fighting for ten years or more; they had just forged deep into Turkish territory over rough terrain. They had then fought a series of major battles, and later were engaged in running skirmishes as they retreated. The army was barely able to evacuate Smyrna, much less engage in violent activities with civilians.

2. The American consul general George Horton became one of the major champions of the Smyrna refugees and relief efforts. On his return to America, he worked tirelessly to draw attention to their plight and to secure aid.

3. This refers to the warehouses controlled by Near East Relief, a nonreligious relief agency that worked to supply food, shelter, education, and medical care for those in need throughout the region. Near East Relief also ran a number of orphanages.

4. Jennings did not realize it, but U.S. battleships were present later on, the USS *Arizona* and USS *Utah* among them. The USS *Mississippi*, renamed the *Kilkis* by the Greeks, served in a largely peacetime capacity, except for a brief period in 1914. During that time, she transported naval aviators to Vera Cruz, when fighting broke out in Mexico. She would be sunk by German bombers during WWII.

5. The actual number of refugees evacuated cannot be verified. Accounts from Jennings and others, including media of the day, vary. Jennings estimates that 250,000 thousand were taken from the Smyrna quay; while a possible total of up to one million were evacuated from Smyrna, surrounding towns, and other parts of Asia Minor. Other accounts say 300,000 from Smyrna alone, and so on.

George Sherwood Eddy

E. O. Jacob and family

CHAPTER 4

Other Voices

A SA JENNINGS'S EFFORTS DID NOT GO UNNOTICED, and soon the world knew of his deeds and of the horrors of Smyrna. Several eyewitnesses, relief workers based in the city, were aware of his actions. In the harbor lay ships not only from America, but also from Great Britain, France, Italy, and Belgium. The officers of these ships recorded in the ships' logs and captains' diaries the events of those chaotic days, including Jennings's role. In addition, as word of Smyrna's plight and Jennings's efforts spread, press dispatches were sent to U.S. media, which later relayed the story to their readers.

Ernst Otto Jacob ("E.O." in his writings) was a traveling secretary for the YMCA stationed in Smyrna at the time of the crisis. Called Jake by his friends, he was a veteran of the Near East, having covered the eastern Mediterranean from Greece to Egypt since 1910. He had spent much of his time within the Turkish empire. From September 1 through September 30, 1922, he kept a diary of events in the city.[1] This diary was later passed to D. A. Davis of the YMCA in Geneva, Switzerland. Here Jacob notes the events of September 24:

"The first batch of Greek ships arrives with Jennings, convoyed by an American destroyer. Turkish authorities give strict orders that they must lie well out in the bay, with embarkation to be by boats and lighters, a terribly slow and tedious process. At the last moment, Griswold, an American businessman, cajoles the harbor master to give permission that ships might tie up to the Aldin Railroad piers, thus vastly facilitating the task. 15,000 out of a mob of 50,000 were taken off by us today in stifling heat and dust amidst indescribable, crushing confusion, robberies and beatings by Turkish soldiers, and sickening wails of mothers, wives and children as sons and husbands were seized for deportation. One consolation carries us through this inferno: some do get away. Outsiders often tell us that all is futile: that in Mytilene they will freeze and starve just the same as here. To my mind the difference is that between heaven and hell. Whatever may be suffered in Mytilene, it will be among friends who will be doing their best to help them. In Smyrna, hunger and exposure are the least of the evils: persecution, deportation, robbery, rape, murder—those are going on now, and the victims are justified in dreading that they will go on until the last of their races are extinguished."

On September 26, Jacob again documents the rescue:

"Seventeen boats. 'Commodore' Jennings of the Y.M.C.A. in charge, load from 35,000 to 43,000 people. A horrible day, but what a relief to see the crammed ships pull out. The Americans, civil and naval, engage in a watchful patrol of all the points where there are Turkish police and soldiers. This by no means eliminates the robbery and beating. It certainly does vastly decrease it. Would that we could dissuade all men of military age from trying to run this half-mile gauntlet. Small chances do they have against four barrages of sharp-eyed police and military officers who ferret out even those in disguise and tear them away from their families. If only they kept to the prescribed age limits! Thousands were taken at the pier alone. ...no less than 50,000 have been sent out—in very truth a life sentence, though probably of short duration."

Howard B. Grose, a doctor of divinity, was another commentator. In a *New York Times* article from July 8, 1923, he offers his account of the rescue:

"For hours, while horror reigned on the crowded quays of the city, Jennings pleaded with and finally demanded that the Greek government do its part in the emergency. He won at last, and all Greek merchant ships in the Aegean were placed under his command. With his own small American flag at the masthead of one of the vessels, he led the fleet into Smyrna under the escort of the U.S. destroyer Lawrence, and the work of evacuating refugees was immediately begun. A total of fifty ships, large and small, including two transatlantic liners, were employed in the work, which continued day and night for the week ending September 30—the final day permitted by the Turkish authorities for taking out refugees. Conspicuous service was rendered by the sailors of the American fleet.

"Commander Powell [commander of the U.S. destroyer *Litchfield*] states: 'The ships were brought into the harbor under the command of Mr. Jennings of the Y.M.C.A., and were escorted and loaded by officers and men of American destroyers. It was only through the energy and zeal and stubborn insistence of Mr. Jennings that these ships were obtained.'"

Dr. George Sherwood Eddy was with the Foreign Division of The International Committee of the YMCA His account, "Can Jennings Work Another Miracle?" also appeared in the *New York Times* on July 8, 1923. He described Jennings's rescue as "the almost unbelievable tale of an unknown little American."

"[I]t was on his birthday that he [Jennings] seemed to hear God tell him to get ships and save those perishing refugees. Permission was granted by the Turkish authorities to take away all the refugees if transportation could be secured in the ten days remaining before midnight on September 30, 1922. The commander eagerly turned the American destroyers into cargo boats to bring food supplies from Constantinople, and tens of thousands were fed in camps along the shore."

Eddy reports Jennings's frustrating go-round with the Greek government regarding use of their ships. He writes:

"At last, driven to desperation, at four o'clock in the afternoon this little man rose up in his wrath and sent an ultimatum to the whole Greek government. He demanded the ships and threatened to decode his message and tell the world what was taking place. After a meeting of the cabinet, the Greek government cabled, handing over not only twenty ships but finally fifty vessels, including all the Greek ships in the Aegean.

"Taking out his little American flag, which had been three times fired upon, and running up a signal flag, 'Follow me,' Jennings hoisted these to the masthead of his flag ship, and with the order, 'full steam ahead,' dashed for Smyrna to rescue the perishing Greeks along the shore. The American naval forces rendered heroic service in loading the ships. On the first day they saved over ten thousand; on the third day they loaded seventeen vessels and took away 43,000 refugees. Before the last day ended, 300,000 men, women and children had been fed and taken safely away to Greek territory."

William T. Ellis wrote of Jennings's exploits and of the role of the American Navy and relief workers for the *Saturday Evening Post* on October 23, 1923:

"So with 'Commodore' Jennings on the bridge of the foremost boat, the flotilla of mercy set sail for Smyrna. At dawn, as prophesied by Jennings, an American destroyer was found loafing about the entrance to the channel; and how could it object if 'Commodore' Jennings and his fleet followed its course through the minefield to the inner harbor of burnt Smyrna, where the once beautiful Bund was heaped high with a human cargo of misery?

"[I]t will never be told how the American navy, officers and men, did stevedoring work in getting that motely mass of misery separated and assorted and aboard the Greek boats. Not even a little chantey survives to tell of the children carried in the arms of American sailors. There was no help available ashore except American—the Greek merchant sailors dared not set foot on the Bund; the British were too closely identified with the ill-fated Greek military adventure to be free to circulate on shore. Only Americans—naval men, missionaries, teachers, and relief workers—were at call for this huge task of evacuation for which Jennings had accepted the responsibility. They must ever share with him the glory of one of the most singular feats of human service in history.

"As pledged by the landlubber 'commodore,' in his message to Athens, all of the ships were returned safely to Greek harbors, after the three hundred and fifty thousand refugees had been transported aboard ship without the loss of a single life. It was efficiency walking hand in hand with audacity and altruism."

The Associated Press picked up the story, broadcasting this article around the world, dateline Mytilene, September 28, 1922: "Amid the scene of disorder and excitement a dramatic figure was A.K. Jennings of New York, of the Near East Relief[2], who is attempting single-handed to alleviate the sufferings and quiet the fears of the distracted fugitives. On the initiative and enterprise of Jennings a steady stream of boats is kept running between Mytilene Island and Smyrna, taking off refugees from the inland and survivors of the Smyrna fire. At first the captains of the Greek boats refused to go to Smyrna, fearing they would be seized by the Kemalists[3], but Mr. Jennings arranged to have them discard their Greek flags and convoyed by American torpedo boat destroyers to Smyrna. Through his resourcefulness

Mr. Jennings doubtless was the means of saving thousands of persons from fire and famine. He has won the admiration of the entire island.

"The untiring devotion of the American bluejackets has stirred the emotion of the population of Mytilene, who are thrilled at the presence of the Stars and Stripes thousands of miles from American shores."

A *New York Times* story, that ran on July 8, 1923, opened as follows:

"When the Aquitania arrived last week, there walked down the gangplank, avoiding reporters, a short, middle-aged American who carried, stored away in his baggage, the highest civilian and military awards of the Greek government[4], and in his mind, the recollection of a unique experience in saving 300,000 lives. The man was Asa K. Jennings, of Utica, N.Y., one time minister, now of the YMCA, who was converted by a whim of fate, from a worker among boys in Smyrna, to, virtually, the Admiral of a fleet of fifty ships, engaged in carrying refugees from the city, after it burned last September.

"Press dispatches to newspapers in this country, at the time of the disaster, credited Jennings with being largely responsible for the rescue of 300,000 refugees. He himself gave an account of his experiences upon his arrival in the Hotel Bristol from the ship. Those who heard it characterized it as a uniquely American experience—the story of a man who, when suddenly confronted by a strange and awful calamity, faces and overcomes it."

The *New York Times* account ends thus:

"That evening he started out with seven ships from Mytilene. Three more followed the same night. The next day 43,000 refugees were loaded in Smyrna, and during the following week the whole 300,000 were evacuated. All of this time, Mr. Jennings said, he did not go to bed, did not take off his clothes and slept only during the rare intervals when he could find a few minutes to set down. During this entire time, as well as for some weeks following, the fleet was at Mr. Jennings' disposal. He directed the movements of each ship, planning the distribution of the refugees over the Greek islands and mainland from Asia Minor. After these had been evacuated from Smyrna, many had to be redistributed so that Mr. Jennings estimated the entire number of people moved as 500,000.

"At the end of the experience, Mr. Jennings found himself known to his fellow Americans as 'The Admiral,' a sobriquet which stuck to him to the day he left the Near East.

"In recounting his experience, Mr. Jennings minimizes his personal participation and stresses the work of the American relief organizations, and the United States Navy, which made the rescue work possible. 'In the Smyrna disaster the United States demonstrated new humanitarian uses to which a navy can be put,' he said. 'The saving of the refugees would also have been impossible, he pointed out, but for the work of the Near East Relief, the Red Cross and the American Women's Hospitals, which with the YMCA, represented the people of the United States.'"

An Associated Press story out of Athens, printed in the *New York Times* on October 14, 1922, includes this account: "The United States Government through its Charge d'Affaires here, Jefferson Caffery, has taken steps for the dispatch to Greece of an American Red Cross mission to handle the refugee situation here. News of this action, coupled with the announcement that the Red Cross has appropriated an additional $300,000 for relief work, has immensely cheered the Greek people. The tragedy of the refugee problem lies in the fact that virtually all able bodied Greeks and Armenians in Asia Minor were deported into the interior as prisoners of the Turks, and that Greece today must succor several hundred thousand women and children who will henceforth have no husbands and fathers to provide for their wants.

"A.K. Jennings of the Y.M.C.A., arriving here from Mytilene, has been informed by wireless that 20,000 more refugees, without food or clothes, are awaiting rescue on the shores of Asia Minor, near Adali and Makri. Steps are being taken to save them. At the time of the Smyrna disaster, Mr. Jennings sent an urgent wireless to the Government at Athens asking for immediate mobilization of a fleet of fifty merchant ships. The Government speedily acquiesced,[5] and all Athens declared today that it was chiefly due to the enterprise of Mr. Jennings that some 300,000 refugees were rescued."

In the story, Jennings is quoted as saying, "Heroic treatment is needed during a long period. There are 80,000 refugees at Mytilene today. Most of them are sleeping in the open air, and every inch of ground seems covered with a human form. At the beginning the babies had only warm water to live on, and at Chios and Samos they did not even have that. That is the awful feature in this tragedy. There are hungry, homeless children and tottering old men roaming about scanning the sea and waiting for help from some land of hope. I am confident that America is that land of hope."

Another Associated Press article, datelined Constantinople, October 13, 1922, addresses the need for funds to help the refugees survive the winter, and recognizes the significant commitment by the United States:

"The exodus of Christians from Turkish territory will include more than 1,250,000 persons, says the appeal issued by Meletios Metaxakis, the Greek Patriarch at Constantinople, asking for aid to facilitate the evacuation and decrease the suffering.

"The Patriarch, in the appeal, says there are 500,000 Christians in Asia Minor, 300,000 in Eastern Thrace and 450,000 in Constantinople. He says the entire fund contributed thus far by the outside world for the care of the refugees is slightly more than $1,000,000 and is tabulated as follows: American Near East Relief, $400,000; Great Britain, $200,000; American Red Cross, $100,000; contributions sent directly to the Patriarch, $250,000; American Women's Hospital, $25,000; American committees in the Near East, $25,000 and the Y.M.C.A. and Y.W.C.A., $20,000. . . . The Patriarch expressed his gratitude to the United States in these words: 'It is a great debt that the Greek people owe to the United States for their help at the beginning of the present emergency. The most striking feature of the American relief organizations in the Near East is their ability to act quickly. 'He gives twice who gives speedily,' says the Greek proverb.'

"The Patriarch mentioned particularly in this connection the work of H.C. Jaquith, director of American Near East Relief, and A.K. Jennings of Syracuse, N.Y., of the Y.M.C.A. The latter commanded the entire Greek fleet of fifty merchant ships in the Smyrna evacuation."

Jennings was also recognized in *The Story of Near East Relief*, which recounts the work of that agency around the world. In its retelling of the Smyrna tragedy, the author writes:

"After the fire, the only solution to the vast unwelcome refugee problem was evacuation. There was only one place they [the refugees] could go and that was to Greece which would not close its doors. The Turkish authorities facilitated the exodus of the women and children, but no Greek ships dared venture into Smyrna harbor for fear of confiscation. The energy and ingenuity of Asa K. Jennings, a member of the local relief committee from the Y.M.C.A., solved the question. Admiral Bristol assured him of the presence and aid of American destroyers at all points of embarkation. The Turkish officials agreed to recognize accompanying ships as under convoy and protection. The Greek government furnished the necessary ships under these conditions. As many as 45,000 refugees were removed from Smyrna daily until the entire surviving Christian population was transferred to the Greek islands of Chios, Samos and Mytilene and to Salonica and Athens.

"The peace time service of the American navy is deserving of the widest possible recognition. It is a chapter in the naval history that has never been as yet adequately told. The American high commissioner in Constantinople, Admiral Bristol, had assigned to him a squadron of destroyers. As many as twenty naval vessels were in the eastern Mediterranean at the time. Regular communication was maintained between Black Sea and Mediterranean ports with relays of destroyers stationed in all the principal harbors. These were the days following the war when commercial transportation was struggling back to service. They were days when peace had not come to the Near East, and ordinary vessels did not dare venture into many of the ports. American business and relief personnel were transported by the courtesy and efficiency of the navy. Radio communications were maintained uninterrupted by means of the destroyers stationed in each harbor of importance in constant contact by radio with the base-ship in Constantinople."

The *Near East Relief* account concludes, "During and following the events at Smyrna, the service of the navy was strikingly conspicuous. Destroyers carried refugees and children to points of safety the night of the fire. Relief supplies and personnel were carried to scenes of need Greek ships brought to embark the refugees were escorted by American destroyers to assure their safe departure from Turkish ports, and the officers and men assisted in the humanitarian and orderly loading of refugee ships. The cooperation of the American high commissioner, Admiral Bristol, was always unstinted, timely and sympathetic, and this spirit was reflected in all of the officers and men."

The *New York Times* continued its coverage of the Smyrna saga with a follow-up story on December 10, 1922. Here are excerpts:

"The work of the flotilla of American destroyers in the Levant during the trying period of the evacuation of the Greeks, Armenians, and others in the exodus from Smyrna and other Asiatic ports has, according to reports reaching U.S. Naval Secretary Edwin Denby, measured up to the very best traditions of the American naval service.

"It is understood that the conduct of and services rendered by the American naval representatives, as well as by the American relief organizations in the Near East, besides earning praise from the Greeks and other nationalities that were assisted, also won the admiration of the Turk nationalist leaders.

"Among the communications received by Secretary Denby dealing with the service rendered are letters written by Admiral Sir Osmond de Brock, K.C.B., Commander-in-Chief of the British Mediterranean fleet, and Cass Arthur Reed, Acting President of the International College at Smyrna. . . . Admiral Brock praises in particular the work of Commander Halsey Powell [U.S.], and the men under his command, of the destroyer *Edsall*."

The British commander's letter was excerpted in the *Times* as follows:

"At the commencement of the evacuation, a limit of time was set for the refugees being permitted to depart, and speed of embarkation was essential. In my opinion, Commander Powell of the U.S.S. *Edsall* is deserving of the greatest commendation. The ships working for the American Relief Committee were under his supervision, and American sailors under his orders provided barrier and gate guards. He was in personal touch and tactful in his dealings with Turkish authorities. I am of opinion that the successful evacuation of so large a number of refugees is largely due to his own personal efforts and also to the officers and men serving under his command."

More than six months later, the Smyrna evacuation was still making news. The *New York Times* ran this story on June 24, 1923, datelined Constantinople:

"The United States has spent $18,000,000 for relief work in the Near East since the Smyrna disaster, according to the Athens newspaper Logos, organ of the Revolutionary Government. The total was divided as follows: Near East Relief, $8,000,000; the American Women's Hospital and other specialized organizations, $1,000,000; the Admiral Coundouriotis fund and organizations supported by Greeks in America, $1,000,000; the Red Cross expended $2,000,000 and individual remittances from America were $5,000,000.

"America's contribution is eight times the amount received from all other countries for Near East relief. Half of the American money was devoted to work in Greece and the rest in Asia Minor, Syria, Palestine, Armenia and Persia. The Logos says the two most striking features of the American administration were, firstly, the honest and efficient supervision insured by the experienced Americans placed in charge of the distributions, and, secondly, that the major part of the money was spent in America for supplies which were transported to the Near East, thus not only helping American producers but preventing the depletion of the Near Eastern markets at a time when the demand greatly exceeded the supply.

"The Greek Government, in recognition of the work of the administration, voted the award of the highest civil honor, the Cross of Saint Xaviour, to one hundred members of the American Relief Missions. The first of these awards, announced today, went to Charles Fowle of Near York,[6] Foreign Secretary of the Near East Relief."

Thus the story of Jennings's efforts, the plight of the refugees, and the tragedy of Smyrna traveled around the world. The crisis was major news. Those involved found their lives changed forever—not just the refugees, but all who lived it, from the relief workers and medical teams to the captains and crews of the ships in the harbor.

End Notes

1. Excerpts from E. O. Jacob's diary were reprinted in several newspaper accounts.

2. The AP story linked Jennings with Near East Relief, but he was with the YMCA. However, both groups worked closely together.

3. The Kemalists were those who support Moustapha Kemal, an army officer who led the Turkish revolt and was in power in Turkey at the time of the Smyrna disaster.

4. The awarding of medals by the Greek government to Asa Jennings is discussed in chapter 9.

5. The Greek government actually did not act speedily to give Jennings his ships. It was fearful of its craft being lost to the Turks, despite protection from American ships and the Turks' promise not to harm the transports. If Greece lost its navy, the Greek isles would be wide open to Turkish naval assault. The Greeks complied only when Jennings issued his ultimatum—threatening to tell the world of their delay.

6. This is probably a typographical error—it should say "New York."

CHAPTER 5

Ships' and Captains' Logs

*What thou seest, write in a book, and send it unto the seven
churches, which are in Asia; unto Ephesus, and unto Smyrna,
and unto Pergamos, and unto Thyatira, and unto Sardis, and
unto Philadelphia, and unto Laodicea.*
                                        —Revelation 1:1.

RESTING AT ANCHOR IN THE SMYRNA HARBOR WERE
numerous ships from five countries: the United States, Great Britain, Italy,
France, and Belgium. Each nation had citizens based in the city of Smyrna
or in nearby towns. The ships had arrived to keep an eye on things as the
Greek/Turkish conflict escalated. When the ships first came into port, the
city was relatively quiet. The Greek army had been routed and the city was
resigned to its fate. The Turkish army would arrive at any time, and life
would change for all within Smyrna's boundaries.

As September progressed, the situation in Smyrna worsened. Vast
numbers of refugees poured into the city and soon the ships' crews could
see a teeming mass of humanity crowded on the quay. Tempers flared
between the Turks and the Greek citizens, creating episodes of violence. By
the middle of the month, fires had broken out and those shipboard watched
in horror as the shoreline of Smyrna was slowly consumed by flames.

The captains of these ships were in a delicate position. The Allies—
Great Britain, France, Italy, and Belgium—had been at war with Turkey
during World War I and relations with the new Turkish regime were

Refugees on board an American rescue ship. The man in the Panama hat in the background (top left) is believed to be Asa Jennings.

sensitive. The United States had not declared war with Turkey during the Great War, and were directed to remain neutral. America's non-action had been guided by President Wilson's sympathetic interest in the relief efforts conducted by American organizations in Turkey. Therefore, when armed hostilities broke out, even though Turkey aligned with Germany, Wilson withheld a formal declaration of war and instead simply severed diplomatic relations. This allowed American relief efforts to continue.

The Turks, for their part, honored the decision and American relief workers were allowed to remain at their stations. In an unprecedented move, monies for the relief work flowed into Turkey even though she was allied with enemies of the United States. Throughout World War I, U.S. agencies, especially Near East Relief, continued to run orphanages, hospitals, and soup kitchens in Turkey.

Thus, in September 1922, the relationship between the United States and Turkey was a complex one, with a delicate peace being maintained. For U.S. ships to act could be interpreted as a political statement. The officers of these ships were well aware of all the nuances involved in their actions. Officially, they were pledged only to protect and evacuate citizens from their own countries. But as the suffering of the refugees increased, the need for humanitarian aid outweighed diplomatic issues. American officers were quick to organize relief efforts, and when Asa Jennings requested ships, the

U.S., British, Italian, and French vessels responded. For their part, the Turks were cooperative in allowing the rescue to take place.

In September 1922, nine U.S. naval ships were operating in Smyrna waters. They were: the destroyers USS *Litchfield*, USS *Lawrence*, USS *Simpson*, USS *Hopkins*, USS *King*, and USS *Gregory;* the USS *Edsall;* the flagship USS *Scorpion;* and the battleships USS *Arizona* and USS *Utah*, plus other smaller vessels. All but the *Utah* and *Arizona* were under the command of Rear Admiral Mark L. Bristol, U.S. High Commissioner for Turkey. Records from the Office of the Chief of Naval Operations, Naval History Division, in Washington, D.C., indicate that the *Litchfield* had a heroic history:

"Litchfield served in humanitarian causes and was an instrument of American foreign policy as Admiral Bristol's destroyers evacuated 260,000 Greek and Armenian refugees after a fire swept Smyrna, Turkey, 13 September. The destroyers also assisted civilian relief agencies attempting to feed and evacuate additional thousands suffering from famine and war."

The USS *Edsall* was similarly recognized in the U.S. Naval Archives:

"She did much for international relations by helping nations to alle-viate postwar famine in eastern Europe, evacuating refugees, furnishing a center of communications for the Near East, and all the while standing by for emergencies. When the Turks set fire to Smyrna (Izmir), Edsall was one of the American destroyers who evacuated thousands of Greeks. On 14 September 1922 she took 607 refugees off Litchfield (DD-336) in Smyrna and transported them to Salonika, returning to Smyrna 16 September to act as flagship for the naval forces there. In October she carried refugees from Smyrna to Mytilene on Lesvos. She made repeated visits to ports in Turkey, Bulgaria, Russia, Greece, Egypt, Palestine, Syria, Tunisia, Dalmatia, and Italy, yet managed to keep up gunnery and torpedo practice with her sisters until her return to Boston for overhaul 26 July 1924."

Commendations are in the U.S. Naval Department files for the other American ships for their work at Smyrna. Yet it is the accounts from the captains' logs and ships' logs that capture the events of that September. In terse but nonetheless compelling language, they describe the horrific situation at Smyrna, the role of Jennings, and the assistance of the U.S. Navy, among others.

◙ ◙ ◙

The flotilla of rescue ships.

Admiral Mark Bristol was a career military officer who had a keen interest in the Near East. He had close ties with missionary educators in the region, often visiting their homes, and frequently presided over activities at functions of American-run schools. In general, he was considered able, friendly, and straightforward, if a bit verbose on occcasion. He had admired the discipline of the Turkish military, and was sometimes accused of being a Turkophile, but others said he attempted to treat each of the ethnic communities in the Ottoman Empire equally. In fact, as early as July 18, 1921, Bristol cabled a protest directly to Moustapha Kemal, asking him to stop the deportations of Greeks from Samsun. He also cabled the Secretary of State, noting that the situation in Turkey was growing critical. The State Department was not pleased with Bristol's actions in contacting Kemal, believing that Kemal should not even be acknowledged. Nonetheless, they couldn't completely disapprove of Bristol's actions if they saved lives. Bristol would play a key role in the rescue, both as admiral and later as U.S. High Commissioner to Turkey.

Admiral Bristol's flagship was the USS *Scorpion*, under the command of Captain A. M. Hepburn, his chief of staff. Hepburn was in command of Smyrna forces until September 16, when he was relieved by Commander Halsey Powell. Admiral Bristol filed the following report with U.S. Secretary of the Navy Denby on March 23, 1924, regarding actions in Smyrna

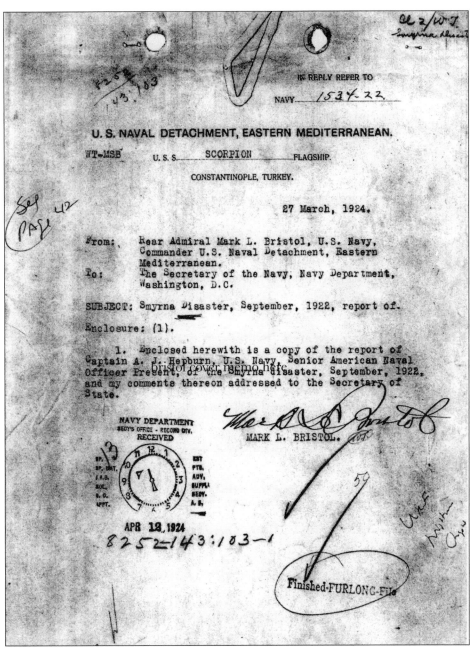

IN REPLY REFER TO

NAVY 1534-22

U. S. NAVAL DETACHMENT, EASTERN MEDITERRANEAN.

WT-MSB

U. S. S. SCORPION FLAGSHIP.

CONSTANTINOPLE, TURKEY.

27 March, 1924.

From: Rear Admiral Mark L. Bristol, U.S. Navy,
Commander U.S. Naval Detachment, Eastern
Mediterranean.

To: The Secretary of the Navy, Navy Department,
Washington, D.C.

SUBJECT: Smyrna Disaster, September, 1922, report of.

Enclosure: (1).

1. Enclosed herewith is a copy of the report of
Captain A. J. Hepburn, U.S. Navy, Senior American Naval
Officer Present, of the Smyrna disaster, September, 1922,
and my comments thereon addressed to the Secretary of
State.

MARK L. BRISTOL.

NAVY DEPARTMENT
SEOY'S OFFICE - RECORD DIV.
RECEIVED

APR 12 1924

8252-143:103-1

Finished-FURLONG-File

The cover memo of a U.S. Navy War Diary, set forth from Admiral Mark Bristol to the Secretary of the Navy on March 27, 1924. This is a declassified Navy document.

Harbor in September 1922. His report also includes extensive excerpts from Captain Hepburn's log. These documents describe the delicate situation U.S. naval forces found themselves in while anchored at Smyrna:

"The first destroyer sent to Smyrna on September 6, 1922 was the USS LITCHFIELD under command of Lt. Commander J.B. Rhodes," wrote Bristol. "As was customary under such circumstances, the commanding officer of the destroyer had a personal conference with me before leaving. Captain Hepburn, Chief of Staff, was present at the conference and the instructions then given were the same as were given to other Commanding Officers proceeding on the same duty. I took occasion to carefully define the position of America with relation to Turkey and cautioned Lt. Commander Rhodes to make himself thoroughly familiar with the international law covering such a situation, but as modified by the existing peculiar conditions. I called his attention to the fact that there would be a number of Allied ships in port and that these Allies were at war with Turkey while the United States was not. This would require the Senior Officer present of the American Naval forces to be very careful not to cooperate with the Allies, while, at the same time coordinating his work with them on a purely humanitarian basis."

The report mentions that other U.S. ships soon joined the *Litchfield*. "The LITCHFIELD arrived in Smyrna on 6 of September 1922. It was reinforced by the SIMPSON arriving that same day, and the LAWRENCE arrived with Captain Hepburn on board on 9 September 1922."

Admiral Bristol's report describes the other ships in the Smyrna Harbor that September. The harbor was busy and ships of every stripe were in port. Because of the recent skirmishes between Greece and Turkey, nations with an interest in Smyrna were keeping a watchful eye on the proceedings. Each country present was concerned for the safety of its citizens still in Turkey.

"When the LITCHFIELD arrived at Smyrna at daylight on 6 September 1922," the report continues, "the following foreign men-of-war were in port: two British battleships and six destroyers, three French cruisers and two destroyers, one Italian light cruiser and one destroyer, two Greek battleships, one light cruiser and two destroyers."

Bristol goes on: "There was one division of Greek troops on board transports ready to disembark for the defense of Smyrna. The commanding officer of the LITCHFIELD, Lt. Commander Rhodes, exchanged the usual calls of courtesy with the foreign men-of-war and with the American Consul General. The British Admiral believed that, in case of rioting, there would be little chance of preventing it, because of the narrow and crooked streets and the general layout of the city."

In these early days of September, it was clear that a crisis was looming. The tension was palpable as waves of retreating Greek troops rushed through the city and panicked civilians joined the flight. Everyone knew the Turkish army was close behind.

Admiral Bristol records the scene:

"At the time of the arrival of the LITCHFIELD, there was already a state of panic in Smyrna. Greek troops were pouring into the city without arms or were selling their arms to the people within the city. There was no fight left in these men. Also, refugees were streaming into Smyrna and all kinds of wild rumors were current of burning and pillaging in the interior. . . . At this time, refugees were obtaining all kinds of floating craft in the harbor to leave the city . . ."

In his log, Captain Hepburn wrote that as they arrived in Smyrna at 8:30 on the morning of September 9, a long, straggling line of Greek cavalry was making its way toward the harbor. There a Greek battleship was waiting to pick up these last troops. Already small craft filled with refugees were also setting sail. Later that day, the Turkish army would arrive. Greek officials had already fled, and Smyrna was entirely without government, but at this point calm. When Turkish troops marched into the city at about 11:30 in the morning, there was a stampede of refugees up the road from the quay and shots were fired. The shots were retaliatory rifle fire from the Turks after a small bomb had been thrown in their midst. According to Hepburn's report, six to eight citizens were killed, but then order was reestablished. Later that day, Hepburn made contact with the commander of this Turkish advance force, General Murcelle Pasha, and asked permission to have guards at strategic locations in the American quarter for the sake of keeping order. Pasha readily agreed, and the two then discussed relief options. Again, Pasha was open to the request and the foundation was laid for future talks.

. . . continued on page 80

BACKGROUND: *Faces of the refugees aboard the rescue ships—a mix of emotions is felt, for while they are rescued, their future is uncertain. Every available surface is filled in order to move as many people as possible.*

BELOW: *Refugee children aboard a rescue ship. These may very well be orphans, as the U.S. Navy rescued several thousand orphans during the Smyrna catastrophe.*

As evening approached, Hepburn watched the town from shipboard. He described the waterfront as dark except for regular city lights. All the shops and cafés, once so vibrant, were closed. Occasionally, the quiet was punctuated by bursts of rifle fire. As feared, looting by some Turkish irregulars and others had begun. On Monday, Captain Hepburn drove through sections of the city. He recorded that the Armenian quarter was in the most disarray, with more than thirty-five bodies in the street. Looting by Turkish civilians was blatant. Hepburn could see that with tensions seething under the surface, an explosion was unavoidable. His report states that, in his opinion, resolving the refugee crisis was paramount to keeping the peace. But how to remove thousands of people?

The Turks now had a military governor in place, Noureddin Pasha, and according to his log, Captain Hepburn arranged for a meeting on September 11. Accompanied by a representative from Near East Relief who spoke fluent Turkish, Captain Hepburn asked about provisions for the refugees. Could they be returned to their homes? Hepburn writes that Pasha's answer was a vehement no, as he blamed the retreating Greek army for devastating the countryside. Pasha's answer was: "Bring ships and take them out of the country. It is the only solution."

At this point, even American citizens had not yet begun to leave Smyrna, but as soon as Pasha passed an edict allowing this exodus, the evacuation began. All American-born citizens and naturalized citizens were free to go, but a passport or other proof of citizenship was required. The citizens of other nations received the same instructions.

Concern was also growing for the American civilians still onshore at Smyrna. Lieutenant Commander Rhodes, of the USS *Litchfield*, landed a party of guards to set up outposts at key locations within the American district. If the situation worsened, American civilians would gather at these points for evacuation. Even before the arrival of the Turkish troops, some killing, looting, and burning had taken place. With the Turkish army now in place and hundreds of refugees fleeing the city, the situation would only deteriorate.

On September 13, as each nation began evacuating its citizens, refugees congregated at the piers, desperate for passage. Captain Hepburn noted that "the quay became thronged with . . . refugees that crowded to the evacuation points in the hope of begging, forcing, or stealing a passage for themselves. Though there was at this time no alarm because of fire, the nervousness of the refugees was such that it was inadvisable to bring a small boat alongside the quay without a sufficient guard to prevent the crowd from swarming into it and swamping it."

About two in the afternoon, three fires broke out at the Armenian compound. As recorded in Captain Hepburn's log, the American naval officer stationed nearby believed these fires were started with the object of smoking out the thousand or more refugees who had taken shelter in the various buildings. Throughout the afternoon the fire spread, gaining strength and heading toward the waterfront. Terrified citizens fled before it. "Returning to the street, I found the stampede from the fire just beginning," writes Captain Hepburn. "All of the refugees that had been scattered through the streets or stowed away in churches or other institutions were moving toward the waterfront. Steadily augmenting this flow were those abandoning their homes in the path of the fire."

Captain Hepburn goes on to capture the scene at nightfall:

"It was now dark. The quay was already well filled with tens of thousands of terrified refugees moving aimlessly between the custom house and the Point, and still the steady stream of new arrivals continued until the entire waterfront seemed one solid congested mass of humanity and luggage of every description.

". . . the appalling nature of the catastrophe began to make itself felt," he continues. "From the Point to the Passport Office, a distance of about a mile, the broad waterfront street appeared to be one solidly packed mass of humanity, domestic animals, vehicles and luggage. Beyond, still separated from the crowd by a few short unburned blocks, the city was a mass of flame driving directly down upon the waterfront before a stiff breeze. Mingled with the noise of the wind and flames and the crash of falling buildings were the sounds of frequent sharp reports, such has might have been made either by rifle fire or the explosion of small-arms ammunition and bombs in the burning area. High above all other sounds was the continuous wail of terror from the multitude. There was no movement of the crowd toward the natural exits to safety in the direction of the Konak[1] or around the Point. The practical destruction of the entire wretched horde, either by fire or drowning, seemed inevitable."

Major C. Claflin Davis, of the American Red Cross, and Mark Prentiss, of Near East Relief, met with Captain Hepburn to discuss rescuing the refugees. They did not have enough boats to convey this great mass

Greek ship while convoyed to anchorage in Smyrna harbor. The first ship, ISMINI, on which I travelled, had wireless which we used constantly. We experienced great difficulty in getting in touch with EDSALL as she seemed to be working constantly with Constantinople. However, we sent radio of our departure and where we wished destroyer to meet us which communication was picked up by EDSALL. Later efforts were picked up by LAWRENCE.

Arrived Long Island about 4.30 a.m. and left about 10:30 a.m. We were met by Captain Wollsson, commanding LAWRENCE, and continued to anchorage in Smyrna harbor.

The Greek battleship KILKIS was ordered elsewhere when we left Mytilene and was replaced by the ADRIATIKIS, under command of Captain Dedes, to whom Captain Theofanides turned over his orders, regarding Mytilene and sending the boats to Smyrna. We may use his radio call for Mytilene if desired.

Other boats are available and ready to leave for Smyrna on same conditions when the word is given. Committee will be ready to receive refugees upon arrival on the Island of Mytilene. The Government of Mytilene is also taking up the matter with the Government at Athens with reference to transporting the refugees elsewhere.

The immediate need for flour at Mytilene is imperative. We must have flour within 24 hours or there will be a food panic and riot on the Island. All are now depending on our promise that flour will arrive immediately. The knowledge that flour has actually been landed will calm all and help us in controlling the situation.

Upon the arrival of the 7 ships leaving Smyrna tonight, approximately 15,000 people, there will be 90,000 refugees on the Island of Mytilene.

Jennings.

Asa Jennings, in the white Panama-style hat, supervises the unloading of supplies for refugees at Mytilene. Also shown is a copy of the telegram sent by Asa Jennings regarding the desperate need for flour in Mytilene. Mytilene was where many of the rescued refugees were initially taken. Jennings notes that by nightfall, there will be 90,000 refugees in Mytilene.

of humanity from shore to their ships, and their ships were already laden with rescued American personnel. Captain Hepburn asked Davis to enlist the assistance of Admiral Dumeanil of the French fleet, whom Davis knew personally. Davis was to request that the admiral assist in pulling a number of large cargo lighters moored at the inner basis to the outer quay in an attempt to save some of the refugees. Dumeanil was unavailable, still involved in evacuating French nationals, so Davis approached Admiral de Brock, of the British flagship. Even though it was well past midnight, within minutes after Davis's return to the *Litchfield*, the British gave the signal for "Away all boats." Boats large enough to be of service, power launches, crews in uniform, and boat officers ranking from captain to midshipman set sail for shore.

After filling to capacity with refugees, they returned to the *Litchfield*, unloading 671 evacuees, according to Hepburn. (This created a heavy deckload, and thereafter, refugees were taken to other vessels lying farther offshore.) After promptly feeding the refugees, the decision was then made to send them to Salonica. Fortunately, the USS *Edsall* was only an hour or two away. She was due to arrive about daylight with some thirty tons of flour for the Disaster Relief Committee. According to Hepburn's report, the refugees were then transferred to the *Edsall* and sent with sufficient flour for several days' rations after landing. On Thursday, September 14, Captain Hepburn recorded these notes in his log:

"The U.S.S. EDSALL arrived just before daylight: went alongside LITCHFIELD and after discharging her cargo of flour, embarked the refugees on the LITCHFIELD and sailed for Salonika about 8:00 A.M. These were the first refugees to leave after the breaking out of the fire, except for those foreigners whose evacuation had been determined upon before the fire and which was already underway by the time the fire had become a general menace."

. . . *continued on page 86*

BACKGROUND: USS Edsall, *flagship of the American fleet.*
TOP RIGHT: USS Simpson
BOTTOM RIGHT: USS Litchfield
BOTTOM LEFT: USS Lawrence
OVAL: *Lieutenant Commander J. B. Rhodes*

The fire continued to burn fiercely throughout September 14, reaching the waterfront about 1:30 in the morning, according to Hepburn's log. The naval war diary of the USS *Utah* reports that at times the heat was so intense that it could be felt by the ships in the harbor. The diary tells us: "On the quay, the heat was so great the refugees took cover under water-soaked carpets and blankets or any other of their belongings which would protect them from the intense heat and keep sparks from their bodies." Eventually, the fire began to burn itself out in places, and the mass of refugees huddled onshore shuttled from one burned-out area to the next.

As Captain Hepburn watched the spectacle, he saw that it was increasingly apparent that all refugees throughout Asia Minor would need to be evacuated. This was an undertaking beyond the scope and capacity of any one organization; it would require international cooperation. He asked Major Davis of the Red Cross to act as his emissary in approaching the commanders of the other vessels for a conference. The French and British commanders declined to attend, but sent their senior officers as representatives.

Meanwhile, several groups of refugees who were under the protection or patronage of American charitable or educational institutions had been located. Near East Relief agreed to pay their passage if passage could be found, and more than two thousand were rescued on the American vessel *Winona* and taken to Piraeus.

At about the same time, Asa Jennings was starting to put his own rescue plans in motion, approaching first the French and Italian ships and later the Greek navy. He and Hepburn would soon cross paths, partnering in one of the great rescue efforts of all time.

By the fifteenth, the fire had burned out to such an extent that the refugees on shore were no longer in immediate danger from the flames. Now their suffering was from the unrelenting heat, hunger, thirst, and continued brutality. New concerns had also arisen, as Jennings reported to Hepburn that large numbers of refugees were being deported into the Turkish interior. Hepburn writes, "From the reports of the relief workers and those who had made the trip to Paradise [Paradise College], it appeared that they [the refugees] were either voluntarily or forcibly being conducted into the interior. One report by Mr. Jennings of the relief committee was very explicit in stating that he had seen a considerable detachment being driven along the road toward Paradise by Turkish troops. It was the universal opinion that all refugees being deported into the interior would soon be beyond any chance of help."

The conference of naval officers was organized for noon on September 15 aboard the Italian yacht *Galileo*, the flagship of Rear Admiral Pepe of the Italian navy. Attending the conference were Rear Admiral Pepe, senior Italian naval officer, Rear Admiral Tyrrwhitty, of the Royal Navy; Captain Perbinquiere, chief of staff to French Admiral Dumesnil; Sir Harry Lamb, the British consul general; the French and Italian consuls; and Major C. Claflin Davis, of the Red Cross.

At the conference, Captain Hepburn, who had spent the most time near the quay and onshore, said he estimated the number of refugees to be between 120,000 and 130,000; this was a huge crowd to be evacuated and provided for, but all present agreed that evacuation was the only course. Admiral Tyrrwhitty advised that nothing could really be done until there were some assurances from the Turkish authorities that relief measures could proceed peaceably. He recommended that a delegation of all the foreign powers present should have an audience with Moustapha Kemal, the Turkish leader. The objective was to obtain Kemal's cooperation in addressing the refugee situation and eventual evacuation. Kemal complied, although he initially set a deadline of just ten days. At the insistence of American Naval officers, this was extended to September 30, and later another extension was granted. Following the meeting, a Disaster Relief Committee was formed.

On Saturday, September 16, the USS *Edsall*, commanded by Halsey Powell, arrived at Salonika with its cargo of refugees. Officers and crews from the *Edsall*, the *Lawrence*, and the *Simpson* worked for more than five days without sleep to rescue refugees. Following is the report from Captain Hepburn's log after receiving Commander Powell's report:

"The EDSALL arrived from Salonika at 6:00 a.m. Commander Powell reported that the Greek authorities had most warmly welcomed him, and had made efficient preparations for the disembarkation and care of the refugees which he brought. Instead of making difficulties about formalities of any sort, or appearing to regard the sudden dumping of these refugees upon the community as a burden, their attitude was that of extreme gratitude for American assistance in rescuing their people and bringing them home. The action of the EDSALL in landing a few day's rations of flour with the refugees was regarded as an astonishing piece of generosity."

In the afternoon of the sixteenth, Captain Hepburn received word that a second conference was being called, for six that night aboard the *Galileo*. As he had already planned to return to Constantinople, he directed Commander Powell to attend in his stead. Meanwhile, Captain Hepburn was asked to aid in the evacuation of two hundred Armenian orphans who had been cared for at an American-run institution. The captain agreed and the orphans were brought aboard the *Litchfield*.

That evening, Commander Powell proceeded to the conference. The results were reported in the U.S. Secretary of the Navy's Annual Report for 1923: "At the first conference[2] of the senior naval officers, the commanding officer of the EDSALL urged the immediate evacuation of the refugees and the necessity for ships. Finally the Turks allowed the Greek ships to enter their ports for this purpose. Here they were permitting the enemy's ships to enter their ports, and although there was no guaranty the ships would not be molested, they never were. The ships were escorted into port by American destroyers and docked, loaded, and dispatched under the supervision of the destroyer officers. The children were carried on board by American bluejackets. Old and decrepit men and women were assisted or carried by those same destroyer men."

The Greek ships mentioned above were the "fleet" secured from the Greek government by Asa Jennings. With Jennings at their head, and escorted by American destroyers, they set about rescuing the mass of refugees on the Smyrna quay. Reports filed from Commander Halsey Powell of the USS *Edsall* to Admiral Bristol, and reports filed with the U.S. Secretary of the Navy, document their rescue work over the next few days. An excerpt from one of Commander Powell's reports follows:

"1. The U.S.S. EDSALL arrived Smyrna at 6 a.m., 14 September; after being at anchor about one hour, went alongside the U.S.S. LITCH-FIELD and embarked 671 Greek and Armenian refugees. At 9:00 a.m., got underway for Salonica. Arrived Salonica 11:30 p.m., went alongside the east Mole and in one and one half hours had disembarked all refugees with thirty bags of flour. The refugees had been given two square meals enroute to Salonica. As soon as their cars and relief were secured, the EDSALL returned to Smyrna, arriving at 7:00 a.m., 16 September.

"2. While at Salonica, I discussed arrangements for obtaining Greek ships for the evacuation of refugees from Smyrna, and reported this to the

Detachment Commander [*Author's note*: Most likely this conversation was with Jennings, whom Powell had been in contact with.]

"3. At the first conference of the Senior Naval Officers after I became Senior U.S. Naval Officer, I urged upon the conference the necessity for the immediate evacuation of the refugees and the necessity for ships. I suggested that Kemal Pasha would probably give permission for Greek ships to enter for the purpose of evacuation. It was agreed that Admiral Pepe would go to Kemal Pasha[3] to obtain this permission. [*Author's note*: Commander Powell was aware of Asa Jennings's efforts to secure ships, having given him a motor launch by which to reach the French ship and others. When Jennings approached the Greeks, he was also in touch with Commander Powell. It was Powell who ultimately wired Jennings that permission was granted by the Turks for the Greek ships to enter the harbor, and Powell also coordinated with Captain Hepburn, Commander Rhodes, and others for the destroyer escort and continued American rescue efforts.]

"4. On 20 September word was received through the Liason Officer that Greek ships could enter if they did not fly the Greek flag. On 21 September received final notification from Izzedini Pasha, Commander First Army Corps that Greek steamers could come to Smyrna, provided they did not fly their own flag and provided they did not tie up to the quay or piers. I sent a member of the Relief Committee to Mytileni to inform the Greeks of this, and also sent a dispatch to Constantinople. [*Author's note*: The member of the Relief Committee is most likely Jennings, who was awaiting such a reply.]

"5. On 24 September seven Greek ships were escorted into the harbor by the U.S.S. LAWRENCE, and by permission of the Captain of the Port were tied up to the piers. The refugees were concentrated and handled, except on the pier near the ships, by the Turkish troops and harbor police. Towards the end of the pier and on board the ships, they were handled by a landing force from the LAWRENCE and EDSALL. 15000 were evacuated this day.

"6. On the 25th no Greek ships arrived.

"7. On the 25th, twelve Greek ships came in under escort of the U.S.S. EDSALL. They were sent immediately to the pier, four at a time, and the same arrangements of embarkation as on the 24th.

. . . *continued on page 92*

"8. I received a note from the British Admiral asking if he could help in any way. I went on board and discussed the situation with him, and it was decided that he would land a large working party to work on the ships and abreast the ships, provided the Turkish authorities welcomed the landing of the British bluejackets. I obtained this permission from the Turks, and the British landed a force at 1:00 p.m."

Commander Powell reports that the refugees were funneled through a set of three gates at the railway yards, each set manned by Turkish forces. It was at these gates that any young men of military age were commandeered by the Turks and deported to the Turkish interior. As the refugees got closer to the piers, the U.S. and British naval forces took over, escorting the refugees to the boats that would ferry them to the ships offshore. It was a stressful, time-consuming task. The steady stream of humanity was moved along as quickly as possible, yet the boats could contain only a certain number of people, so delays were inevitable. Added to this were the cries of those being separated from their sons, brothers, and husbands, and the general lament of a people who had already suffered so much. Ill, hungry, frightened, they were now being herded toward who knows where. Commander Powell notes that the lack of a common language added to their fear as they did not understand the directions of those trying to assist them. Still, leaving the hellish quay was the goal they all sought, and getting on one of the boats provided some glimmer of hope.

Although Commander Powell reports some brutality from the Turkish forces (and others), he also points out that there were a great many instances of compassion during the evacuation: "Two sides of the Turks nature were evidenced nearly every day of the evacuation; one . . . was the robber and more or less of a brute, the other was a soldier doing his duty with a very humane side to him. I have seen them pick up a hat, and an old man, or assist a cripple or an elderly woman. I have had stories brought to me where one soldier got down on all fours over a little child to protect it from the onrushing mob. It would have undoubtedly been crushed to death if he had not done this. Another report was that of one of the harbor police carrying a little child up and down the dock for quite sometime until he found its mother."

Powell also mentioned the growing concern for the state of the refugees: "The physical condition of the refugees appeared to be worse day by day, they needed more help and there were more stretcher cases," he wrote.

"There were several cases of child birth immediately after arrival on board the ships. There was one on the dock. There were several deaths in the railroad yard and on the pier. There were many stretcher cases sent on board who did not look as though they would live to Mytileni."

Powell's report concluded with commendations for all those involved in the rescue effort:

"13. The British forces were the greatest help, and it is estimated that the evacuation could not have been finished in the time allowed but for the part they took in it. The bluejackets with two services, worked as one service, and although the Captain of the "CURACOA" was on the pier every day, practically all day, he consulted me in all decisions, and asked my advice in many changes he wished to make, and in general made me feel that I was in charge. There was never a hitch or misunderstanding of any kind. Admiral Nicholson was always ready to assist in every way, and I consulted him daily . . .

"15. I cannot too highly commend the work of Dr. Lovejoy, who during her stay in Smyrna was on the dock daily during the evacuation from early in the morning until late in the afternoon or into the night. She gave good advice in handling women who were in very serious condition, and I think in a few cases which happened, assisted in delivering babies which were born, and undoubtedly saved several lives.

"16. I wish to invite the attention of the Commander, U.S. Naval Forces in Turkish Waters to the excellent work of the officers of the U.S.S. EDSALL, and to the cheerful work and behavior of the men. The men did everything from carrying a bundle of rugs or a stretcher case, to taking a cripple on their backs, or a baby in each arm for a sickly mother . . ."

Soon after these hectic days of rescue, Admiral Bristol sent the following report to the Secretary of the Navy, describing the rescue efforts, as led by Asa Jennings:

"There was also one member of this Committee who is not prominently mentioned in this report who afterwards by his efforts and energy contributed as much individually as any other one person to the successful evacuation of the Christian refugees from Smyrna and the surrounding country. This was Mr. A.K. Jennings of the Y.M.C.A. It was he who went to Mytilene and demanded of the Greek Admiral that the Greek ships, about 27, then lying idle in Mytilene be sent to Smyrna to evacuate the refugees. He virtually delivered an ultimatum to the Greek Admiral that unless the ships were made available for evacuation of the refugees, he, Jennings would publish the facts to the world that the Greeks and the Greek Government refused to render this assistance to Greek refugees in Smyrna. The permission was given and Mr. Jennings cooperated with our destroyer captains in Smyrna by seeing that those Greek ships were dispatched from Mytilene to Smyrna, while the American destroyers conveyed these ships into harbor and were responsible for their conduct to the Turkish government."

Rescues from Other Islands

American ships, and those from other nations, did not rescue refugees just from Smyrna. Refugees were scattered about a number of communities throughout Asia Minor, and all were in need of aid. From the United States, the ships USS *Utah*, the USS *Bulmer*, the USS *MacLeish*, the USS *Edsall*, and *SC#96*, a sub chaser, participated in evacuating people from outlying towns, including Moudania.

On September 10, fires had been set in some of the villages surrounding Moudania; by September 11, all of the villages were burning. With the fires growing closer, tens of thousands of refugees crowded the waterfront in Moudania, according to Admiral Bristol's diary. Steamers arrived to evacuate the citizens of other countries and the retreating Greek army. Witnessing this sent the refugees into a panic. It was obvious that they would soon be left to fend for themselves.

"Ten bodies were seen in the water near the dock, probably having fallen overboard in attempting to get on steamers," Bristol writes. "Twelve men and women who were clinging to piles were removed by Sub. Chasers. . . . By the 11th conditions had become indescribable and looting on a small scale had commenced. All the baggage and furnishing so laboriously got thus far by the refugees were abandoned in an effort to save themselves. The water supply was shut off, the people themselves having broken the pipe in their craze for water."

The thousands of refugees entering the town created "chaotic conditions." In his war diary Bristol writes, "Food and water are scarce and immediate relief is necessary to prevent thousands of deaths. The streets are littered with the belongings of refugees who have abandoned everything in an endeavor to save themselves. It is estimated that there are 40,000 refugees in Moudania alone."

Miss J. L. Jillson[4], of the American Foreign Mission Board, approached Admiral Bristol about assistance for the refugees in Moudania. She had operated a school in Broussa, Turkey, for many years and urged that something be done. According to Bristol's account, he ordered the sub chaser *SC #96* to return her to Moudania and provide assistance.

Over the next several days, U.S. ships, Greek ships, and a variety of "ships for hire" evacuated the refugees from these outlying towns.

Aid from Other Nations

Ships and crews from Great Britain, France, and Italy also brought assistance during the refugee crisis. "The [British] Naval Review," produced by the Naval Society in August 1923, gives an extensive account of the situation in Smyrna. According to the "Review," on August 31, 1922, the following British ships were at Constaninople: *Iron Duke*, the admiral's flagship; the *Benbow*, and the *King George V*; the *Ajax*, a hospital ship; the *Maine*; and several destroyers.

On September 3, the report includes the following:

"The cypher offices were now kept busy. After two years of uninteresting labour, a succession of signals came through, giving a complete precis of the situation.

"The Greeks were on the run. Ushak was in flames, and the retirement was drawing near Alashehr. The Kemalists were using aircraft and cavalry with effect. Refugees were making towards Smyrna, the only outlet, and blocking the roads. The Greek High Command stated an effort was to be made to reform the two Greek corps of the Southern Army near Alashehr, but, doubtful of stemming the advance, were talking of evacuation."

When news of the Turks' imminent arrival came, preparations were quickly made for evacuating British subjects. By September 4, it was clear that the Greek high command and civilian officials were fleeing Turkey. With the arrival of the other British ships (the aforementioned *Iron Duke* and *King George V*), plus the French *Waldeck Rousseau*, some citizens began to believe that the Allies would take control and stop the Turkish advance. A strange calm prevailed, as an almost fatalistic atmosphere touched the citizenry. The city, according to "The Naval Review," became deathly quiet, with a stillness that "seemed almost uncanny."

. . . *continued on page 98*

French warships at Smyrna
BACKGROUND: Jean Bart; TOP RIGHT: Hova;
BOTTOM RIGHT: Tourville; TOP LEFT: Somali;
MIDDLE LEFT: Taureg; BOTTOM LEFT: Edgar Quinet.

TOP: *The Greek ship Kilkis, formerly the American battleship, USS Mississippi.*
BOTTOM: *The Italian warship Venezia.*

The Allies, however, had no intention of making a stand, and on
September 4, the British colony began to be evacuated. At that time, a
number of other refugees were also taken aboard. The HMHS *Maine,* the
SS *Bavarian,* the SS *Antioch,* and the SS *Magira* were among those ships used
to transport evacuees.

On September 4, it was also reported to the British command that
five thousand refugees had arrived by rail and that fifteen thousand were

expected the next day. "The Naval Review" notes that the food situation in town was already critical, and with that many mouths to feed, starvation would become an issue within days. By the forenoon, refugees began arriving by rail and road, filling the streets. "They appeared to have no plans or projects, and were sitting in the streets where they arrived," reads the report. "They are all women and children. They are as yet not arriving in the large numbers expected, and the reason given for this is that they are being held up on the rail and road, and military traffic is getting the precedence. If so, their outlook is poor, as the Turks have little sympathy if they catch them up."

By 10:30 on the fifth, the harbor was "unusually full," according to the "Review." Two British destroyers, the *Senator* and the *Sparrowhawk,* have arrived, along with the French ships the *Ernest Renan*, the *Edgar Quinnet*, and two other destroyers; the Italian ship *Venezia* and two destroyers; and several Greek ships, the *Kilkis,* the *Lemnos,* and the *Helle,* plus five or six torpedo boats that are always on the move.[5] A variety of merchant vessels from Britain, Italy, and Greece are also in port.

According to "The Naval Review," a group of British officers went ashore that afternoon and witnessed a pitiful sight:

"But the worst sight of all was the refugees from all of the villages around. Never possessing much—a hut and a bit of land—they work the land, sow seeds, and the corn and vegetables they reap and grow keep them on into the next year, when they begin over again. They have nothing much to bring—a small bundle and themselves.

"But it was sweltering hot, and these old and young women, old men and boys, who had footed it for miles in their rags come along.

"A woman, bare of feet, whose back is bent in order that a child may cling on, a smaller one on her shoulder, yet another (maybe four years of age) clinging to her skirts, all with a crucifix around their necks—trudge in. Perspiring is no word for her condition. She literally drops her life-blood with every step she takes. But on—on! She has probably lost relatives before in a massacre by the Turks. Her hunted look and the fierce determination on her face as she passes haunts one still: she and her children shall be safe if possible: at any rate she will struggle for them. But where to go? They make for the Palace of the Metropolitan of the Greek Church, and there, inside the quadrangle, between the Palace and the Cathedral, a sight met our eyes that can never be forgotten—a living hell, and yet so close to God's acre.

. . . *continued on page 105*

UNITED STATES SHIP ."LITCHFIELD" #336   **Friday**   **22nd**, **September**, **1922**
                                                 (Day.)   (Date.)   (Month.)

ZONE DESCRIPTION.. minus-2   REMARKS.

Commences and until 4:00 a/m.

   Moored to dock at Eastern quay at Seloniki, Greece, disembarking refugees.
At 12:53 finished disembarking refugees, Mr. J.B. Harris and Mr. W. Harris re-
ported aboard for passage to Smyrne,. At 12:55 got underway and stood out of
harbor S.S. 15 knots. At 1:10 set course 130 (PSC) 126 True. At 1:26 passed
Naziki Gas Buoy on Stbd beam dist. 7/8 mile. At 150 C.C. to 180 (PSC) 176
True. At 2:17 passed Panomi point light abeam dist. 4 1/4 miles and C.C. to
140 True 144 (PSC). At 3:59 sighted Kassandra point light bearing 110° true.
Average Steam 230 Average Revolutions 169.

                                        W.D. Taylor,
                                        Lieut. U.S. Navy.

From 4:00 p.m. to 8:00 p.m.

   Steaming as before. 4:02 C.C. to 165° (PSC). 4:20 standing into Maytelinef
Harbor on various courses and speeds, 4:30 anchored in 9 fathoms of water with
30 fathoms of chain on stbd anchor. 4:33 Captain left ship. 4:40 Commanding Officer Greek Auxiliary Adriaduon paid official visit, 4:45 left ship. 5:30 board-
ing Officer Italian Destroyer Solferiono paid official visit. 7:03 made preparations for getting underway. 7:05 Captain returned with Mr. Jennings of Near
East Relief as passenger to Smyrna, Turkey. 7:21 hove in and underway, on boilers
#1&2. Stood out of harbor on various courses ans speeds. 7:32 C.C. to 145° (PSC)
an went ahead at speed 20 knots. 8:00 passed Greek predreadnaught Kilkis bound
North. C.C. to 180° (PSC) . Average Steam 230 Average Revolutions 175.

                                        F.M. Shannonhouse,
                                        Ensign, U.S. Navy.

UNITED STATES SHIP "LITCHFIELD" #336   **Wednesday**, **27th Sept**, **1922**. 19
                                                (Day)   (Date.)   (Month.)

ZONE DESCRIPTION.. minus-2   REMARKS.

                                        Ensign, U.S. Navy.

From 4:00 a.m. to 8:00 a.m.

   Moored as before, at 4:30 made all preparations for getting underway, at
5:00 got underway on various courses and speeds and stood out to Pelican Spit.
At 6:00 stood in from Pelican Spit escorting refugeeships into Smyrna Harbor. At
7:15 anchored off Railroad pier in Smyrna Harbor. in 6 1/2 fathoms of water with
35 fathoms of chain out on stbd anchor. At 7:30 a patrol consisting of 30 men and
3 Officers left the ship for duty on railroad pier embarkation point of refugees
At 7:35 a patrol of four men left ship for duty at Standard Oil Co. Average Steam
225, Average Revolutions 112.

                                        H. Corman.
                                        Ensign, U.S. Navy.

From 4:00 p.m. to 8:00 p.m.

Anchored as before. At 4:30 the S.S. Nicholas Athanas Culis stood out with refugees. At 4:35 the S.S. Poymeah stood out with refugees. At 4:50 the S.S. Grand
Duke Alexander Michealoritch stood out with refugees. At 4:55 the S.S. Trake
stood out with refugees. At 7:35 turned on both 24" searchlights and kept them
trained on the railroad pier where refugees were being embarked. At 7:40 a patrol
consisting of 30 men left the ship to relieve the patrol on the railroad pier.

                                        H. Corman,
                                        Ensign, U.S. Navy.

Excerpts from the declassified ships' logs of the USS Litchfield

UNITED STATES SHIP "LITCHFIELD" #336 ——— Wednesday, 27th Sept. 1922. 19

ZONE DESCRIPTION minus-2   **REMARKS.**

Ensign, U.S. Navy.

From 4:00 a.m. to 8:00 a.m.

Moored as before, at 4:30 made all preparations for getting underway, at 5:00 got underway on various courses and speeds and stood out to Pelican Spit. At 6:00 stood in from Pelican Spit escorting refugeeships into Smyrna Harbor. At 7:15 anchored off Railroad pier in Smyrna Harbor. in 6 1/2 fathoms of water with 35 fathoms of chain out on stbd anchor. At 7:30 a patrol consisting of 30 men and 3 Officers left the ship for duty on railroad pier embarkation point of refugees At 7:35 a patrol of four men left ship for duty at Standard Oil Co. Average Steam 225, Average Revolutions 112.

H. Corman.
Ensign, U.S. Navy.

From 4:00 p.m. to 8:00 p.m.

Anchored as before. At 4:30 the S.S. Nicholas Athanas Culis stood out with refugees. At 4:35 the S.S. Poymeah stood out with refugees. At 4:50 the S.S. Grand Duke Alexander Michealoritch stood out with refugees. At 4:55 the S.S. Trake stood out with refugees. At 7:35 turned on both 24" searchlights and kept them trained on the railroad pier where refugees were being embarked. At 7:40 a patrol consisting of 30 men left the ship to relieve the patrol on the railroad pier.

H. Corman.
Ensign, U.S. Navy.

UNITED STATES SHIP "LITCHFIELD" #336 ——— Thursday, 28th September, 1922

ZONE DESCRIPTION minus-2   **REMARKS.**

From 4:00 a.m. to 8:00 a.m.

Anchored as before. At 5:30 made all preparations for getting underway. At 5:40 got underway on various courses and speeds and stood out towards Pelican Spit. At 6:20 stood in from Pelican Spit escorting 11 relief vessels into Smyrna Harbor. At 7:00 anchored off railroad pier in Smyrna Harbor in 6 1/2 fathoms of water with 30 fathoms of chain on stbd anchor. At 7:30 patrol consisting of 30 men and 3 Officers left the ship for duty on railroad pier, embarkation point of refugees. At 7:45 patrol of 4 men left the ship for duty at the Standard Oil Co.

H. Corman.
Ensign, U.S. Navy.

Meridian to 4:00 p.m.

Anchored as before, six steamers loaded with refugees stood out. At 3:35 French Destroyer Hova stood out.

W.D. Taylor
Lieut, U.S. Navy.

Excerpts from the declassified ships' logs of the USS Litchfield

UNITED STATES SHIP "LITCHFIELD" #336   Friday,   29th, September, 1922 19

ZONE DESCRIPTION minus-2   REMARKS.

From 4:00 a.m. to 8:00 a.m.

    Anchored as before. At 5:00 USS MAC LIESH stood out. At 5:50 British Stea-
mer Wesley Hall stood in. At 7:00 sent patrol of two Officers and fifteen men
to dock to assist loading refugees and one Officer and 12 men to Cordilio to
assist loading refugees. Five Greek Steamers stood in during watch to take out
refugees.

                                                    W.D. Taylor
                                                    Lieut, U.S. Navy.

Meridian to 4:00 p.m.

    Anchored as before. Six Greek steamers got underway and stood out with
refugees. At 2:33 USS MAC LIESH stood in and at 3:05 anchored off the railroad
pier. Cantania, J. RM1c, reported on board fr. the USS EDSALL, for transfer to
the Base Hospital for treatment.

                                                    H. Corman,
                                                    Ensign, U.S. Navy.

From 4:00 p.m. to 8:00 p.m.

    Anchored as before. Three Greek Steamers got underway and stood out
carrying refugees. At 4:30 the Cordilio patrol returned to the ship. At 4:45
a patrol consisting of 13 men left ship for duty on railroad pier. At 4:55
the Standard Oil Co. Patrol returned to the ship. At 6:25 the railroad pier
patrol returned to the ship. At 7:10 turned on both 24" searchlights and trained
them on railroad pier.

                                                    H. Corman,
                                                    Ensign, U.S. Navy.

Excerpts from the declassified ships' logs of the USS Litchfield.

UNITED STATES SHIP EDSALL (219)   Sunday, 24 September, 1922, 19
                                    (Day.)   (Date.)   (Month.)

ZONE DESCRIPTION   (-2).   REMARKS.

Meridian to 4:00 p.m.

    At 2:00 U.S.S. LAWRENCE stood in convoying seven Greek merchant ships,
all ships anchoring off point.

                                    Chas. J. Maguire,
                                    Ensign, U. S. Navy.

4:00 p.m. to 8:00 p.m.

    Greek merchant ships went alongside dock at the point and approximately
15,000 refugees embarked under direction of Near East Relief with assistance of American sailors and Turkish troops. Ships then stood out to sea
under escort of U.S.S. LAWRENCE.

                                    Chas. J. Maguire,
                                    Ensign, U. S. Navy.

8:00 p.m. to Midnight.

    At 8:00 extra patrol used for embarkation returned to ship. At 9:00
U.S.S. LAWRENCE stood in and anchored off starboard bow. Passengers from
shore, mail, etc., were transferred to U.S.S. LAWRENCE which got underway
at 10:15 and stood out of harbor for Constantinople.

                                    Chas. J. Maguire.

UNITED STATES SHIP EDSALL (219)   Sunday, 24 September, 1922, 19
                                    (Day.)   (Date.)   (Month.)

ZONE DESCRIPTION   (-2).   REMARKS.

4:00 a.m. to 8:00 a.m.

    Landed patrol of ten men at 7:45 for protection of Consulate.

                                    T.B. Perry,
                                    Lieutenant (jg), U.S. Navy.

Meridian to 4:00 p.m.

    At 2:00 U.S.S. LAWRENCE stood in convoying seven Greek merchant ships,
all ships anchoring off point.

                                    Chas. J. Maguire,
                                    Ensign, U. S. Navy.

4:00 p.m. to 8:00 p.m.

    Greek merchant ships went alongside dock at the point and approximately
15,000 refugees embarked under direction of Near East Relief with assistance of American sailors and Turkish troops. Ships then stood out to sea
under escort of U.S.S. LAWRENCE.

                                    Chas. J. Maguire,
                                    Ensign, U. S. Navy.

8:00 p.m. to Midnight.

    At 8:00 extra patrol used for embarkation returned to ship. At 9:00
U.S.S. LAWRENCE stood in and anchored off starboard bow. Passengers from
shore, mail, etc., were transferred to U.S.S. LAWRENCE which got underway
at 10:15 and stood out of harbor for Constantinople.

                                    Chas. J. Maguire,
                                    Ensign, U. S. Navy.

Excerpts from the declassified ships' logs of the USS Edsall.

UNITED STATES SHIP __EDSALL__ (219)   Thursday, 28 September, 1922   19
                                            (Day.)   (Date.)   (Month.)

ZONE DESCRIPTION __(-2).__   REMARKS.

__4:00 a.m. to 8:00 a.m.__

    At 5:45 U.S.S. LITCHFIELD stood out and at 7:00 stood in again onvoying 12 Greek ships at their own request. Landed 30 men and 2 officers on pier to assist embarkation of refugees and at 8:00 commenced evacuating refugees.

                                                   Thos. J. McGuire,
                                                   Ensign, U.S. Navy.

UNITED STATES SHIP __EDSALL__ (219)   Friday, 29 September, 1922   19
                                            (Day.)   (Date.)   (Month.)

ZONE DESCRIPTION __(-2).__   REMARKS.

__Commences and until 4:00 a.m.__

    Anchored in Smyrna Harbor in 7 fathoms of water, 45 fathoms of chain on starboard anchor. Boiler No. 1 in use for auxiliary purposes.

                                                  K.C. Caldwell,
                                                 Ensign, U.S. Navy.

__4:00 a.m. to 8:00 a.m.__

    At 4:50 U.S.S. MacLEISH got underway and stood out and escorted in Greek ships. Landed 50 men and 3 officers to assist in embarkation of refugees.

                                                    K.C. Caldwell,
                                               Ensign, U.S. Navy.

Excerpts from the declassified ships' logs of the USS Edsall.

"Old wrinkled women, lying on pavement, in rags, or propped up against a wall, asleep. Babies in their mothers' arms, or sometimes two or three on an old sack, in a row, looking like waxen images. Will they never waken again, one wonders? The mothers in many cases staring blankly in front of them, but ready to spring at the first person who would dare harm their child. Women with hair all over the place, and wild eyes. The events have been too much for them: but they are safe, from sheer exhaustion they could not move or do harm if they would.

"And then one came upon the prostrate form of the woman previously seen. She had brought her children to safety, but could no longer care for them. The two smaller ones slept by her side, while the eldest one climbed over her body which showed no signs of life.

"Words failed to convey even the smallest part of the misery seen that day. And this was war. God in his mercy grant us peace."

On September 6, the first of the British refugees left on the SS *Magira*, along with seventy-nine women and children from the refugee ranks. The SS *Antioch* left with another load at 11:30 in the morning. The log of the *Ajax* shows that on September 9, she took 180 refugees on board. The log of the USS *Edsall* reports that the British admiral offered assistance. The offer was accepted and British sailors worked alongside Americans in coordinating the loading of the refugees both onshore and on U.S. vessels. Commander Powell of the *Edsall* specifically commends British forces for their teamwork in the effort.

It should also be mentioned that the relationship between the Turks and the British was an uneasy one, as they were technically at war. There was little regard between the two nations during the time of these events. At one point the Turks even fired upon a British vessel, although this may have been the action of irregulars. When the British commander Admiral W. S. Nicholson offered to assist in the evacuation, the U.S. naval authorities had to apply to the Turkish authorities for permission. The Turks granted this, but with the provisos that British naval forces could not land except on the deck where the refugee ships were being loaded and that U.S. naval forces must at all times be between British forces and the shore. Admiral Bristol's report from his flagship, the USS *Scorpion* says, "In this connection it must be remembered that when this request was granted, the feeling of the Turkish Nationalists against the British was most intense and bitter, and every minute it looked as if the British and the Turks would begin fighting around Constantinople."

The French had several ships in harbor during the Smyrna crisis. These were under the command of Admiral Dumesnil, and were used primarily to evacuate French citizens from Smyrna and surrounding communities. If the British walked a delicate line due to more antagonistic relations with the Turks, the French walked a similar line for entirely different reasons. The French wanted to maintain strong relations with the Turks for economic reasons; they did not want to make any move that might cause a breach. French troops went ashore without incident at Moudania to protect the French railroad, and their presence may have helped calm events in that region.[6] Admiral Dumensil's report records that the British torpedo boat Speedy "had to cast off hurriedly from there [Moudania] on September 18 in order to avoid an intentional or chance bombardment of the Kemalist batteries . . ." Dumensil also notes that an American sub chaser supported them with "devoted assistance" and "spontaneously put itself at the disposal of Commander JOUBERT in the difficult times at MOUDANIA."

The captain's log of the French vessel *Somali* describes the gradually deteriorating situation at Moudania. The captain is Lieutenant Commander Cazlis, and his eloquence painfully evokes the frustration and fear of those dark days. The *Somali* was sent to relieve the *Touareg* in the evacuation of citizens from Moudania. People from nearby Broussa and other villages are pouring into Moudania ahead of the Turkish army. Some Greek citizens have guns and are threatening to use them against the advancing Turks. Chaos reigns on land and sea. From captain's log:

"The night is rather bad at the roadstead at Moudania. The American chaser [sub chaser #96] narrowly misses going ashore, swept along by a steamer, and another big ship is run aground. It will leave dry ground with great difficulty the next day, though helped by a salvage vessel.

"September 9 . . . The general evacuation rushes headlong. The refugees congest the wharves and all the plots of land adjacent to the station and the workshops. The trains stop on the outside on account of the bottling up. The steamers take in freight with feverish haste. There is nothing more than a semblance of order...

"September 10 . . . At night, I ascertain that the villages are on fire everywhere from Guemleck to the approaches of Moudania, that the panic increases on land, that public order begins to be less sure. I fear the burning of Moudania tonight and some acts of pillaging . . .

"September 11 . . . In the morning, they can't put a locomotive on its way for lack of personnel and water. Besides, the route is cut, for a bridge has blown up. Moreover, the rumor is afloat that Proussa and also Guemlek are occupied by Turks. . . . In the meantime toward 10:00, a panic occurs without reason. The refugees trample each other and several are crushed. Some women and children are drowned of their own free will. The steamers are taken by storm at the wharves. They get under way in haste. One of them, the 'THESALONIQUE,' in consequence of a false maneuver (for an anchor gets caught in the framework of the wharf), crushes a certain number of persons and drowns others while easing off its entangled cable; on the other hand, in order to restore public order, there is a threat made with a revolver. Having jumped into my ship's boat and pushed at some distance in order not to be assailed, then having gone back on board, I am present at painful scenes like a helpless spectator. I return to land when calm returned and I no longer meet with authorities again. I reassure the refugees."

Meanwhile, in his report, the admiral also records the violence of the Smyrna harborside on September 13 through 15. During evacuation attempts, small boats from the French ship *Jean Bart* were used to transport citizens. Shots were fired from the shore and a young French lieutenant was wounded while loading one of the craft. This was also the time of the great Smyrna fire, and at one point a barge burst into flames, having been set alight by sparks blowing from the shore. The barge drifted into the harbor, a virtual "fire ship" threatening the other ships in port. The steamship of the *Jean Bart* put out the barge fire, to the relief of the other sailors.

In his log, Admiral Dumesnil writes, "I state to the Military Commander that the Admirals and the Consuls General of France, Great Britain, Italy and the United States are going to attempt a common effort in order to provide for the food for the refugees; but I am desirous of knowing first if the local authorities have envisaged some measures and in what order."[7]

In addition to evacuating French citizens, the admiral put his ships to work evacuating refugees from Belgium, Poland, Czechoslovakia, and Yugoslavia, and the consuls general of Spain and Belgium. They also assisted in the evacuation of Greek refugees, according to his report:

"I have indicated to you that we had embarked during the night of the fire about 1,200 Armenians or Greeks whom I fed, then transported to PIRAEUS on a French steamship chartered for this occasion.

"Quite a big number of others have been able to leave on some French commercial ships by paying for their passage; but in general, my means of transport for this category of refugees were quickly quite insufficient in order to participate effectively in the English evacuation, then in the American evacuation that is in progress via Greek cargo boats."

The admiral's log is quite specific in recording the assistance of the American and British vessels during the rescue of refugees. In it the admiral writes: "The American Colony of MOUDANIA generou[s]ly exerted itself for the refugees and our Commanders took pleasure in paying homage to its [the American Colony's] attitude." And, ". . . the torpedo boat "HOVA" was able to ensure the departure from Tshesme on an English cargo boat of 5,500 Christian, Armenian or Greek refugees."

A telegram sent from the *Jean Bart* to the minister of the Navy, high commissioner at Constantinople states the following regarding the rescue of Greek refugees from Smyrna: "Refugees evacuated yesterday, September 26 43,000 by Greek ships. Today September 27 30,000 by Greek ships and an English ship. 1,200 French protégées by "DEDAIGNEUSE" and "ALEXANDRE MIKAILOVITCH" total for two days about 74,000 Stop. All these refugees to Mytilene Stop. Impossible to estimate how many of them were left in the city and the suburbs. Stop...NAVY PARIS. HIGH-COMMISSIONER informed. 1050/27/9" [*Author's note*: The "Greek" ships are the rescue fleet led by American Asa Jennings, and escorted by American destroyers, transporting refugees from Smyrna to Mytilene.]

A later telegram sent from *Jean Bart* contains this information about the Smyrna rescue efforts: "6—The Greek cargo boats continue to remove a lot of people. We estimate at 53 thousand the total number of persons having left SMYRNA since the beginning of September. Today there are leaving about 30 thousand via seventeen ships. It is difficult to know the number stayed it is estimated 30 or 40,000 by the Americans. It can increase if the means for leaving continue to be important." [Again, this is part of "Jennings' Armada."]

A telegram sent from the *Edgar Quinet* to the *Jean Bart* said: "In a meeting of the High Commissioners of France, Great Britain, Italy and America held yesterday the following information has been given concerning the undertaking of help to the refugees of Smyrna. The Greek government authorizes their transport to Metelin [Mytilene], Salonica and Cavalla. The British Government has promised to suscribe 5,000 pounds sterling if other governments participate in the undertaking. The great American [charitable] societies have given 50,000 dollars. Apart from ten Greek cargo boats that have begun the evacuation, 12 to 15 English boats are ready to be directed to Smyrna in 48 hours; they will bring some supplies. These means of transport seem sufficient."

Italy also had several vessels in Smyrna harbor, including the *Venezia*, and the yacht *Galileo*, which served as the flagship for Admiral Pepe, and was also the site of the council of naval leaders regarding the situation at Smyrna. The logs of the American captains and British captains indicate that Admiral Pepe was helpful in convincing the Turks to allow the Greek merchant ships, with American escorts, to rescue the refugees at Smyrna. A number of Greek ships also assisted in the transport of refugees from Smyrna, Makri, Finike and Adalia.

The Italians also aided in rescuing refugees from various locations. Following is the captain's log from the Italian torpedo boat *Euro*, led by Lieutenant Commander Ugo Fucci:

"The evacuation of Makri occurs by sea. The Turks do not take steps with appropriate means. Whoever has money can be evacuated on sailing ships paying Five banknotes per person [equal to about 70 Italian lire]. The sailing ships are all directed to Rhodes and leave full of people. It is not difficult to deduce that they make some huge undertakings. Whoever does not have money waits for some Greek steamships to come, whose arrival is stated previously.

"Each refugee, before embarking, is subjected to a minute search. There were confiscated gold under any form and jewels; even some ornaments that the Greek women wear in the form of buttons of silver or gold or of gold on their clothes were taken away. The luggage [was] ransacked. I was told that birth certificates, contracts, and other documents were torn to pieces, [with their] saying that they are not valid because the refugees will not especially return any more to Turkey. All that is perfectly legalized by the presence of the Turkish authorities who sit permanently on the quay to be present at the aforementioned operations.

"It has to be noted that a great part of this people were born in these places, and they tell me that some of them do not understand the Greek language. Women and children are leaving. Men, not even one, (are not leaving) because they are interned. It is the ruination of an entire people! They are leaving and do not know where they are going, leaving houses, fields, dragging them(selves) in great part misery and troubles. And yet some are leaving, singing (that they are) happy to be rescued finally from the Turkish incubus!"

Lieutenant Commander Fucci records that he is at Finike for about two hours on September 15th—11:30 to 13:45 (1:45). "Here too [there is] an exodus of refugees. I don't go ashore. On the morning of the 16th, I am at Adalia. Evacuation and scenes and identical behavior at Makri. On the 17th arrive two American Chf. Torpedo Boats, the 'Lawrance' and the 'Parrot' which undertake the direction of evacuation from the quay aboard two big Greek steamships. On the evening of the 14th, the evacuation is carried out. I leave on the following morning . . . I am at Makri on the 22nd. Here too the evacuation is finished. The city is deserted, the greatest part of the population being Greek. A graveyard! I have the impression that Makri has stopped living economically.

"The greatest part of the trades of the industries, agriculture, etc. were controlled by Greeks . . . All is silence."[8]

(The Greek steamships with American naval escorts mentioned by Lieutenant Commander Fucci are undoubtedly part of the Asa Jennings rescue fleet, which sailed to surrounding towns, as well as Smyrna.)

End Notes

1. Konsk may be Konak, or governor's palace.

2. This wasn't really the first conference, as one had been held the day before, which Captain Hepburn attended. This was the second conference, but the first attended by Captain Powell.

3. Most likely refers to Moustapha Kemal. In Turkey, the term *Pasha* is a title of rank or honor placed after the name. It indicates a high military or government official. Moustapha Kemal was head of Turkish forces and the Nationalist movement.

4. Jeannie Jillson, a worker with the American Foreign Missions board.

5. The "Naval Review" and several other ships' logs call this ship the *Kĭltis*, but Jennings calls it the *Kĭlkis* in Abernethy's account in chapter 3. It is undoubtedly the same ship.

6. This refers to the fires, the panic of the refugee,s and the firing by Kemalist troops upon the British craft.

7. Admiral Dumesnil's log was translated from the French by Dr. Richard E. Clairmont, assistant professor of classics at the University of New Hampshire.

8. Lieutenant Commander Fucci's log was translated from the Italian by Dr. Richard E. Clairmont.

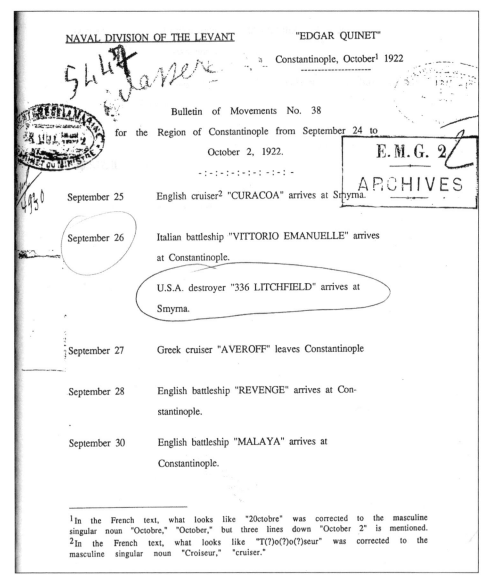

NAVAL DIVISION OF THE LEVANT   "EDGAR QUINET"

Constantinople, October[1] 1922

Bulletin of Movements No. 38

for the Region of Constantinople from September 24 to October 2, 1922.

E.M.G. 2

ARCHIVES

- : - : - : - : - : - : - : - : - -

September 25   English cruiser[2] "CURACOA" arrives at Smyrna.

September 26   Italian battleship "VITTORIO EMANUELLE" arrives at Constantinople.

U.S.A. destroyer "336 LITCHFIELD" arrives at Smyrna.

September 27   Greek cruiser "AVEROFF" leaves Constantinople

September 28   English battleship "REVENGE" arrives at Constantinople.

September 30   English battleship "MALAYA" arrives at Constantinople.

---

[1] In the French text, what looks like "20ctobre" was corrected to the masculine singular noun "Octobre," "October," but three lines down "October 2" is mentioned.
[2] In the French text, what looks like "T(?)o(?)o(?)seur" was corrected to the masculine singular noun "Croiseur," "cruiser."

Excerpts from the log of the French warship Edgar Quinet, *noting the movement of American ships. The logs of the* Edgar Quinet *and the other French war ships present at Smyrna were obtained from the French Marine Nationale, Navy History Archives in Boite Postale, France.*

p. 3

Telegram received by "JEAN BART"

From: "EDGAR-QUINET"

Passed on by: HIGH-COMMISSIONER Constantinople (Coded)

In a meeting of the High Commissioners of France, Great Britain, Italy and America held yesterday the following information has been given concerning the undertaking of help to the refugees of Smyrna. The Greek government authorizes their transport to Métélin,[3] Salonica and Cavalla. The British Government has promised to subscribe 5,000 pounds sterling if the other governments participate in the undertaking. The great American societies[4] have given 50,000 dollars. Apart from ten Greek cargo boats that have begun the evacuation, 12 to 15 English boats are ready to be directed to Smyrna in 48 hours; they will bring some supplies. These means of transport seem sufficient.

---

[3] Probably "Mitylene" although the French spelling, I should think, would be "Mitylène."

[4] That is, charitable societies.

Telegram sent from the French warship Edgar Quinet *to her counterpart,* Jean Bart *during the Smyrna crisis.*

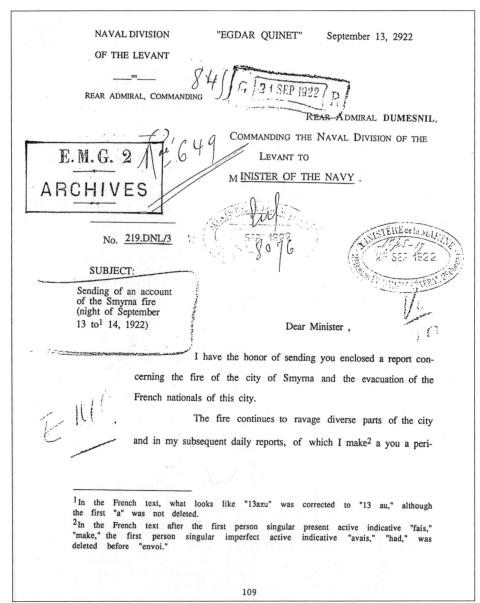

NAVAL DIVISION   "EGDAR QUINET"   September 13, 2922

OF THE LEVANT

REAR ADMIRAL, COMMANDING

E.M.G. 2

ARCHIVES

REAR ADMIRAL DUMESNIL,

COMMANDING THE NAVAL DIVISION OF THE

LEVANT TO

MINISTER OF THE NAVY

No. 219.DNL/3

SUBJECT:

Sending of an account
of the Smyrna fire
(night of September
13 to[1] 14, 1922)

Dear Minister ,

I have the honor of sending you enclosed a report con-

cerning the fire of the city of Smyrna and the evacuation of the

French nationals of this city.

The fire continues to ravage diverse parts of the city

and in my subsequent daily reports, of which I make[2] a you a peri-

---

[1] In the French text, what looks like "13azu" was corrected to "13 au," although the first "a" was not deleted.

[2] In the French text after the first person singular present active indicative "fais," "make," the first person singular imperfect active indicative "avais," "had," was deleted before "envoi."

109

A series of three French naval documents regarding the evacuations and the Smyrna situation.

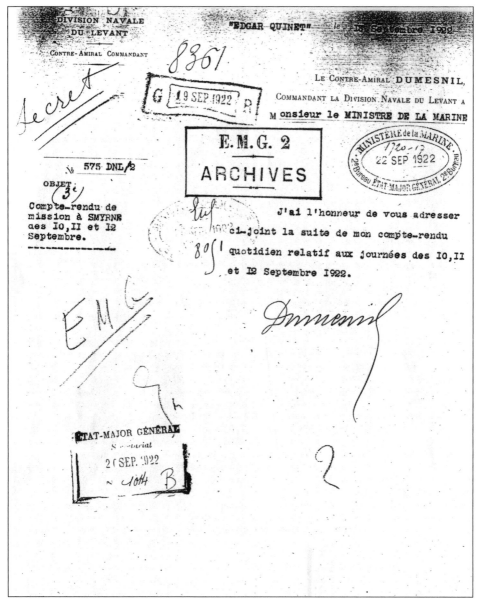

A series of three French naval documents regarding the evacuations and the Smyrna situation.

DU LEVANT
:-:-:-:-:-:-:-
CONTRE AMIRAL
Commandant
—o—

OBJET :
Rapport Mensuel
— — — —

SECRET

Mois de Septembre 1922

30 sept.

Le Contre Amiral DUMESNIL
Commandant la Division Navale du Levant

à

1930-12

Monsieur le Ministre de la Marine

Monsieur le Ministre,

I.- J'ai l'honneur de vous adresser le rapport mensuel
de Septembre 1922 de la D.N.L.

 Ce rapport ,en ce qui concerne les événements
importants qui se sont déroulés en Asie-Mineure et qui ont
motivé ma venue à Smyrne,se réfère naturellement aux diver-
ses correspondances par lesquelles je vous ai tenu au courant
de mon action entre le 4 et le 16 Septembre ,et de ma lettre
n°227 DNL/3 qui résume cette action dans la série des événements qui se sont déroulés du 4 au 25 Septembre,tant à Smyrne
qu'à Constantinople et en Marmara.

II.- Au 30 Septembre ,la <u>situation politique</u> paraît
assez claire

 Bien que tous les détails de la révolution grecque
ne soient pas parvenus officiellement à notre connaissance,
l'abdication du roi Constantin en faveur du Diadoque semble
chose faite; le changement de régime et la constitution d'un
gouvernement provisoire paraissent s'être effectuées sans
effusion de sang.Après avoir renié la France le peuple
       fait..../...

A series of three French naval documents regarding the evacuations and the Smyrna situation.

H.M.S. "Diligence", Friday 15th day of September, 1922.
From Smyrna, *To* Constantinople, *or At* Constantinople

Hours	Patent Log	Distance Run: Miles	Distance Run: Tenths	Standard Compass Courses	Deviation of Standard Compass	Revolutions per minute	Wind: Direction	Wind: Force	Weather	State of the Sea	Height of Barometer and Attached Thermometer	Temperature: Air	Temperature: Wet Bulb	Temperature: Sea
A.M.														
1		00 11	7 6	N. 11 E.	Nil	65								
2		11	6	– – –	–	66								
3		11	0 6	N. 46½ E	–	66								
4		5 4	8 9	– – – – – –	–	66	E.S.E	2-3	b.	2-3	30.04 80	74	73	71
5		6	7 9	N. 72 E. – – –	–	66								
6		10 1 3	7 9 9	N. 60 E N. 2 E As req	–	66.5								
7		3 2 3	6 2 4	N. 56 E – – – – – –	–	67								
8		8 5 5	5 0 4	N. 48 E – – – N. 68 E	–	67.7	E.N.E.	1-2	b.	1-2	30.04 83	75	75	72
9		1	6 2	As req – – –	–	68.2								
10		10	3	N. 68 E	–	65.5								
11		11 5	6 8	– – – – – –	–	65.8								
12		5	7	N. 77½ E	–	64.5	S.b.E	1-2	b.c.	1-2	30.05 80	79	77	71
P.M.														
1		5 15	5 5	N. 77½ E N. 82½ E	Nil	62								
2		11 2	0 7	N. 82½ E – – –	–	62								
3		8	3	N. 75 E	–	62								
4		11	0	– – –	–	62	N.E.	1-2	b.c.	0-1	30.02 84	85	77	71
5		11 5	0 5	– – – – – –	–	62								
6		2 1 2	7 5 0	N. 62 E As req Var	–	60.7 Var								
7			7											
8							Lt airs	0-1	b.c.		30.06 84	79	75	70
9														
10														
11														
12							Calm	0	b.		29.90 77	74	70	70

Position: 8.0 a.m. / 8.0 p.m. — Latitude — Longitude

REMARKS

A.M.

0145. Tenedos Lt. N. 28 E.
[illegible] sea boats crew.
0253. Tenedos Lt abm 4'. 0257 a/c N. 46½ E.
0300. Advanced clocks 30 mins
0425 a/c N. 72 E.
0503. C. Helles Lt. abm. 0505 a/c N. 60 E.
[illegible] sea boats crew
0610. a/c N. 2 E. 0625. Passed H.M. Ships Ajax, Concord, Tribune, Senator, Swell, Pegasus off Chanak
0630. a/c as req for rounding Nagara Simsau. 634. C/H 56 E.
0645 a/c N. 56 E 0717. C N. 48 E. 0733. Karaburun Lt. L. W/T + S.S.O. 0825. Zindjir Bozan buoy abm a/c N. 68 E
65 revs. 0852. a/c to avoid merchant ship
0901. Resumed co.
Hands employed as req
1130 a/c N. 77½ E. 1132. Khairsiz Ada abm 2'. 1139 62 revs

P.M.

1230 a/c N. 82½ E.
Hands make + mend clothes
1415 a/c N. 75 E.
1717. San Stefano Lt. abm 1.7' 1730 a/c N. 62 E.
1745. Co as req for entering Bosphorus. 1753, 34 revs
1803. Dressed ship with mast head flags (Italian [illegible]) 1805. Co + speed as req for securing to No. 8 buoy 1853. Secured to No. 8 buoy
Fleet anchorage. "[illegible]" sailed
Gave leave to P.W. till 2300. P.O.'s + till 2400
15 of [illegible] till 0700

Distance run through the Water	Course and Distance made good	Latitude	Longitude	Number on Sick List
224.8	134 (8) Var. 206'	D.R. – Obs. 40 41½ N	D.R. – Obs. 27 36½ E	18

Variation	True Bearing and Distance	Currents in the 24 hours ending at Noon
1½ W.	Khairsiz Ada Lt. 236° 5.5'	–

Provisions received	lbs.	Fresh Water	Tons	Fuel	Tons
Fresh Meat		Received		Expended for all purposes: Coal	47
Vegetables		Distilled		Oil	–
Bread		Expended	22	Remaining: Coal	305
		Remaining	2	Oil	–

Excerpts from the ships' logs of the British vessels HMS Cardiff, *HMS* Speer *and HMS* Diligence. *All three ships were in Smyrna waters, and the logs record the search for refugees and the arrival of the U.S. destroyers.*

H.M.S. " *Cardiff* ", Sunday 24ᵗʰ day of September, 1922.

From *Smyrna*, To *Constantinople* or At *Constantinople*

Time	Patent Log	Distance Run — Miles	Tenths	True Course	Revolutions per minute	Wind — Direction	Force	Weather	State of the Sea	Height of Barometer and attached Thermometer	Air	Wet Bulb	Sea	REMARKS
		138												
0100	-3....	10	0	as reqᵗ	215									12.30 Co as reqᵗ passing through Dardanelle. 1.0 Reduced speed as reqᵗ
0200		13	0	— —	140									1.30 Stopped off Chanak. H.M.S Marlborough communicated by boat.
0300		20	0	— —	215									1.45 Proceeded Co as reqᵗ for Dardanelle 3.10 Eski Fanar Burnu abᵗ ¾' Shaped Co 66° 215 Rev.
0400		16	8	66°	215	S.W	2	6	1	30.04 / 67	72	72	65	4.0.0
0500		16	5	— —	176									4.19 Rⁿᵈ speed to 140 Rev. 5.0 Nara Burnu Boᵗ abᵗ 5'
0600		12	0	— —										5.30 Kharsis Ada It abᵗ 2 m. 5.48 % 78°
0700		15	0	— —	160									
0800		15	0	— —	160	S.S.E	2	6	1	30.15 / 70	69	67	64	8.0.0 %
0900		as	reqᵘⁱˢⁱᵗ	138										8.5 & 9.40 Co & speed as reqᵗ searching for traces of survivors missing from H.M.S. Speedy.
1000		5	0	74°	159									9.40 Shaped Co 74°. 160 Rev.
1100		15	0	— —	160									11.35 S.Stefano It abᵗ 2' Co & speed as reqᵗ approaching Bosphorus
Noon		8	5	as reqᵘⁱˢⁱᵗ		S	2	6	0	30.16 / 72	75	73	64	Noon

Distance run through the Water	Course and Distance made good		Latitude	Longitude	Number on Sick List	Provisions received — lbs.	Fresh Water — Tons
292 2	as reqᵘⁱˢⁱᵗ		D.R. / Obs.	D.R. / Obs.	5	Fresh Meat	Received
Time kept at Noon	True Bearing and Distance		Currents in the 24 hours ending at Noon			Vegetables	Distilled 13 / Expended 4
3 hrs						Bread	Remaining 37

Time				True Course	Rev	Wind	Force			Barometer	Air	Wet	Sea	REMARKS
1300		as	reqᵘⁱˢⁱᵗ											Stopped 1.0 Steamed alongside oiler British Beacon in Haidar Pasha Bay.
1400														
1500														3.45 Slipped from oiler & proceeded as reqᵘⁱˢⁱᵗ to Fuel Jetty.
1600		as	reqᵘⁱˢⁱᵗ			N.N.E	6	6		30.15 / 76	76	74		4.40 Stopped & moored in 20 fms in No 3 Berth. 6 sh on each.
1700														
1800														
1900														
2000						N.	2	6	c	30.15 / 75	71	71		8.0.0
2100														
2200														
2300										30.09				
Midt						E.N.E	2	8		30.09 / 72	71	65		

Excerpts from the ships' logs of the British vessels HMS Cardiff, HMS Speer and HMS Diligence. All three ships were in Smyrna waters, and the logs record the search for refugees and the arrival of the U.S. destroyers.

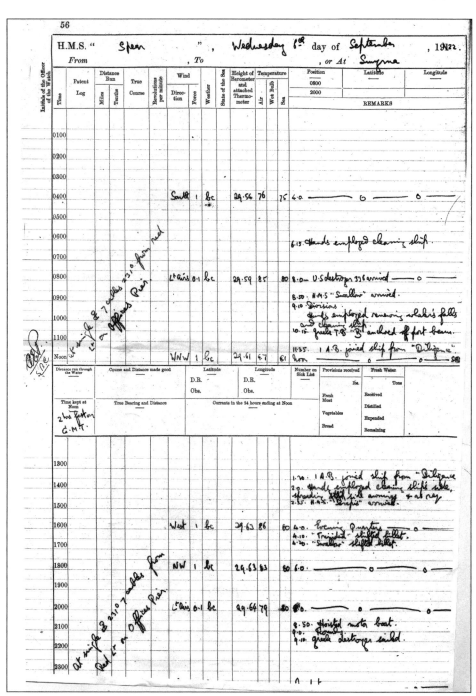

Excerpts from the ships' logs of the British vessels HMS Cardiff, HMS Speer and HMS Diligence. All three ships were in Smyrna waters, and the logs record the search for refugees and the arrival of the U.S. destroyers.

CHAPTER 6

The Japan Connection

SOME YEARS AFTER THE SMYRNA TRAGEDY, STORIES began to circulate that the Allied ships had *not* assisted in the evacuation, and that instead it was Japanese ships providing the primary means of escape. This misleading report has persisted even to the present day.

No one can know for certain at this juncture how the misconceptions started, but a number of books and articles about the rescue continue to perpetuate them. In 1971, Marjorie Housepian Dobkin wrote a book called *Smyrna 1922: The Destruction of a City*. Dobkin is an American of Armenian descent, and her book focuses on the brutal treatment of the Armenians during the taking of Smyrna, but also addresses the crisis overall. She claims, "The appearance of the [USS] *Simpson* on Thursday morning [September 14, 1922] raised a waver of excitement, but the initial cheers turned sour when word spread that only American citizens had been brought out. Later in the day, a Japanese ship arrived whose passengers praised the exceptional kindness of the captain and crew; they had thrown cargo overboard to make room for refugees. There was no other traffic from Smyrna all day."

Further on she records the memory of a refugee: "'The water was filled with bodies,' he said recently [refugee Karekin Bizdikian]. 'The Turks were going through the crowd with swords, robbing people, snatching girls, doing what they pleased. The French, American, and British ships were not making a move to help these people.'"

Smouldering Smyrna echoes Dobkin's story. Written in 1995 by Lydia Kouroyen Karagianis, of Laconia, New Hampshire, the book recounts her mother's story. Her mother was a young girl in Smyrna at the time of the tragedy. The book makes similar statements regarding help from Japan. Karagianis writes, "Only one warship out of the whole assorted fleet at anchor in the outer harbor could not countenance the barbarous inferno any longer, and that ship, was strange as it may seem, Asiatic, a Japanese ship. To the Japanese, no statute, no code, stood higher than human life."

The theme continues in *Demetrios the Survivor*, by Jasmine P. Andrews. Written in 2000, the book is a work of fiction but based on actual experiences by Andrews's family in Turkey. Andrews writes: "There were many merchant and foreign naval ships in the harbor of Tsesme. Not one ship offered to take the desperate refugees on board. Men tried to swim to ships only to be sprayed with hot water or kicked off the ships." The story goes on to relate how a Japanese ship offered assistance. "His crew had thrown many crates overboard to make room for his human cargo."

When I asked these authors where they got their information regarding Japanese involvement, none was able to provide written verification. In all of these accounts, the Japanese ship is never named, nor are any of the officers. No specifics are provided.

In 2001, the Dragatsis family set down its clan's history in the booklet *The Dragatsis Family 1745-2001: An American Experience*. It was written by Christos Dragatsis of Joliet, Illinois. The family also suffered through the Smyrna tragedy, and notes of ancestors' recollections appear in the booklet. The document includes the Americans and some other nations as providing assistance, but still focuses on Japan as a primary rescuer: "For days, they mingled on the wharfs of Smyrna, hungry and tired while the city of Smyrna was burning. Tens of thousands of refugees filled the city. Finally boats from Japan, Italy, America, France and England evacuated the refugees to the Greek islands and to the mainland."

Another proponent of the Japan theory is Stella L. Jatras, whose late husband was a career diplomat with the U.S. State Department. Jatras began writing letters to the *Washington Times* during the Clinton administration. She was urging the president to support House Resolution 596, which would have recognized the massacre of Armenians in Asia Minor during and after World War I. (The bill was defeated.)

Jatras brought up the crisis at Smyrna, and on October 20, 2000, wrote the following in one of her letters to the editor:

"Another interesting note in history is that during the 1922 Turkish genocide, there were ships in the Smyrna (now the Izmir) harbor from

Great Britain, the United States, France, Japan, and Italy, among others. To escape the massacring Turks, the Christian population swam out to these ships.

"The ships' crews, however, hit the hands of those trying to board so they would fall back into the sea or literally pushed them back into the sea. Their excuse? They did not want to offend the Turkish government. Only the Japanese captain took pity on the victims and allowed them on board."

As a source, Jatras cites, *Greek Fire*, a book by Nicholas Gage. (Gage is known for a number of compelling books, among them *Eleni*, the story of his mother's murder at the hands of the Germans during World War II.) *Greek Fire* is the story of the long love affair between the Greek shipping tycoon Aristotle Onassis and the opera singer Maria Callas. In it he writes: "Foreign battleships—English, American, Italians and French—were anchored in the harbor, sent by the major powers initially in support of Greek forces but later told to maintain neutrality. They would or could do nothing for the 200,000 refugees on the quai. The pitiful throng—huddled together, sometimes screaming for help but mostly waiting in a silent panic beyond hope—didn't budge for days. Typhoid reduced their numbers, and there was no way to dispose of the dead.

"Occasionally a person would swim from the dock to one of the anchored ships and try to climb the ropes and chairs only to be driven off. On the American battleships the musicians on board were ordered to play as loudly as they could to drown out the screams of the pleading swimmers. The English poured boiling water down on the unfortunates who reached their vessels. The harbors were so clogged with corpses that the officers of the foreign battleships were often late to their dinner appointments because bodies would get tangled in the propellers of their launches."

In his bibliography, Gage cites Dobkin's book as his source for the Smyrna information, and also acknowledges Onassis' personal accounts of the tragedy regarding the deaths of his relatives.

Even today, tales of Allied mistreatment and apathy persist, along with the legend that only Japanese ships intervened. Several speakers who lecture on Smyrna continue to include these stories in their talks. George Makredes is a businessman who frequently lectures on Smyrna. He resides in Massachusetts, but his family was originally from that part of Greece. One of his standard talks is entitled "The Smyrna Holocaust: Betrayal and

Barbarity." In it, Makredes says, "Mutilate, rape, murder and loot? . . . And how many died in the streets by gunfire, and on the quay, where waves of humanity were huddled, panic-stricken, trampled on by fire-crazed horses, pushed into the sea, or incinerated alive, awaiting rescue from foreign naval ships which looked the other way? How many hundreds of bodies floating lifeless in the harbor waters, chose slipping under the silent deep over the inferno and horror raging above . . . How many gave up hope after swimming out to one of the 'neutral' ships from Britain, France, Italy, United States and Japan only to be denied and driven away with scalding water or a severed line? . . .

"And how many perished in forced death marches into the Anatolian interior? God only knows their true numbers."

Among his sources Makredes cites Dobkin and Karagianis. Many of the books and accounts noted earlier credit each other.

It is interesting that none of the few published accounts seems to have corroborated its statements by actually researching and reading ships' or captains' logs from any of the numerous ships present from five countries. Nor, it seems, did any of the authors read any of the media accounts of the day. If they had, they would have seen over and over again, the true story of aid coming from many countries, and the inspiring effort of one man in particular, Asa Jennings. One could say, "Well, of course, the logs of the American ships will say they helped." Yet the logs of ships from other nations record the same thing. One might also say, "Of course the ships would not record any poor behavior," yet the logs of all the ships do not hesitate to be critical of certain actions by other nations. It is unlikely that a captain from one nation's vessel would not record the inhumanity supposedly displayed toward the refugees by another country's sailors—the dousing with scalding water, the pushing off with oars, and so on.

One speaker has argued that the ships of Great Britain, France, Italy, and the United States were "neutral," and that is why he claims they did not help. Yet the neutrality issue is not strictly true. Technically, Great Britain, France, and Italy were at war with Turkey; only the United States was neutral. All of the nations present were walking a very delicate line in terms of trying not to escalate a conflict with Turkey, at the same time contributing humanitarian aid to the Greeks, Armenians, and others.

Some might ask, why was the United States neutral? Why didn't she, or any other nation, make a move to get involved militarily? The answer appears to be that both the United States and other nations wanted to avoid precipitating World War II. The peace at the time of the Smyrna crisis was uneasy at best. There were many unresolved issues among the combatants of World War I. Adding to the tension was the desire by many of the nations for control of various territories within the Ottoman Empire, not to mention control of the straits. If any country had taken sides militarily with Turkey or Greece, the others would have quickly followed suit, and war undoubtedly would have broken out as they fought to secure their claims.

No one wanted an armed conflict coming so quickly upon the heels of the Great War, which had claimed many young men and drained every country's resources. A war in the Near East would have been especially costly for the United States, not just in terms of possible loss of life, but in sheer logistics as well. Once again, the fighting would have taken place more than halfway around the world, and the cost of moving men, machines, fuel, arms, and supplies seemed prohibitive. The United States had no land claims in Asia Minor and no unfinished business from World War I, so there were no real grounds for launching a military strike against Turkey.

Many of the accounts mentioned in this chapter give the impression of a contingent of uncaring naval officers from powerful nations who stood idly by while Smyrna burned. Yet these same naval officers held a conference aboard the Italian flagship *Galileo* for the main purpose of providing aid and rescue to the refugees. This conference was suggested by American officers, and not only attended by all nations present, but also documented by their captains' logs. If the nations present had no interest in saving the refugees, why did every single log document each nation participating to varying degrees in evacuating the Greeks? And even those who did not play a large-scale role in evacuating refugees sent food to aid them.

And what of Asa Jennings? His dramatic actions did not go unnoticed by the local naval commanders—the Americans documented his efforts quite specifically—and the media of the day gave him extensive coverage. His selflessness also did not go unrecognized by the people he saved, as we shall see. How could his "rescue fleet," the main vehicle for removing the refugees, be overlooked?

The support of these nations, specifically the Americans, continued after the immediate evacuation. Food, money, materials, and hands-on help were provided in great quantity. The Americans alone contributed

$18 million in relief aid, according to The *New York Times* of June 24, 1923, dateline Constantinople.

And what about the Japanese? Were Japanese naval ships present? Were they the heroic rescuers? This is truly a puzzle, for research shows that not only were Japanese naval ships not the primary rescuers of the Greeks, but Japanese naval ships were not even present in Smyrna Harbor during September 1922, never mind leading the rescue.

This is documented by three Japanese government agencies that responded to questions about the role of any Japanese ships during the evacuation at Smyrna in September 1922. The agencies are the Military History Department, the National Institute for Defense Studies, and the Japan Information and Culture Center at the Embassy of Japan.

A letter from the National Institute for Defense Studies in Tokyo, dated March 9, 2000, from Captain (retired) Noritaka Kitzzawa, says the following:

"In reply to your letter of January 27, 2000, in 1922 Japanese Naval Ships operated in the Pacific, Atlantic and Indian Ocean. So Japanese Naval ships did not visit in the Mediterranean Sea."

The Military History Department in Tokyo, sent this communication on June 22, 2002: "This library has every day's Japanese Naval ships station in 1922. From this book, in the September 1922, there is no Japanese Naval ship in the Mediterranean Sea."

Copies of these letters are included in this chapter, as are letters from the Japan Information and Culture Center, Embassy of Japan. Here is an excerpt from a letter sent by the Honorable Izumi Seki, deputy executive director of the center, on January 28, 2000:

"We have searched the data bases of the Defense Agency, the National Institute for Defense Studies, and the Diplomatic Record Office of the Ministry of Foreign Affairs, and were unable to find any information. We have also tried the Nippon Yusan Kaisha Maritime Museum, but were unable to come up with any leading clues. The only information we found in the Nippon Yusan Kaisha Maritime Museum that might be helpful to you is that Nippon Yusan was the first private ship operator of Japan to create an annual ship route to the port of Smyrna in 1924." This is not until two years after the terrible events of September 1922.

Mr. Seki's letter goes on to say that he also reviewed the databank of the Asahi Shimbun Public Relations Desk (Asahi newspaper), which featured articles on the Smyrna massacre from September to December 1922, but there was no mention of any Japanese ships rescuing the Greeks.

Therefore, it seems safe to say that no Japanese military ships were involved in this epic evacuation, much less played a leading role. It is also unlikely that a fleet of Japanese merchant vessels was present. None of their government agencies, and none of the media accounts of the time, mention their ships even being in those waters; they also do not mention any rescue activities regarding the trapped Greeks. If such rescue efforts had indeed been mounted by the Japanese navy or by Japanese citizens, the accounts would have been recorded in captains' logs and later publicized.

It is especially ironic that Japan was frequently cited as the main rescuer when in fact, Japan sympathized with the Turks. This information came to light through a confidential memo from U.S. Rear Admiral Mark Bristol, who was commanding the American naval detachment in Smyrna, to the Secretary of the Navy in Washington, D.C. (See facing page.)

So where did the stories of Japanese rescue ships come from? At this date, most likely the origin will never be known. Perhaps Japanese fishing boat or merchant ship was present in a nearby harbor; it is possible that such a vessel provided some help. But clearly there were not a large number of Japanese ships heading the rescue.

Some Greeks are beginning to search for the truth and have questioned stories of what happened at Smyrna, including Japan's sympathies lying with the Turks. Following is a letter from Professor Stavros Stavridis, a historical researcher from Melbourne, Australia, who frequently writes about Smyrna.

"Dear Mr. Papoutsy,

"I apologise for not answering sooner [as I] was on holidays until today. I will respond to your inquiry based on rechecking some of the documentary evidence. I honestly thought the Japanese did assist in the evacuation of refugees from Smyrna to mainland Greece and Greek Islands. I checked the war diaries of Admiral Mark Bristol, the U.S. High Commissioner in Constantinople and naval intelligence reports, for the period September-October 1922 and could not find one shred of evidence on Japanese assistance.

"Bristol sent copies of his war diary and naval intelligence reports to Secretary of State Charles E. Hughes and these documents list the names and origin of American, British ships, etc. that went to Smyrna and other

. . . continued on page 130

JAPAN SUPPORTS TURKEY –
URGES ALLIES TO NOT GET INVOLVED

Wednesday, 20 of September, 1922

In the afternoon I received a call from the Japanese High Commissioner, Mr. Uchida. He came as usual for information but I had very little to give him. He is well known to be very close to the Turks here in Constantinople, and at the same time I know his people very well and their proclivity for using other people as a source of information. He tried to lead me out on the subject of the critical situation here, and I admitted the situation looked grave to me and almost anything might happen, but I was careful not to express my opinion about what might happen or what the Allies should do. He, himself, volunteered that it would be a great mistake for the Allies to bring on a war here with the Nationalist Turks and that the Allies without big reinforcements could not hope to stand off a determined attack by the Turkish Nationalists. I simply asked him if he really thought the Allies hadn't sufficient forces and he said quite decidedly that that was his idea. This is not the first time that Uchida has shown his sympathy with the Turks. When he first came and one of the first times that we had a talk he expressed the idea that Japan is interested in the freedom of the Straits from her interest in Russian affairs. I have always been inclined to believe that he was interested in favor of the Turks because Japan does not desire to antagonize Bolshevik Russia on account of the interests in the far east of Japan in Siberia. There was some other side talk along the same line with Uchida and I became more than ever convinced that he was not in sympathy with the policy of England.

Consul General G. Bie Ravndal called to pay his respects and report his return from leave of absence. He suggested the idea of a plan for the protection of American lives in Constantinople if there were any disturbances. I told him that we were drawing up such a plan at the present time, further that I felt that I had naval vessels enough to handle the situation as far as protection of American lives were concerned, but I could not undertake the protection of American property, and in fact, without a large military force the protection of American property would be impossible if there was any real attack on our property. I told him that I had been through such experiences a good many times and our plan would cover the situation without any trouble. He suggested that during the Greek war he had been a member of a committee to arrange for the concentration of Americans in certain quarters.

FROM: Rear Admiral Mark L. Bristol
             Commander U.S. Naval Detachment
             Eastern Mediterranean

TO: The Secretary of the Navy
             Washington, D.C.

Letter from Admiral Mark Bristol to the U.S. Secretary of the Navy, noting Japan's political leanings during the Smyrna crisis.

Captain (Ret.) Noritaka Kitazawa
Military History Department
National Institute for Defense Studies
2-2-1 Nakameguro, Meguro-Ku
Tokyo 153-8648 Japan
9th March 2000

Mr. Chris and Mrs. Mary Papoutsy
P.O. Box 322
Rye Beach, N.H. 03871
U.S.A.

Dear Mr. Chris and Mrs. Mary Papoutsy

I reply to your letter of January 27, 2000.
In 1922 Japanese Naval Ships (Training Squadron) operated in The Pacific, Atlantic and Indian Ocean.
So Japanese Naval ships did not visit in The Mediterranean Sea.
As to merchant ships, this library has no materials and I can no give you any information on your request.

Yours Sincerely

Noritaka Kitazawa

Letter, March 9, 2000, from the Japanese Military History Department, National Institute for Defense Studies, regarding the involvement of Japanese ships in the rescue of the refugees.

Captain(Ret.) Noritaka Kitazawa
Military History Department
National Institute for Defense Studies
2-2-1 Nakameguro, Meguro-Ku
Tokyo 153-8648 Japan
22nd June 2000

Mr. Chris and Mrs. Mary Papoutsy
P.O. Box 322
Rye Beach, N H 03871
U.S.A.

Dear Mr. Chris and Mrs. Mary Papoutsy

I reply to your letter of May 9, 2000.
This library has every day's Japanese naval ships station in 1922.
From this book, in the September 1922, there is no Japanese naval ship in the Mediterranean Sea.

Yours Sincerely

n. Kitazawa

Noritaka Kitazawa

Letter from Japanese Military History Department on June 22, 2000.

JAPAN INFORMATION & CULTURE CENTER
EMBASSY OF JAPAN

Lafayette Centre III, 1155 21st Street, NW
Washington, DC 20036
Tel: (202) 238-6900
Fax: (202) 822-6524
http://www.embjapan.org/jicc.html

January 28, 2000

Mr. & Mrs. Chris Paputsu
P.O. Box 710 Rye Beach
New Hampshire, 03871

Re: Inquiry about the ship ported in Smyrna

Dear Mr. & Mrs. Chris Paputsu,

Thank you for your letter dated October 29th concerning the ship ported in Smynar. We regret to report that we were unable to find the name of the ship you requested.

We have searched in the databases of the Defense Agency, the National Institute for Defense Studies, and the Diplomatic Record Office of the Ministry of Foreign Affairs, and were unable to find any information. We have also tried the Nippon Yusen Kaisha Maritime Museum, but were unable to come up with any leading clues. The only information we found in the Nippon Yusen Kaisha Maritime Museum that might be helpful to you is that Nippon Yusen Kaisha was the first private ship operator of Japan to create an annual ship route to the Port of Smyrna in 1924. Therefore if it actually existed it should have been a non-annual liner ship of a private company.

In the Asahi Shimbun Public Relations Desk (Asahi Newspaper) databank, we were able to find articles of the Port of Smyrna massacre in several articles ranging from September to December of 1922, although there was no mentioning of any Japanese ships assisting in a rescue effort of the Greeks.

We have exhausted all of the resources we have at hand to find this information, but could not find any significant information for you. We apologize for any inconvenience it may cause, and for the delay in our response. If you have any more questions that we might be able to answer, please feel free to contact us again at 202-238-6949. Thank you for your patience.

Sincerely,

Izumi Seki
Deputy Executive Director
JICC, Embassy of Japan

Letter, January 28, 2000, from the Japan Information & Culture Center regarding the same.

Turkish seaports to remove refugees. What is interesting is that Bristol does record in his war diary that S. Uchida the Japanese high commissioner in Constantinople, was sympathetic to the Turks; Uchida was interested in freedom of the Straits. Japan was competing with the Soviets for influence in the Far East and Tokyo may have (had) interest in expanding its trade with Russia in the Black Sea. The State Dept. and British Foreign Documents may contain some important details that could shed some light on this issue."

Professor Stavridis later conducted further research into the matter; what he found reinforces the case for the possibility that a Japanese merchant ship or fishing vessel was present. He found several old newspaper accounts that quoted a handful of survivors as praising help by a—that is, one—Japanese ship; the story of cargo being thrown overboard to make room for refugees is repeated. But no account can name the ship, and several describe it as a merchantman or freighter (which is consistent with the cargo story). This would also explain why the name is not officially recorded anywhere, as it would be with a military vessel.

Professor Stavridis also checked the *Japanese Times and Mail*, a Japanese newspaper published in English in Yokohama, for clues regarding Japanese shipping movements between September and October 1922. Again, no Japanese ships of any kind were noted as being in Smyrna Harbor. However, there were Japanese ships plying various trade routes in Asia Minor, including the route between Marseilles and Port Said. Stavridis suggests that perhaps one of these ships diverted course for Smyrna, and that is possible.

We will probably never know if a Japanese merchant ship provided aid at Smyrna; quite possibly one did. But again, clearly a Japanese military fleet was not present, nor was Japan the main rescuer of refugees from this catastrophe.

The Surveys

The Hellenic Communication Service is a nonprofit, charitable venture. It provides free Internet news and information for Greeks and Greek communities in the United States and worldwide. The site receives more than one million visits each year.

. . . *continued on page 134*

Hellenic Communication Service Survey

Smyrna, September 1922: Searching for the Truth about the Evacuations

The publishers of Hellenic Communication Service are completing research on the evacuation of refugees from Smyrna in September 1922, as the title of this online survey indicates. Results of the research will be released in an upcoming book to be published sometimes in the next two years. Considerable work has been expended on this topic and your personal input would be greatly appreciated. Please take a moment to indicate your *perception* of the tragic events of that fateful month; these impressions may be based on facts, direct personal knowledge, or information gleaned second-hand by family members or friends involved in the evacuation.

1. From September 1 to September 30, 1922, which countries, in your opinion, offered the most assistance in evacuating the refugees from the quay of Smyrna?

Directions: Rank your three top choices by placing the numbers 1, 2, and 3 next to the names of your selections below.

Country	Checkmark
Italy	
Greece	1
France	
Japan	2
Britain	
Sweden	
United States	
Russia	
Canada	
Spain	
Australia	
Other (specify)	

2. To which locations were most of the refugees initially evacuated?

Directions: Place a check mark next to your chosen location below.

Location	Checkmark
Pireaus	
Rhodes	
Lesvos	
United States	
London	
Other (specify)	

3. How many refugees, in your opinion, were evacuated from Smyrna during September 1922?

Directions: Mark only one number below.

Number of Refugees Evacuated	Checkmark
50,000	
300,000 to 700,000	
One million	
Other (specify)	CIVILIANS – NOT MANY

GREEK ARMY– MOST OF IS

4. Where did you receive the information that informed your answers to the survey questions?

Directions: Mark all that apply below.

Method	Checkmark
Word of Mouth	
Books, literature	
Other (specify)	LECTURE / BOOK REVIEW

5. From what part of Greece does your family originate?

CRETE

6. Please provide us with any other written comments relevant to the evacuation of refugees from Smyrna during the month of September 1922. Your remarks will be greatly valued.

BARNES & NOBLE, TEL. 603- 422- 7733
BOOK AVAILABLE:
"SMYRNA INCIDENT"
BY DOCTOR MARGERY HOUSEPIAN DOBKIN
WAS PROF. AT HUNTER COLLEGE.
SHE RESEARCHED THE STORY TO RESOLVE CONFLICT BETWEEN
FAMILY ARMENIANS AND TURKISH FRIENDS.
NOTE: AMERICAN SEC. OF STATE WAS FORMERLY OF STANDARD OIL.
HIS ORDERS TO U.S. NAVY WERE–DO NOTHING TO OFFEND THE TURKS.

7. Please provide us with your name and postal address so that we can mail you a copy of our forthcoming book about Smyrna in appreciation for your participation in the survey.

Name: GEORGE J. SIGANOS

Address: 445 OCEAN BLVD.

City: HAMPTON   Zipcode: 03842

State: N. H.

Country: U. S. A.

CHRIS & MARY Properantey

Thank you for your participation in this important survey. Please return to

Hellenic Communication Service
PO Box 6748
Portsmouth, NH 03802-6748

pp 131-133: Three filled-out copies of Hellenic Communications Surveys. Responding are George Makredes, Bill Ameredes (former president of the Asia Minor Hellenic American Society of Ohio), and George Siganos. Surveys were distributed in Greek and English. (Shown reduced)

Hellenic Communication Service Survey

Smyrna, September 1922: Searching for the Truth about the Evacuations

The publishers of Hellenic Communication Service are completing research on the evacuation of refugees from Smyrna in September 1922, as the title of this online survey indicates. Results of the research will be released in an upcoming book to be published sometime in the next two years. Considerable work has been expended on this topic and your personal input would be greatly appreciated. Please take a moment to indicate your *perception* of the tragic events of that fateful month; these impressions may be based on facts, direct personal knowledge, or information gleaned second-hand by family members or friends involved in the evacuation.

1. From September 1 to September 30, 1922, which countries, in your opinion, offered the most assistance in evacuating the refugees from the quay of Smyrna?

Directions: Rank your three top choices by placing the numbers 1, 2, and 3 next to the names of your selections below.

Country	Checkmark
Italy	
Greece	
France	#1
Japan	#3
Britain	
Sweden	#2
United States	
Russia	
Canada	
Spain	
Australia	
Other (specify)	

2. To which locations were most of the refugees initially evacuated?

Directions: Place a check mark next to your chosen location below.

Location	Checkmark
Piraeus	
Rhodes	
Lesvos	
United States	✓
London	
Other (specify) GREECE	

FRANCE

Suggestion: Should heart-rendering numerical order

3. How many refugees, in your opinion, were evacuated from Smyrna during September 1922?

Directions: Mark only one number below.

Number of Refugees Evacuated	Checkmark
50,000	
300,000 to 700,000	
One million	
Other (specify)	✓

4. Where did you receive the information that informed your answers to the survey questions?

Directions: Mark all that apply below.

Method	Checkmark
Word of Mouth	
Books, literature	✓
Other (specify)	

5. From what part of Greece does your family originate?

Mother – Ganohora near Constantinla
Father – Porton – Augyropolia (Grandfather & from Metaloya (Matsa)

6. Please provide us with any other written comments relevant to the evacuation of refugees from Smyrna during the month of September 1922. Your remarks will be greatly valued.

Many left from Smyrna but the majority, in my opinion left from Porton & other cities; Bruda Ceomus alletate Palemor Barugales

7. Please provide us with your name and postal address so that we can mail you a copy of our forthcoming book about Smyrna in appreciation for your participation in the survey.

Name: Bill N. Amerodes
Address: 81 Fischurst Rd.
City: Munroe Falls
State: Ohio   Zipcode: 44262
Country: U.S.A.

Thank you for your participation in this important survey. Please return to

Hellenic Communication Service
PO Box 6748
Portsmouth, NH 03802-6748

Chris & Mary Papanty

FROM:
Georg Makreon

Hellenic Communication Service Survey

Smyrna, September 1922: Searching for the Truth about the Evacuations

The publishers of Hellenic Communication Service are completing research on the evacuation of refugees from Smyrna in September 1922, as the title of this online survey indicates. Results of the research will be released in an upcoming book to be published sometime in the next two years. Considerable work has been expanded on this topic and your personal input would be greatly appreciated. Please take a moment to indicate your *perception* of the tragic events of that fateful month; these impressions may be based on facts, direct personal knowledge, or information gleaned second-hand by family members or friends involved in the evacuation.

1. From September 1 to September 30, 1922, which countries, in your opinion, offered the most assistance in evacuating the refugees from the quay of Smyrna?

   Directions: Rank your three top choices by placing the numbers 1, 2, and 3 next to the names of your selections below.

Country	Checkmark
Italy	
Greece	
France	
Japan	1
Britain	
Sweden	
United States	
Russia	
Canada	
Spain	
Australia	
Other (specify)	

2. To which locations were most of the refugees initially evacuated?

   Directions: Place a check mark next to your chosen location below.

Location	Checkmark
Piraeus	✓
Rhodes	
Lesvos	
United States	
London	
Other (specify)	

3. How many refugees, in your opinion, were evacuated from Smyrna during September 1922?

   Directions: Mark only one number below.

Number of Refugees Evacuated	Checkmark
50,000	✓
300,000 to 700,000	
One million	
Other (specify)	

4. Where did you receive the information that informed your answers to the survey questions?

   Directions: Mark all that apply below.

Method	Checkmark
Word of Mouth	
Books, literature	✓
Other (specify)	

5. From what part of Greece does your family originate?

   ALATSATA & TSESME, ASIA MINOR

6. Please provide us with any other written comments relevant to the evacuation of refugees from Smyrna during the month of September 1922. Your remarks will be greatly valued.

7. Please provide us with your name and postal address so that we can mail you a copy of our forthcoming book about Smyrna in appreciation for your participation in the survey.

   Name: GEORGE MAKREDES SR.

   Address: 1074 MASSACHUSETTS AVENUE

   City: ARLINGTON   Zipcode: 02476

   State: MASS

   Country:

Thank you for your participation in this important survey. Please return to

Hellenic Communication Service
PO Box 6748
Portsmouth, NH 03802-6748

Chris & Mary Papanity

In 2000-2001, Hellenic Communication Service conducted a survey to find out what impressions people had of Smyrna. Who did they think came to the aid of the refugees? Where were the refugees taken? How many did they think were evacuated? News of the survey was posted on the company's Web site, and surveys could be downloaded. Additional hard copies of the survey were sent out, using mailing lists provided by the Center for Asia Minor Studies in Athens. I interviewed a few individuals in person; I traveled to Greece specifically for this purpose.

Analysis of the several hundred responses revealed that 27 percent believed that Greek ships provided the most assistance in evacuating the refugees from the Smyrna quay in September of 1922. This corroborates Asa Jennings' rescue fleet of Greek ships with American escorts. However, 23 percent believed Japanese ships were involved; 21 percent cited Americans as the rescuers; 10 percent named France; 7 percent named Great Britain and Italy; and 5 percent believed Russian ships had aided in the rescue.

Respondents indicated that Lesvos, Piraeus, and Rhodes were where the majority of the refugees were taken. As to how many refugees were evacuated, respondents were divided in their estimates, with reports ranging from 50,000 to one million. (see surveys in previous pages)

Lecturer George Makredes participated in the survey, and his response indicated that he believed Japan offered the most assistance in evacuating the refugees from Smyrna; that most were taken to Piraeus; and that about 50,000 refugees were evacuated. The survey asked respondents to indicate where they or their family were from, and Makredes' family originated from Alatsata and Tsesme in Asia Minor. The survey also asks where people received the information that they based their answers on, and Makredes indicated books and literature. As noted earlier, in his lectures he frequently cites Dobkin and Karagianis, whose books credit Japanese ships as the heroic rescuers. The point here is not to target Mr. Makredes, but rather to illustrate how once a story gets started, it can expand and evolve to influence even the most respected speakers and authors. Researchers appear to focus on the same few works, never going far enough or deep enough to unearth the whole story. Family memories (often passed down only orally) can merge with tales told by others, who heard them from someone else, and so on, until very little real fact remains. The one truth, corroborated over and over, is the veracity of the horrific tales of abuse. The outcry of the victims continues to ring through time.

Most of the respondents were relatives, descendants, or friends of those affected by the Smyrna tragedy, not actual survivors. However, interviews were conducted with a few eyewitnesses.

Eyewitness Accounts

In 2001, I journeyed to Greece to conduct interviews with survivors and eyewitnesses to the Smyrna tragedy. Among those was George Katramopoulos, a survivor of the exodus. He was interviewed at the Athens home of his daughter, the renowned Greek journalist and reporter for the Kathimerini newspaper *Eleni Bistikas*. The interview was conducted in Greek. The English-language translation appears below.

Questions

1) Were you evacuated from Smyrna during September (or October) 1922?
2) If you were, on which ship were you evacuated? Do you remember its name and registry (to what country did it belong?)? For example, was it a French, Greek, British, or Japanese ship?
3) If you were evacuated, where did the ship take you?
4) How long did you have to wait on the quay before being evacuated?
5) What did you see with your own eyes regarding the treatment toward refugees by sailors and officials of the various ships in the harbor, the American, French, Italian, Japanese and British vessels?
6) The ships of which countries assisted most in the evacuation of the refugees, according to your own experience?
7) Is it true what many people say, that only the Japanese vessels assisted the refugees?
8) Do you have any written diaries or letters from this time frame that we could come and look at?
9) Have you ever been interviewed by anyone regarding this subject? (Note: I left reference to Japanese ships in the questions to see what kind of response that evoked.)

Answers and comments, translated by Mary Papoutsy into English:

"Dear madam and sir . . . Thank you for selecting me to inform you about the events during the Smyrna Catastrophe and the expulsion of the Greeks by the Turks in 1922. Note, however, that my bad vision is not aiding me but my memory is very good and thus I am in the position to give you the information, replying to questions and completing the answers to your questionnaire.

I am answering the questions in the order you have them.

1) September—9-13-1922.
2) Old Russian cargo ship
3) In Macedonia, Gulf of Thessaloniki
4) Around 5 to 6 hours.
5) The only assistance came from American organizations, which indeed continued to aid us for some time. If my memory does not play tricks on me, the president of such an organization was the American Senator Morgenthau, in whose honor a street of Athens is dedicated.[1]
6) Only cargo ships charted by American organizations and the Greek government.
7) No Japanese ships were present.
8) I have published two books with memories from Smyrna.[2]
9) I have often given televised interviews about the Catastrophe (These interviews have been on Greek television.)

Athens, 5-8-2001—Katramopoulos, George"

On September 8, 2005, we visited the home of Mrs. Filio Haïdemenou, a survivor of the Smyrna holocaust. Mentally sharp, Mrs. Haïdemenou is "106 years young" and in good health. She lives with her daughter and son-in-law in Nea Filadelfia, an Athens suburb. Mrs. Haïdemenou is the author of the recently published book *Three Eras, One Life—Grandmother Filio from Asia Minor* (Treis Aiones Mia Zoi), and the founder and president of the folklore museum Laografiko Mouseio P.P. I. E. D.-Filio Haïdemenou.[3]

The interview was conducted in Greek. Mrs. Haïdemenou stated that she clearly remembered her evacuation from Smyrna in a small boat. She was fifteen years old at the time. "It was the Americans," she stressed. According to her, the Americans rescued the majority of the stranded refugees from the quay. She also said there were no Japanese or Chinese ships in Smyrna Harbor.

In an excerpt from her book, she recalls, "Two days and nights we remained standing at the shore, waiting to board some boat. Thousands of people, without hope and in abject poverty, with eyes vacant from what we had seen, and with hearts bleeding painfully from the deaths of our loved ones. Carts unloaded dead bodies next to us where they were stumbled upon. In the evening, the Turks began to rape and commit terrible acts against the women they found; the Americans turned on their searchlights and trained them on us to stop the evil deeds somehow. Voices were heard: 'Women and children board first!'" (translated from the Greek by Mary Papoutsy)

We also uncovered eyewitness accounts recorded in a book by Demetrios I. Archigenes, called *Witnesses of the Asia Minor Catastrophe*. The book was published in 1973 in Athens by a private printing house, the Estia Nea Smyrnis, an Onassis family foundation. Mary Papoutsy translated some of the accounts from the Greek.

The account of witness Anestos Serras:

"Outside of Smyrna, near the wagonpath, was the monastery complex called 'Koulas' occupied and owned by the Catholic Church. Catholic nuns there ran a home for the blind and an orphanage. Witness indicated that the nuns saved many lives during the Catastrophe, and had even offered to take the witness' immediate family, but not his extended family, with them when they were evacuated by French troops. Anestos declined the offer, and somehow managed to make his way—through much danger—to the harbor. Eventually, he was rescued and transported away by an 'English' ship, called the Litchfield." (*Author's note*: The full account appears on pages 22-33 of Archigenes' book. The English ship called the *Litchfield* is actually an American ship.)

Although Smyrna 1922 was unquestionably a time of horror, with evil deeds committed by many, it was also a time of heroism. Many people from diverse nationalities, ranks, and walks of life came together to aid the Greek refugees. Naval personnel and civilian personnel worked side by side to mount a rescue, provide food and medical aid, and see the refugees established in new locations. The crimes of Smyrna should not be forgotten, nor should the good works of those tragic days.

Πώς να σε ξεχάσω, Σμύρνη αγαπημένη...
Ο Γ. Θ. Κατραμόπουλος υπογράφοντας το πρώτο του βιβλίο (πάλι από την «Ωκεανίδα»), που έκανε επτά εκδόσεις και μπήκε στη λίστα των «μπεστ-σέλλερ».
(Φωτογραφία Γιάννη Μπαρδόπουλου)

LEFT: *George Katramopoulos, Smyrna survivor and survey respondent. He is the author of several books about his experience during the Smyrna catastrophe.*

BELOW: *Smyrna survivor Mrs. Filio Haïdemenou with Mary and Chris Papoutsy.*

CENTRE D' ÉTUDES D' ASIE MINEURE
FONDATEURS:
MELPO ET OCTAVE MERLIER
KYDATHINÉON 11, ATHÈNES 105 58 GRÈCE
TEL.: 210 3239225 - FAX: 210 3229758
e-mail: kms@otenet.gr

Athènes 17. 2. 04

Reg. No: 28

Chris Papoutsy
Publisher
Hellenic Communication Service
PO Box 6748
Portsmouth
NH 03802-6748,
USA

Dear Sir,

I have been informed, by S. Th. Anestides, of the important work the Hellenic Communication Service has been undertaking on the memory and tradition of Asia Minor Hellenism.

Please find enclosed 18 questionnaires of the Hellenic Communication Service's survey entitled "Smyrna, September 1922: Searching for the Truth about the Evacuations". These were completed in the last two months in the Center of Asia Minor Studies from visiting researchers and readers. The number of questionnaires completed could have been significantly higher, had been not hindered by mainly two reasons. Firstly, the relatively small number of visitors lately consisted of the same people on a daily basis and, also, a number of them had very little or no knowledge of the English language. The Center is always willing to contribute further to your research program. We will continue to kindly ask our visitors to take some time to complete the questionnaire. We reserve ourselves to be of greater contribution to your research in the near future.

Best regards

Stelios A. Kapsomenos
Researcher

Letter from the Center of Asia Minor Studies regarding the surveys.

End Notes

1. I believe he refers to Henry Morgenthau, a former U.S. ambassador, who was appointed by the League of Nations to head the Greek Refugee Settlement Committee in Athens.

2. George Katramopoulos is the author of *One Era, Two Homelands, How Could I Forget You, Dear Smyrna*, and *The Smyrna of Her Compatriots*.

3. Approximate translation of Mrs. Filio Haïdemenou's museum, World Cultural Foundation of Hellenism in the Diaspora "Andreas Papandreou," in the Municipality of New Philadelphia.

CHAPTER 7

The Plight of the Refugees

*Although the world is full of suffering, it is also full of
overcoming it,*
— *Helen Keller*

*I*F LIFE WERE A MOVIE, THEN THE REFUGEES WOULD have
sailed off into the sunset and all would have been instantly resolved. But
this was not the case; for the rescuers, the challenge of helping these people
was expanding rather than shrinking. For the refugees themselves, life was
still filled with turmoil. The immediate danger was gone, but new fears were
on the horizon.

With the collapse of the Greek army, the writing was on the wall—the
Turks would regain control of the region and Greek citizens would be driven
out. Consequently, Greeks from all over Asia Minor began fleeing toward
the coast, racing for their lives ahead of the victorious Turks. As a result,
nearly a million people were evacuated from Smyrna and surrounding
towns, creating one of the largest exoduses in history. Initially, the flight
from Turkey was somewhat orderly. Refugees journeyed to the coast by
rail and bus, laden with suitcases and bundles of goods. Some came from
outlying towns with carts piled with their possessions.

"Refugees from anywhere within 150 miles inland herded seaward
toward Smyrna. At first, they came in orderly trainloads or in carts with
rug-wrapped bedding, some little household equipment, and perhaps even
a few animals. But as the distant military momentum speeded up, the influx

became a wild rabble of ten, then twenty, then thirty thousand a day. Their increasingly scanty possessions betokened a mad and yet madder stampede from the sword of fire, until September 7 saw utterly destitute multitudes staggering in," wrote Melville Chater in *History's Greatest Trek*, by Constantine Hatzidimitriou's, *American Accounts Documenting the Destruction of Smyrna by the Kemalist Turkish Forces, September 1922*.

The fact that these people were being driven from their homelands was tragic, but with an orderly evacuation, they might have brought enough resources with which to start a new life. But once panic ensued, carts and bundles were left behind, and families fled with what they had on their backs. Some retained a few pitiful bundles of clothing or household goods, but no more. Those who did retain their money, or anything else of value, were fodder for the thieves who prowled the quay.

The refugee population was unique in that it was largely women and children, the ill and the elderly. All able-bodied men between the ages of roughly sixteen and fifty (what was then considered military age) had been conscripted into the interior of Turkey, most never to be seen or heard of again. Families were shattered as fathers, brothers, sons, and fiancés were torn from the arms of their loved ones. The air was filled with the sound of wailing and screams; even the ships offshore could hear the lamentations. Those on the quay knew that imprisonment and death awaited their loved ones. For themselves, their fate remained unknown. Whatever life held in store, it would not happen here, in their own country, but rather in some new place.

Among the evacuees were scores of pregnant women. "Never have I seen so many women carrying children," said Dr. Esther Lovejoy, chairman of the executive board of the American Women's Hospitals and president of the Medical Women's International Association, in the *New York Times*, October 19, 1922. Dr. Lovejoy worked tirelessly among the refugees, caring for their needs and delivering babies. "It seemed that every other woman was an expectant mother," she said. "The flight and conditions brought on many premature births, and on the quay with scarcely room to lie down and without aid, most of the children were born. In the five days I was there more than 200 such confinements occurred."

Even those who had started the trek in decent condition were weakened by days without food and water, and the heat of a relentless sun. Adding to their physical difficulties was their state of mind. These people

Thousands of refugees pack the port of Mytilene as they await transport to other locations in Greece.

▼ *Refugees trek to the sea.*

Desperately needed flour arrives in Mitylene via American ships.

American sailors transport ill and elderly refugees along the rail lines.

had suffered and witnessed untold horrors. They had been robbed, beaten, and raped; women had seen their children raped, their husbands murdered or taken away. All possessions were gone—stolen or left behind. Life as they had known it no longer existed. And what of the future? Was there a future?

Many found enough strength of purpose to fight for survival; others were barely clinging to life. Their bodies functioned, but their minds were elsewhere, imprisoned by the horrors they had experienced. Today, we know this as post-traumatic stress syndrome and treatment is available, but in the 1920s, there was little to be done.

Then there was the language barrier. These refugees were terrified, and though their rescuers tried to reassure them, the lack of a common language made that difficult. Eventually, actions spoke louder than words, but until the rescuers' benign intentions sunk in, chaos reigned. The evacuees were not sure if they were being saved by friends or handed over to yet a new enemy.

Who Were the Relief Agencies?

Philanthropic agencies had been providing aid and services to the people of Asia Minor long before the Smyrna crisis. They organized schools and colleges, offered medical care, taught trades, and generally helped their host communities any way they could.

Among those present was the Constantinople chapter of the American Red Cross. The Red Cross was formed at a conference in Geneva, Switzerland, in 1863 as an international relief organization. The brainchild of Henri Dunant, its mission was to create societies of volunteers to help the wounded in wartime. An amendment to the conference in 1864 provided for Red Cross workers to enter battlefields in order to aid wounded troops. During peace, the Red Cross (known as the Red Crescent in Muslim countries) provides disaster relief and medical aid where needed. It also trains volunteers.

In 1881, Clara Barton, called America's "angel of the battlefield" for her fearless work on Civil War fronts, organized the American chapter of the Red Cross. By World War I, many Red Cross workers, both men and women, took to the battlefields of France and Germany. Among them was Dr. Esther Lovejoy, the first American Red Cross woman in France.

More than five thousand orphans were evacuated from Kharput, in interior Turkey, to spare them from ostracization or enslavement by the Turks. The orphans, accompanied by workers from Near East Relief, journeyed by donkey, camel, and on foot to orphanages in Syria and Greece.

As time passed, the healing mission of the Red Cross spread around the world. Asia Minor was one such location. After the war, Dr. Lovejoy found herself, along with other relief workers, providing medical care in the region. Her skill and composure would serve her well during the Smyrna crisis.

The Young Men's Christian Association (YMCA) and Young Women's Christian Association (Y.W.C.A.) were also active in Smyrna, involved in providing education and in other community efforts, such as sports, music, and social activities. The YMCA was formed in London in 1844 to promote good values among young men; a women's branch with a similar mission was established in 1855. The American branch of the YMCA opened in 1851, and in 1866 the women's branch got underway in Boston. Asa Jennings and many of the heroes of Smyrna were with the YMCA.

But by far the predominant organization present was Near East Relief. This group was founded in 1915 as a special philanthropic committee. Incorporated by an act of Congress, its primary mission was to provide aid to Near Eastern countries and those territories within the boundaries of the Great National Assembly, Turkey's new parliament. Since its inception, Near East Relief representatives worked tirelessly in Syria, Constantinople, the Caucasus, Persia, and elsewhere in the region. They built and staffed schools, orphanages, and hospitals and brought humanitarian aid wherever possible. Near East Relief did not have a religious agenda, and thus members were well received even in Muslim countries. They also kept themselves strictly apolitical—no national from Turkey, Persia, Armenia, Russia, or Greece served on the committee—it was strictly American in makeup. When Near East Relief went into Russia, the government was initially suspicious, believing the workers to have political aims with the goal of undermining Bolshevism. However, after seeing their good works, the Bolsheviks supported the organization. The Turks, too, at first believed that Near East Relief would supply aid only to Christians, but by their actions, the organization demonstrated that this was not the case and won the respect of both Turks and Greeks. The Turkish government had such admiration that it invited Near East Relief to stay following the war. Members of Near East Relief played a key role in the evacuation of refugees from throughout Turkey, and saw to their care during the months following the rescue.

Individual Americans also contributed greatly. Among them were Dr. Wilfred Post, of Washington, D.C., and Charles Claflin Davis, of the Red

TOP: *Orphans at play in the shadows of the Temple of Jupiter in Athens.*

LEFT: *An American nurse comforts orphans from Smyrna aboard the American destroyer USS* Litchfield.

BELOW: *A refugee camp is set up near the ancient Temple of Theseus in Athens.*

Cross. An account from the *New York Times* of September 20, 1922, tells of Post's heroic efforts:

"Dr. Post shed lustre on his profession and country by ministering to the suffering and dying, until exhausted, he was taken aboard an American destroyer. He refused to stay on the destroyer, however, and returned to shore. His supplies of medicines was soon exhausted. He seized an automobile and with an American sailor as chauffeur, was making his way to the pharmacy in town when Turkish soldiers stopped him and attempted to seize the car. The bluejacket reached for his revolver and shot one of the assailants through the heart and was about to kill the others when they threw up their hands. The doctor and the sailor then proceeded on their mission.

"Another gallant American was Charles Claflin Davis of Boston[1], who for ten days and nights did not close his eyes giving succor to the survivors and pleading with Kemalists to adopt a more merciful attitude. He organized relief committees and was such a splendid, tender and loveable character that even the Turks revered him."

A Wave of Humanity

None of the relief agencies was prepared for the onslaught of humanity that swept down on the coastal towns ahead of the oncoming Turks. The collapse of the Greek troops and the swift advance of the Turks were so sudden that no one was prepared for the catastrophic turn of events. Within ten days, the Turks had defeated the Greeks and marched two hundred miles, occupying Smyrna and sending the Greek army fleeing in disarray. The civilian non-Muslim population for miles around was racing to escape, and within a few days Smyrna and nearby towns were choked by more than one million refugees.

According to the book, *The Story of Near East Relief,* "The fate and flight of the civilian non-Moslem population, commonly called the Smyrna disaster, aroused the sympathy and interest of the world and necessitated the immediate marshaling of relief forces to fight the new enemies of starvation, disease and exposure among 1,400,000 refugees. . . . There was no opportunity for special preparation, nor to secure additional personnel or supplies, for only a few days elapsed between the collapse of the Greek army and the onrush of refugees into the city of Smyrna. A local relief

committee was immediately formed composed of American residents. . . .
It soon became apparent to the local committee that its resources were
wholly inadequate to cope with the increasingly desperate situation, for the
numbers of refugees mounted by the tens of thousands daily."

Nonetheless, the swift actions of those relief workers present and local
citizens did make a difference. In *The Blight of Asia*, George Horton writes,
"A Provisional Relief Committee was organized on the spot and a sufficient
sum of money contributed to begin operations. All the leading American
firms offered lorries and automobiles and their personal services. Bakers
were hired and set to work, stocks of flour found and purchased, and in a
few hours this organization was feeding the helpless and bewildered refugees
who were crowding into the city. But for the American colony in Smyrna
thousands would have died of starvation before a Relief Unit could arrive
from Constantinople."[2]

Two of the most emotional efforts involved rescuing orphans from
Turkey. An Armenian orphanage in Smyrna, had been supported by American patronage. Now the children needed to be evacuated, and members
of Near East Relief and the Red Cross were working to make that happen
with all haste.

On September 16, Admiral Bristol writes, "With great difficulty these
children had been kept together on the quay, and the American teachers
and officials of the institution [the orphanage] were of course unwilling
to desert them. Some of the older girls, it was reported, had already been
carried off by Turkish soldiers. The number of orphans and attendants
was represented originally as 'about 200,' as it turned out there were a few
more than 520."

Even more dramatic was the heroic trek undertaken by relief workers
from inland Turkey. Realizing that the interior of Anatolia, from Konia to
Kharput, and from the Mediterranean Sea to the Black Sea, was destined
to be Turkish, relief workers knew they must get the children out. The
orphans in their care were from minority populations (primarily Greek and
Armenian) and would no longer be tolerated. Although they might not be
molested, they would never transition to productive, happy lives in such an
environment. Syria agreed to accept children from orphanages in Kharput
and Malatya. The long journey was between three and four hundred miles
over rough terrain. Older children walked; little ones rode on donkeys.
Supplies were loaded onto camels. More than five thousand children made

this long trip. Other orphans were ultimately transferred to Greece. In every instance, workers from Near East Relief and the Red Cross walked with the children every step of the way, and stayed on to establish new homes for their care.

One of the most heroic rescues was undertaken by Dr. Mabel Elliott, of the American Women's Hospital Association, who also distinguished herself by her medical service on the quay. Prior to the fall of Smyrna, she was stationed at the relief hospital in the Cilician city of Marash. This was a mountain outpost with a large Armenian population that had been under the protection of the French after World War I. In January 1920, the Turks laid siege to the city and the French were forced to withdraw. Soon after, the people were also forced to flee, desperately trying to escape the Turks through mountain passes covered with snow.

At 10:30 on the night of February 10, Dr. Elliott and her charges left Marash. She describes their epic journey:

"It was difficult going as soon as we left the buildings behind us, for the darkness blinded us and we did not follow the road, but went across rough fields, guided by hundreds of other marchers as lost as we were. We were not taking the long road to Aleppo, but were to strike out over the mountains in an attempt to reach Islahai.

"Such a night; A turquoise sky flooded with moonlight over a white world, and across the snow, stretching as far as the eye could see, a line of camp fires, horses, wagons, soldiers, refugees, camels, donkeys, carts, all a mixture and confusion of sound and sight. We sat down to rest by a fire of straw and got colder and colder. The poor soldiers kept coming in with their frozen, wet feet to get a taste of fire, which was hardly warmer than candlelight. We had rested less than three-quarters of an hour when the order came to march. We did not stop again until late the next morning, and by that time we had begun to pass children and some women, dropping in the snow, unable to go on.

"[O]n again, with no pause and no more food until we reached El Oghly at three o'clock that afternoon. . . . We slept in a mud house that night—At five in the morning we were on the march again. . . . From the top of a mountain the sight of that column was one never to be forgotten. Four battalions with their guns and a train of 300 camels, and behind that, a stream of refugees going up and down the hills into the far, blue distance.

"That night we camped at Bel Puvar. At five o'clock, in the darkness, we were awakened—we must start at once; there was a blizzard. The swirling snow was so thick that we could see only a few feet, and that with difficulty. Four thousand men were trying to get into line, more than 5,000 refugees were struggling in the confusion and terror. Screams of horses, shrieks of women who could not find their children, wails of children wallowing in the snow alone, creaking of gun carriages, shouts of officers and men, sudden looming up of camels that grunted and bit, all coming out of a swirling whiteness. I thought of my nurses, of my patients from the hospital, women with new-born babies, struggling in the madness. Impossible to find anyone, to do anything. We got somehow into a frantic line and started on the long tramp. It lasted fourteen hours. In a very few hours we were passing the dying all along the way.

"The column was quite quiet. There was hardly a sound for hours, except the scream of someone falling. Always, just when endurance broke, they screamed once as they fell. The column went on silently, leaving them there.

"Armenian women have a way of carrying children on their backs, holding the two hands clutched against the mother's breast and the child's weight on the bent back. When children are carried in this way, almost always one sees their little bare feet, side by side. Working with refugees I see this perhaps a hundred times a day, and never without remembering the road to Islahai. That morning we passed hundreds of mothers, carrying their children in this way. First a vague darkness in the swirling snow, then the mother's bent body, and the child's little bare feet. I would reach out and tuck them up in a corner of shawl or blanket as I went by. I do not know how many hours we had been walking, when I found the first dead child on its mother's back. I walked beside her, examining it; she trudged on, bent under the weight, doggedly lifting one foot, then the other through the snow, blind and deaf to everything. The child was certainly dead and she did not know it. I spoke to her, touched her, finally shook her arm violently to arouse her. When she looked up, I pointed to the child and said 'Finish.' The mother seemed to not understand at first, trudged onward for a few steps, then stopped and let go of the child's hands. The body fell, and the mother went on, blind and deaf as before, all her life in that lifting of one foot after the other through the snow.

"This was the first one. There were perhaps fifty more after that, always the same. No complaint, no protest, a little time to understand what had happened, and then a dumb letting go of the hands and the weight. Strength was so exhausted in these women who had carried their children so far, that there was no emotion left, simply the last shreds of animal endurance. If I had not spoken to them, they would have carried the dead until they dropped and died in the snow.

"In time I, too, was a blind machine moving forward, tucking in no more feet, examining no more children. We had been walking ten hours, and I was probably one of the most fortunate of the thousands of women who followed the French out of Marash. I had more reserve strength on which to draw. Still, there was little of it left in the end. I thought of nothing, cared for nothing, simply struggled onward and tried to keep my balance. It seemed to me that we three were walking on a very narrow ledge between two precipices, and that if I lost my balance and fell we would all go down thousands of feet . . .

"We had been going on thus blindly in the darkness when we heard a high, long whistle. The whole column, thousands of throats, answered it with a terrible sob. A train whistle! Islahai!

"Five thousand Armenians had left Marash, and perhaps a third of them lived to reach Islahai. . . . To understand the lives of these Armenians, remember that the evacuation of Marash was not an isolated calamity. . . . These people had lived through the deportations of Turkey during the war [World War I]; for six years they had been suffering and dying as they suffered and died on the road to Islahai. It was those few months of anxious peace in Marash that was the novelty to them; those few months of patiently beginning again to rebuild ruined houses and broken lives. And the evacuation of Marash was the beginning of the old story again—the beginning of the wanderings and sufferings which are not ended yet. For those who lived to reach Islahai went on to Smyrna, and Izmit, and the villages of Anatolia that were held by the Greeks."

As Dr. Elliot foretold, the refugees from interior Turkey were fleeing toward the coast to escape the Turks. Soon they arrived at Smyrna and other coastal cities, only to find new horrors awaiting them.

American naval officers were quick to address the growing refugee crisis. Admiral Bristol organized the Disaster Preparedness Committee to deal with the Smyrna situation; a similar group was later formed to handle

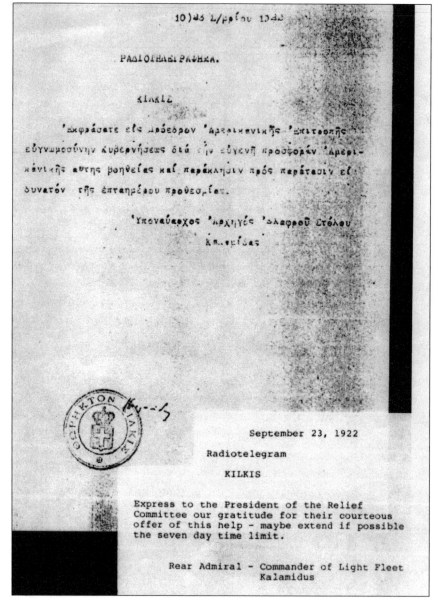

Copy of telegram from Greek Rear Admiral Kalamidos to Near East Relief, thanking the group for its efforts.

refugees from Moudania and that area. Captain Hepburn, who had extensive familiarity with the situation, represented Admiral Bristol in many instances. Other members of the committee were Mr. Stearns, one of Bristol's secretaries (as he was chair); Major Claflin Davis, of the Red Cross; Mr. H. C. Jaquith, representing Near East Relief; Mr. H. E. Boyd, representing the YMCA; Mr. W. R. Monteser representing the Joint Distribution Committee; and Miss Ruth Woodsmall, of the YWCA. There were also representatives from the American Board for Foreign Missions and local businessmen. All these organizations noted contributed to the relief effort. Each association spent its own money but each reported its expenditures to the committee, so there was no overlap.

On September 23, 1922, the Smyrna committee met with Admiral Bristol presiding. He spoke to the committee and recorded the following:

"I had been directed by the Department to form a joint plan to handle the refugees but finding the Allies too busy with other affairs to give this their attention, I had taken the responsibility of directing destroyers at Smyrna to go ahead with the evacuation to the islands in the Aegean Sea or to any other place where they could be landed . . .

"At present time, we are serving 20,000 rations a day. I stated that Near East Relief had appropriated $25,000, the Y.M.C.A. $5,000, the Jewish Joint Distribution Committee $10,000[3], and the Y.W.C.A. $10,000, and I had just received a telegram which was badly garbled stating that our Government was appropriating money for relief but I could not state the details in regard to this appropriation.

"I stated that at Moudania the Disaster Relief Committee was materially assisted by French military and naval forces and had succeeded in evacuating all the refugees in that place. The Turkish soldiers behaved quite well and the assistance rendered by the French was very excellent. Miss Jillson deserved a great deal of commendation for the way she worked out the place, and the success of the operation was greatly due to her actions. I was glad to hear from Miss Jillson that Lieutenant Addoms [U.S.], commanding the Sub-Chaser [Sub-Chaser 96 played a key role in the evacuation], had rendered every assistance possible to make the move a success."

That same Saturday, Dr. Esther Lovejoy and Dr. Mabel Elliott both formally became involved with the relief effort, Dr. Lovejoy's hospital association donated $10,000 for relief, and she renewed her personal assistance to the Smyrna refugees. Dr. Elliott joined the committee. As a veteran of relief work in Asia Minor, her skills, combined with Dr. Lovejoy's battlefield experience, would prove invaluable.

By the next day, Admiral Bristol was already reporting 30,000 rations handed out, as numbers of refugees continued to swell. Ships were continuing to remove refugees to Mytilene, but feeding the refugees en route and upon arrival was a problem. According to Bristol's records, on September 24, a ship loaded with five thousand refugees was only allowed to take fifty bags of flour on board. The Turks would not allow any more flour to be removed, so the ships saw to the refugees' needs with what supplies they had.

Care for the refugees was also affected by a lack of trained workers, especially medical personnel, and some relief workers were new to Asia Minor and less experienced in dealing with the Turks. "The Relief Committee suffered for lack of trained workers. In some cases, Turkish authorities assisted the relief work while in others they interfered. Those members of the committee who were businessmen in Smyrna knew how to handle the Turks and seemed to have no trouble getting assistance from them," wrote Admiral Bristol on September 24, 1922.

Over the next few weeks, Admiral Bristol and his officers continued to deal with a wide range of challenges, including the evacuation of refugees, caring for those still in Turkey, caring for those en route, and aiding in their resettlement. Resources were tight even though word of the refugees' plight was spreading and financial support was beginning to arrive.

On Monday, the twenty-fifth, at noon, Admiral Bristol attended a meeting of the Allied High Commissioners at the British Embassy at Yenikeny, about twenty miles east of Smyrna. Present were Sir Horace Rumbold, British High Commissioner, Senator Marquis Garroni, Italian High Commissioner at Thalapi; General Maurice Pelle, ambassador from France; Mr. Neville Henderson, counselor of the British High Commission; and a lieutenant commander (not named) who acted as a liaison officer for Admiral de Brock, of the British flagship the *Iron Duke*.

The focus of the meeting was continued evacuation action of the refugees at Smyrna, and discussion of ways to aid the refugees while they awaited evacuation, during transport, and after. Rumbold read a dispatch from the foreign office that the British Board of Trade would send fifteen British ships to assist in the evacuation of refugees from Smyrna, and also that the British government had appropriated 50,000 pounds sterling for relief work—on the condition that other countries would contribute a like amount. Rumbold also reported that the League of Nations had voted 100,000 francs to be used by Mr. Fridtjot Nansen, a representative from the league, for immediate relief.

Admiral Bristol reported that American destroyers were evacuating refugees as fast as possible and taking provisions to Smyrna to supply those still awaiting rescue.

"Likewise, before this I had directed our destroyers at Smyrna to evacuate refugees as fast as possible, and in order to facilitate the work of the destroyers they were being ferried to the Mytilene Island or other islands in the Aegean Sea where we had been informed that five or six hundred refugees on each island could be accommodated," he wrote.

Bristol noted that the evacuation situation was expanding due to a possible war between Turkey and Thrace. Turkey was seeking to annex Thrace, and if this happened, refugees who had been transported from Marmara to Thrace would need to be evacuated all over again. The same held true for refugees who had been taken to Silivri, Erekli, and Rodosto, as these communities were also under threat of Turkish reclamation. Bristol urged that these people be evacuated now, before things became even more complex.

His colleagues agreed, although it was also voted that rescuing the Greeks from Smyrna, where danger was already present, was the priority. The other rescues would take place soon thereafter.

Admiral writes in his report of September 25, 1922: "Then the question was raised about where the refugees should finally be evacuated to, and I stated that unofficially we had understood that refugees could be sent to Salonica and Cavalla without limit, and in rather limited numbers to several islands in the Aegean Sea. At this point, the British Naval Officer present stated that they had a radio from their Minister in Athens confirming this information. Thus it was decided to evacuate as rapidly as possible from Smyrna to Mytilene and then transfer the refugees from there to the mainland later and as rapidly as possible. These refugees should preferably be taken to Salonica and Cavalla and to the Greek ports."

On September 28, 1922, local YMCA workers reported to Bristol that their organization back home was starting a drive to provide funds for refugee relief. Other organizations would soon follow.[4]

During the days and weeks to come, brave and skillful relief workers were worth their weight in gold.

Jeanne Jillson was especially highly thought of by Admiral Bristol for her courage and resourcefulness. She was a member of the American Foreign Mission Board, and had operated a school in Brusa,[5] the former Turkish capital. At the start of the crisis, she boldly volunteered to go to Moudania to assess the situation and organize the rescue. Admiral Bristol granted permission and she set out on sub-chaser 96. Admiral Bristol wrote of her, "Miss Jillson was willing to take all risk, and I was very glad to have her go down because of her knowledge of the language and of the people and through her we could get a better picture of the situation than we have at the present time."

Miss Jillson had also visited Silivri and Erekli in mid September and reported that the situation there was not yet urgent, although there were about 20,000 refugees in each location. According to her report to Admiral Bristol on September 20, "[T]hey were being looked out for and many of them had continued on into villages in the interior. At these places, the local people were organizing their own relief and there was plenty of bread, very cheap, and there was plenty of water. At Rodosto, there were about eighty thousand refugees, of which at least thirty-five thousand were still there."

Rodosto, however, was not in good shape, with no facilities for baking bread and a failing water supply. The bakeries had either been burned or had their water shut off, and as water was needed to grind grain, they were rendered useless. Local wells were simply overcome by the volume of people.

On the other hand, Bristol wrote with some frustration of Mr. A. C. Ryan, chairman of the Disaster Relief Committee of Moudania, believing that he was not doing all he could in that area. Bristol had previously thought Ryan quite capable, but commented that he believed him to be afraid of the Turks, even though "three of his own compatriots, all women, go fearlessly into the district and are living there opening up their schools and carrying on work."

Meanwhile, the situation in the communities accepting refugees was becoming dire. On September 24, 1922, Admiral Bristol wrote: "Conditions in Mytilene were reported to be very bad. The Governor reported that about 75,000 refugees had arrived in the island, only a three day food supply was available on 21 September, prices were extremely high, exchange bad, and profiteering serious. Warehouses, churches, Schools and many homes were thrown open to the refugees. The authorities at Mytilene indicated their willingness to receive all refugees providing supplies and food were furnished."

Asa Jennings sent a similar report to Bristol regarding the situation in Mytilene:

"The immediate need for flour at Mytilene is imperative," he wrote. "We must have flour within 24 hours or there will be a food panic and riot on the Island. All are now depending on our promise that flour will arrive immediately. The knowledge that flour has actually been landed will calm all and help us in controlling the situation.

"Upon arrival of the 7 ships leaving Smyrna tonight, approximately 15,000 people, there will be 90,000 refugees on the Island of Mytilene."

Impact on Surrounding Communities

The ships departing Smyrna and surrounding towns sailed to the ports of Mytilene, Salonica, and Cavalla and the islands of Crete, Chios, and Euboea. These were all major harbors. Mytilene is both an island and a port,[6] and is famed as the historic home of the legendary poetess Sappho, the poet Arion, and the philosopher Theophrastus. Salonica[7] was the principal port of Macedonia. A larger community, it was a literate, cultured city and considered the gateway to Europe. Cavalla, located northwest of Salonica, though not as heavily populated, was a hub for that region. Later, some refugees were relocated from these communities to cities such as Athens. With the exception of Athens and Salonica, these were relatively small, historic towns where the primary means of income were fishing, shipping, trade, and farming. Local villages supported shops and eateries, and some small factories, such as those for rug making. There was not an overabundance of material riches or natural resources in any of these locales. Yet suddenly these towns were overwhelmed by thousands of refugees. The evacuees needed to be fed, housed, and treated for illness and injury. Somehow, they had to be absorbed into these communities and given the means to rebuild their lives. It seemed a daunting task and would require a commitment of several years.

Henry Morgenthau summed up the situation in his compelling book *I Was Sent to Athens*. Morgenthau was an eminent American businessman,

Two portraits of Henry Morgenthau, American ambassador. Morgenthau was sent to Athens to supervise and aid in the relocation of the refugees.

lawyer, and, in later years, diplomat and public statesman. His circle of contacts included American President Woodrow Wilson, British Prime Minister Lloyd George, and future prime minister Winston Churchill. Morgenthau served as U.S. ambassador to the then Ottoman Empire (later Turkey) from 1913-1916, and during the Smyrna crisis was vice president of the Relief Committee for the Middle East. From 1923 to 1928, he was appointed by the League of Nations as president of the Greek Refugee Settlement Committee.

Morgenthau wrote, "Suppose that something like this had recently occurred: that twenty-six million men, women, and children had suddenly and unexpectedly arrived by steamer at the ports of Boston, New York, Philadelphia and Baltimore. Suppose, further, that this mighty host was well-nigh starved, was penniless, was without any worldly possessions beyond the clothes they stood in, their bodies covered with vermin and filth and ravaged by typhoid and smallpox. Imagine these twenty-six million beings (chiefly women, children and old men) to be absolutely dependent upon American charity for immediate food, for shelter, and for medical attention. Imagine that they must depend entirely upon America for an opportunity to make their homes and their livelihoods for the rest of their days.

"Now imagine that America had magnificently met this challenge to its humanity and resourcefulness, had fed these starving, sheltered these homeless, healed these sick, found work for the less capable among them, financed a new start in life for them, built modern group homes for most, found land for farmers, sold them seed and implements and animals at cost—in brief, had rehabilitated twenty-six million wrecked human lives, and had done all this within six years from the date they landed on her shores. Would not the world resound with praise of American humanitarianism, American bounty, American energy and resourcefulness?

"Exactly such an achievement, not in absolute numbers but in percentages, has been accomplished by Greece in the last six years—and yet the world at large has heard almost nothing about it!"

Population statistics for Greece in 1920 illustrate the enormity of the refugee problem. With a total population of slightly more than five million, Greece's absorption of more than one million refugees swelled the nation's overall numbers by more than 20 percent. Added to the challenge was the fact that Greece was now a brand-new republic. During the Smyrna crisis, a political revolution had occurred and Greece transitioned from monarchy to republic. This infant government now faced the seemingly insurmountable task of absorbing this wave of humanity.

And yet it did. George Horton writes in *The Blight of Asia*:

"If ever the Four Horseman of the Apocalypse rode down upon a nation it was when this appalling host appeared upon the shores of Greece, that was trampled by the flying hoofs of their chargers and scourged by the spectral riders of War, Famine, Pestilence, and Death. But the little Greek nation of only five million souls met their brothers in distress with unshaken courage and with open arms. Every home in Greece threw wide its doors and took in some of the refugees. In Athens, more than five thousand rooms in private houses were open to them. Public schools were turned into hospitals, town halls were used as barracks, even the beautiful National Opera House in Athens was filled with refugees, each of its velvet-lined boxes becoming the home of a whole family, while scores more slept upon the floor of the auditorium and on the stairways. Relief work was organized on every side. In Athens, the famous Old Palace on Constitution Square was turned into headquarters where bread was distributed daily to thousands of refugees, where lists of names were posted for the purpose of reuniting families that had been separated in the chaos at Smyrna and where the general direction of all relief measures was centered."

The Greeks immediately granted their compatriots citizenship, and were quick to set into motion plans for helping them with work, homes, and assimilation into normal life. By October, Greece had established a nongovernmental agency to deal with the growing horde of refugees, and had raised a large sum of money for this purpose. The success of the unofficial national relief work was due in large part to the efforts of Epaminondos Charilaos, a leading industrialist and self-made man. He enlisted the cooperation of Mr. Étienne Delta of the Red Cross and many other patriotic Greek citizens. Together, they organized the Refugee Treasury Fund and an executive board of three members.

The fund administered all private donations and government provisions and coordinated twenty subcommittees at Piraeus, Volos, Salonica, Larissa, Patras, Edessa, and other locations. The executive board could order the execution of any work, determine how the work would be done, and fix the cost. By eliminating layers of bureaucracy, work was accomplished quickly and efficiently.

The fund not only handled the emergency needs of the arriving refugees, in the form of blankets, medicine, and clothing, but also coordinated their permanent settlement. Over time, they distributed clothing, food, and medicine (primarily from America, according to Morgenthau's report), as well as funds for fuel for cooking meals. They also arranged the transport of all goods to the outlying camps. Hospitals were expanded or built and supplied; delousing stations were set up; sanitation needs were addressed; tent cities were established while housing was built and resettlement arranged. They distributed soap, other cleaning supplies, and cooking utensils, and arranged for transport of the ill or those who were moving elsewhere.

According to Morgenthau, the fund was immensely effective because of its quick, early insights into the needs of the refugees; having anticipated what necessities were essential in advance, it was able to plan and act promptly.

The first permanent urban settlement was constructed at Pangrati. Everything necessary was thought out and then provided. Engineers and technical staff were hired, along with work inspectors. The settlement included schools, baths, workshops, parks, gardens, squares, roads (with plans for extensions), sanitation, water supply, power plant, and housing. A machine and carpentry shop were also located on the premises. Never before had modern Greece undertaken such a massive construction project, so there were no precedents for guidance. Nonetheless, construction was soon completed and well done; the first refugees moved into their new homes in April. So successful was the Pangrati effort that similar settlements were created at Volos, Patras, Eleusis, Salonica, Edessa, and other areas.

According to data provided by Mr. Charilaos to Morgenthau, out of a total of seventy-seven contractors, thirty-four were refugees, and out of a total of 5,900 laborers, 5,488 were refugees.

On October 31, 1923, the Relief Treasury Fund was disbanded, and Morgenthau took control as resettlement efforts continued under the auspices of the International Relief Settlement Commission of the League of Nations.

While this was going on, Near East Relief, the Red Cross, and other humanitarian agencies stepped in with food, money, and hands-on help. Through September, October, and November 1922, relief personnel were dispatched to all the centers where refugees were temporarily segregated, and where the simplest necessities of life were lacking. Supplies were sent from Near East's emergency warehouses in Constantinople, and food-stuffs were diverted from anywhere they were not critically needed. The committee knew that a mass resettlement program would be required and that mass feeding would be needed for at least a year. It was a task of international magnitude and far beyond their capability alone. The Red Cross responded to the plea for help, and in December 1922, by special commission, appropriated $3 million for a period of six months. This allowed Near East Relief to focus its resources on the children, as the Red Cross managed the care of the adults.

Typhus and cholera were at first rampant in the camps, and it took heroic measures to stem the tide of death in the Selimieh Barracks in Constantinople. One American doctor and ten Greek doctors died in the effort. According to the American Red Cross, 60 percent of the refugees suffered from eye infections, and the death toll among the babies and young children was at first quite high.

According to Near East Relief, it cost four or five cents per day to feed the multitude rations of bread and a soup of rice, potatoes, vegetables and beans, with olive oil added for fat. The children were given milk each day, for extra nourishment and as protection against illness. Smallpox was also initially epidemic, and during the first two months the death rate was 140 a day in the refugee camps, as those already weakened by their ordeal had no strength to fight off illness. But thanks to food, medical care, daily health inspections, and strict sanitation rules, after two months the death rate was reduced to fifteen per day. And each week, each month, more refugees moved out of the camps and into society.

There was great concern with winter coming on as to how the refugees would be cared for and housed. Near East Relief, the Red Cross, and others shared in this massive effort through the first winter, feeding the displaced in Greece, Constantinople, and other Black Sea ports. At the height of the effort, they were caring for 1,400,000 refugees. They also oversaw the care of 18,000 orphaned children scattered about at thirteen institutions in Greece. The food the refugees received from the American Red Cross and Near East Relief was in many cases the first food they had eaten in two weeks.

The American Red Cross sent surgical supplies to fourteen hospitals in the region, and hundreds of thousands of articles of clothing, many donated from various women's groups.

By 1923, Near East Relief began to withdraw from general relief activities due to diminishing funds and the increasing role of the International Relief Settlement Commission and others. Over the next seven years, the commission, working with the Greek government and other relief agencies, would see the refugees established in new homes and new lives.

Meanwhile, the U.S. Navy continued its support in a variety of ways. Sailors built bake shops and auto repair shops. They transported vital supplies of food and other goods. They also provided critical communications services. The Annual Report of the Secretary of the Navy for 1923 states, "[T]he destroyers furnished the means of communication. All communication in Anatolia was disrupted and in many cases stopped entirely. The destroyers furnished the chain of communication from Trebizond, Samsun, Constantinople, Athens, Smyrna and other ports." Without this service, relief and resettlement operations could not have moved with the haste required.

Far from abandoning the refugees, the United States maintained a major presence for some time. American Red Cross, YMCA, YWCA and Near East Relief workers were active in resettlement for the next decade, supplying funds, goods, and hands-on aid (see chapter 4). The U.S. Navy maintained a fleet of from six to twenty destroyers in Smyrna waters for more than a year. At the end of October 1923, six remained, offering assistance wherever needed.

Lives of the Refugees

Not only were the refugees hungry, ill, and lacking shelter, but they had also suffered an extremely devastating blow to their morale. Many of the citizens from Smyrna had been among the intelligentsia of Asia Minor. They were people of property and wealth, culture and education. They held important jobs, had lovely homes, and entertained in society. Others were members of the solid mercantile class. They owned land and property, and ran businesses, shops, and restaurants. They had their own homes and lived successful lives. Now all was lost—land, wealth, community standing, the country of their birth. They were faced with abject poverty; and the greatest battle of their lives.

There were also cultural implications. The Greeks of Turkey were different from the Greeks of Greece. These Greeks were direct descendants of the Ionian Greeks who settled the Aegean coast of Asia Minor more than a thousand years ago. Around the fifth century B.C., Alexander the Great (one of the greatest of all Greeks) set about conquering the fertile plains and rich cities of Asia Minor, including Asia Minor Egypt, Palestine, Syria, Babylonia, Mesopotamia, Persia, and northwest India. As he marched through what is now the Near East, he established cities and left behind garrisons of Greek soldiers. These soldiers were the ancestors of the modern Greeks of Asia Minor. Even though the Turks returned to power more than seven hundred years ago in that region, they could not stamp out the influence of Greek culture in art, literature, philosophy, and public works.

Over time, the two cultures mingled, and the region was enriched by their blending. Prior to the Smyrna catastrophe, the Greeks comprised a sizable population in Turkey. In Constantinople alone, there were between 300,000 and 400,000 permanent residents. They were a strong, dynamic part of the population, largely controlling the banking, shipping, and general mercantile business. Morgenthau writes in *I Was Sent to Athens*, "Some of the Greeks in Constantinople were among the most brilliant and cultivated people I have ever met anywhere in the world. Highly educated, fluent linguists, and very prosperous, they would have adorned any society. Some of them were the only non-diplomatic residents of Constantinople who were admitted into the diplomatic social circles."

Thus, to become penniless refugees, living in tents and driven to accept the most menial work, was a huge emotional shock. The fact that so many overcame these circumstances is a testament to the Greek spirit.

Nearly every writer about the Smyrna catastrophe mentions that once rescued, these refugees never clamored for handouts—they asked for work. They were eager for any opportunities that made them self-supporting again. As they waited, they turned their camps into functioning villages; they planted trees and started gardens in an effort to ease the harsh appearance of their surroundings. It was a moving sight to see rows of tents with two or three flowering plants out front, providing a splash of color against the drab canvas.

By far, most of the workforce was young women, as nearly all the younger, able-bodied men were gone. Morgenthau reported that many of these women single-handedly supported families of three or more. They worked at anything they could find—in the shops, in rug factories, as domestic servants, washerwomen, cleaning women, or taking in knitting and sewing. Some worked eight, ten and twelve hours a day. In the evening, women sat outside in groups, visiting and sewing as they talked, either mending clothes or making lace, which they sold. They also quickly made curtains for their windows and covers for their tables, creating a bit of beauty for their surroundings.

Rose Sartinsky survived the Smyrna disaster and eventually became Henry Morgenthau's secretary while he oversaw the refugee resettlement. Among her duties was visiting the camps and reporting on progress. The following stories are from her reports, after visiting the Koundouriotis camps outside of Athens on May 9, 1924, and the 7th Boys School, also near Athens, on May 31, 1924.

Erano Housetian, his wife, three daughters, and two young sons were among those struggling to start over. They lived in a spotless tent. The ground was covered by mats, and mattresses formed crude divans. They found stools a table and a set of shelves so the place had a homey feel. Erano, one daughter, and both sons found some work so there was hope, but regrets remained. Rose wrote, "One of the daughters, a beautiful young girl of about 18, was making a dress for her younger sister. I asked her if she was pleased with her present life. 'Yes,' she said. 'Compared to others we are rather fortunate, as none of our family has been killed or kept prisoner, and we are also able to earn our living, but I can never forget our house with its big garden all around. It was so well furnished and we had plenty of dresses to wear. I had my trousseau ready; I had been working on it for years and years and now everything is burnt.'" With tears in her eyes, the girl asked if Rose thought they could ever return home; sadly, Rose had to tell her no.

Rose wrote of another woman who created a tidy home out of a stone grotto. When she and her husband arrived at the camps, it was late fall and all the tents were taken. While they waited for a tent, they needed a place to live and thought the grotto might work. Digging with their bare hands, they expanded the grotto into a large room. They furnished it with crates, and Rose said it was surprisingly comfortable. The husband was only able to find work breaking stones, which he did for eight to ten hours a day. The wife was worried, however, as her husband was over sixty. The work was so fatiguing that he would not be able to continue much longer, and then they would have to find something new.

Some women were able to smuggle out their jewels, and brooches and rings were sold to buy better living quarters (a room or two in a big house) or some amenities. In nearly every home, a candle was kept burning in front of an icon—in prayer for a loved one trapped in Turkey, or in hope that they might be able to return to their former homes.

Rose wrote, "[E]very family, even the poorest, has its ikon; those who can afford it have more, and the watch light is always burning. Those who are safe thank God for it and place some hope in the future; others, who have some members of their family still in the hands of the Turks, pray for their safe return; and those, the more numerous, whose many a beloved one has been killed, pray for their souls. Their faith never fails them, and I have seen a woman whose husband and two sons were killed, who was living in a hut by herself, with not even a chair to sit on, but she never forgets to light her watch light before the ikon and never did she utter a word of protest. 'God took from me everything I possessed, husband, children, house. Such was His will and my only hope now is that I may soon be called to meet them.'"

A few families were able to bribe the Turks, and thus secured the freedom of their loved ones. But even in those cases, the ending was not always a happy one. Many of these men returned battered and ill, often dying from consumption. They were unable to resume work, and their only solace was that they spent their remaining days with their families.

Most of the widows had to leave their children at the school, at the orphanage, or with elderly friends or relatives while they went to work. Nonetheless, Rose noticed that even in these trying times, the clothes of the children and the women, though worn, were always clean and tidy. Some older children were forced to give up their schooling as they were desperately needed to work.

Rose recorded the plight of one such family:

"Another woman of more than 65 is taking care of her two grandchildren, while the mother is working as a servant and supporting the whole family. The little girl is not more than 12 years old, she has a sad, melancholic look and one can see in her eyes the whole drama of the family. There is none of that childish care freeness left in her. The answers she gave me were too serious, too sorrowful for her age, and I cannot forget her eyes, full of tears when to my question as to where her father was, she pointed to the sky with her little finger and said 'There.' . . . This little girl is now

A receiving station for more than 1,400,000 refugees at Salonica.

Exiles from Turkey en route to a refugee colony.

Milk is distributed to refugee children in the camps.

Selimieh Barracks in Constantinople housed 11,000 refugees in 1923. Typhus and other epidemics took a deathly toll. (brick building)

Another refugee holding area. (tent city)

Health inspections were a daily occurrence in every orphanage.

working at a shirt factory all day long. For the present she only gets [three drachmas] a day because she is just learning and her only hope is that she will soon learn to work sufficiently well and get a raise in her pay which will enable her to help her mother. Thus at the best period of life, when as a rule the children think of nothing but play, and those who are going to school, consider it a hard job to study, hundreds of children like this little girl spend all their sunny days in the prison-like atmosphere of factories with the only expectation that some day they will be able to help their mammas."

Rebirth

One of the fascinating tales to come out of the Smyrna tragedy is of the revitalization of Athens. Prior to the catastrophe, some had considered the capital a bit staid—orderly, familiar, well established in its routine. Athens was successful but not growing, not bursting with ideas and new life. After Smyrna, after thousands of refugees took root in Athens and its outskirts, all that changed. At first, Athens was plunged into poverty at the sudden influx of homeless people, all with great needs. But gradually a miraculous thing happened—Athens was transformed. With so many Greek cultures merged into one, the city truly became the capital of the Greeks. Morgenthau wrote: "Overnight all this [Athens] was changed. Now the streets were thronged with new faces. Strange dialects of Greek assailed the ear. The eye was caught by outlandish peasant costumes from interior Asia Minor. Sidewalks were crowded. Avenues that had been pleasantly ample were now filled with peddlers' carts of refugees who were trying to make a living by selling a few strings of beads or bits of finery. Cobblers set up their stools and trays along the most fashionable thoroughfares. The great rock of the Acropolis, that rises with almost sheer sides at the very heart of Athens, looked down upon a strange sight as it had been since the days when Pheidias was adorning the Parthenon at its summit. At its base sprung up a new Agora, a marketplace, packed with tiny shops displaying all the varieties of small merchandise that refugees could scrape together for sale."

Athens was reborn.

The people rescued from Smyrna and surrounding towns arrived dirty and battered, with torn clothes and tattered emotions. They came with nothing except perhaps a few bundles of clothes, a basket of crockery, or a packet of cherished family photos tied about their waists. They came with nothing except resilience. Before the tragedy of Smyrna, her citizens were part of a thriving community. There were culture and art, places of higher learning, and bountiful agriculture. The many ethnic groups that comprised Smyrna had blended their strengths and creativity into a beautiful, vibrant city. Now, Smyrna was gone. Her structures remained, but her soul was scattered to the winds of the Aegean.

The wind dispersed her citizens, like so many seeds, among new communities. And there, against all odds, they thrived and grew, bringing their gifts of intelligence, artistry, and resourcefulness to fruition. Out of tragedy came a kind of rebirth that spread among the many small towns of Greece, rejuvenating a nation.

End Notes

1. This is the aforementioned C. Claflin Davis, chairman of the Disaster Relief Committee of the Red Cross, Constantinople chapter.

2. "Relief Unit . . . arriving from Constantinople . . ." refers to the arrival of Red Cross units from their base there.

3. Admiral Bristol's war diary and other documents use the names of several of these agencies interchangeably, notably the Jewish Joint Distribution Committee or the Joint Distribution Committee, and the American Board for Foreign Missions or the American Foreign Missions Board.

4. Chapter 4, Other Voices, details the extensive aid provided by American charities and the U.S. government.

5. Also spelled "Broussa"; this is the ancient Turkish capital. Mudania is also seen spelled "Moudania" in many articles of the day.

6. Mytilene is both the island of Mytilene and the port. The two are used interchangeably, both at the time of the rescue and today.

7. Frequently spelled as "Cavalla" at the time of the rescue; today it is spelled as "Kavala." Thessalonica was often shortened to Salonica in writings at the time of the rescue; today it is known as Thessaloniki.

CHAPTER 8

The Truth Behind the Treaty of Lausanne: A Broken Peace

In the Beginning

*T*HE REGION AROUND SMYRNA IS A LAND OF EPIC battles, mighty warriors and legendary kingdoms. This is the country immortalized by the Greek poet Homer, poet of *The Illiad*. It is the land of tragic Helen, lost Troy, and valiant Achilles. The plains of Troy lie on the Asia Minor coast, just south of the Dardanelles and northeast of the island of Mytilene. In Homer's time (eighth century BC), not only the Ionian coast but also the southern shore of the Black Sea were populated by Greeks. Later, that influence spread even farther.

Greek ships plied the waters of the Aegean, Ionian, Adriatic, and Mediterranean Seas; Greek farms sprawled across the fertile fields; cities were enhanced by the influence of Greek civilization. The region flourished, producing art, literature, science, and architecture such as the world has never known. The region's diverse ethnic groups formed a rich tapestry of knowledge and culture.

This vibrant heritage is an essential part of the Asia Minor Greeks. The history of their ancient lands feeds their souls. It is as much a characteristic of these people as hair color or facial features. Although this region endured centuries of conquest and change (Roman, Arabian, Tartar, and, finally, Ottoman Turk in the fifteenth century), the Ionian Greeks gifts for commerce and trade, art, and culture always survived. Greek civilization flourished under even the harshest regime. For more than four thousand years, they enriched their adopted homelands and were simultaneously nourished by them. This symbiosis brought vitality to Asia Minor, as both art and economy thrived.

When the Smyrna catastrophe drove the Greeks from their ancestral lands, something dynamic was lost. Not only were a people horribly wronged, but an entire region was changed as well. One of the most culturally exciting parts of the world was extinguished, its ethnic diversity destroyed as surely as if engulfed by the flames of Smyrna.

The Desire for the Straits

The conflict that led to the Smyrna disaster was frequently called the Greco-Turkish War, although war was never officially declared between Greece and Turkey. This conflict was short, lasting from just 1920 to 1922, yet it led to sweeping changes throughout Asia Minor, changes that resonate even today. The official end to the war was decreed by the Treaty of Lausanne of July 1923, which was signed by the Allied powers, Turkey, and Greece. However, the Treaty of Lausanne is one of the most controversial in history. Although Turkey repeatedly violated terms and treaties going back to the Treaty of Sèvres, massacred entire populations, and drove others from their homelands, she was still allowed to negotiate terms, rather than have them dictated. And the terms she won allowed her to hold on to key lands, continue her ethnic cleansing, and retain military power. The issue of massacres and pogroms was never addressed by military or civilian court.

How could such a thing happen? To understand the infamy of the Treaty of Lausanne, one has to look back to where it all began, including a brief glimpse of ancient history. In the time of ancient Greece and Alexander the Great, Greeks controlled what is now Italy, modern Greece, the islands of the Aegean, the aforementioned settlements throughout Asia Minor and northern Africa, and the regions of Thrace, Macedonia, and what is now Turkey. Today, Italy is of course, its own country; Greece is confined to its peninsula (originally Greece and Macedonia), the islands of the Aegean, and a curving slice of what was once Thrace. Greece is bordered to the north by Albania, the former Yugoslavia, and Bulgaria. These last three countries were all once part of the vast Ottoman Empire. Across the Aegean from Greece lies Turkey, and along its coast is the tragic city of Smyrna, now called Izmir. North of Smyrna and the Greek island of Mytilene, lay the Straits of the Dardanelles, which are bounded by Turkish lands. This narrow waterway connects the Aegean Sea (and ultimately the Mediterranean, as the Aegean flows into the Mediterranean) with the inland Sea of Marmara, which is surrounded by Turkey. The Sea of Marmara is then connected by another set of straits, the Straits of the Bosporus, to the Black Sea and the vastness of Russia.

The modern history of this part of the world centers on competition for control of the Straits of the Dardanelles. This vital waterway is an enormously important gateway, connecting multiple countries and bodies of water. It links two continents—Europe and Asia Minor—and is ultimately a pathway to the world. The Straits are vital for commerce and travel, and, during times of war, are strategic passages for supplies, communications, and access to valuable territory. For centuries at least half of Europe has at one time or another pursued control of the Straits. Turkey's premier city of Constantinople (now called Istanbul) sits high on the Anatolian Plateau, right at the junction of the Sea of Marmara and the Bosporus. Constantinople has always been of strategic importance because it commands the main crossing from southeast Europe to Asia. In *Turkey at the Straits*, James T. Shotwell and Francis Deak explain the situation: "To at least half of Europe there is no single international problem of greater importance than the control of a few short miles of waterway that connects the Black Sea with the Mediterranean, those narrow Straits which separate Europe from Asia . . . the strategic importance of Constantinople was throughout its history based as much upon the control of shipping as upon the territory over which it ruled in Asia and Europe."

For centuries, the Ottoman Empire (Turkey) controlled the straits. The Turks had seized control during the tenth century, and this powerful foothold allowed them unprecedented expansion into Asia Minor and even parts of Europe. It could be argued that the Ottoman Empire succeeded in part due to control of the straits. However, ruling these straits came with a cost. Time and again wars were waged as other nations sought control, or, fearing that the Ottoman Empire would shut down the straits, attempted to block such a move. Russia yearned for dominion over the straits in order to expand her Black Sea trade; Great Britain fought to protect her passage to India; other nations joined in to see what spoils might be plucked from the Ottoman Empire, which was gradually weakened with each confrontation.

The Lure of Oil

The other economic motivator influencing control of the Ottoman lands was oil, the black gold that the industrialized world hungered for with an insatiable appetite. Turkey controlled the oil-rich fields of Mosul, in what is now Iraq, until 1914, when the region was occupied by the British. The Turks withdrew their troops during 1914, but never their claim to the region, and for many years disputed Great Britain's occupation. After World War I, peace negotiations were to determine what part of the Ottoman Empire each victorious nation would receive. In the interim, Great Britain had tried to establish the new Kingdom of Iraq by placing the deposed king of Syria, Baghdad Faysal, on the throne. The kingdom would encompass the Ottoman provinces of Baghdad, Basra, and Mosul, although the status of these provinces had not yet been determined by any international agreement.

Under the Treaty of Sèvres, the weak sultan of the Turkish government agreed to give up much Ottoman territory, including all claims to land in Mesopotamia (Iraq). In August 1920, the treaty was signed and the Fertile Crescent came under British and French mandate. Mosul was awarded to the British, and made part of the new Iraq. France gave up its interest in Mosul in exchange for a 25 percent share of Mosul's oil and control of Syria.

The celebrating over receipt of these lands had barely begun when the agreement was contested. The Turks, outraged at the reduction of their empire, had deposed the sultan, and Moustapha Kemal, head of the Nationalist movement, was in control. He declared the treaty void (with the change in government, the sultan's agreement was nullified) and demanded new terms, including reconsideration of the Mosul lands. During the Treaty of Lausanne talks, the rich prize of Mosul tantalized the Western powers, especially Great Britain, which had once had it in its grasp. The Mosul fields would give Turkey a powerful bargaining chip when negotiations began.

Decline of the Ottoman Empire

As early as the 1700s, the wars and a succession of weak rulers were taking a toll on the Ottoman Empire. Bit by bit lands were lost. Greece, which had come under the Ottoman thumb back in the 1400s, saw that the timing was right and in 1821 began her long fight for freedom. This War of Independence came to a successful conclusion in 1832,[1] although it did not bring freedom to all Greeks. The Greeks of Macedonia, Thrace, the Aegean islands, Asia Minor, and Constantinople remained under Ottoman rule. The new kingdom of Greece bided its time, vowing one day to achieve freedom for all Greeks. They not only sought liberation from the rule of the Turks, but also hoped for restoration of ancient Greek lands. In 1868, the Ionian islands were added to Greece, ceded to her by the British. In 1881, parts of Epirus and Thessaly were added.

Ninety-five years after independence, Greece had her long-dreamed-of opportunity. During the First Balkan War, of 1912, Bulgaria, Greece, Serbia, and Montenegro united in a fight to take over Turkey. They succeeded in wresting a considerable amount of territory from the Ottoman Empire, and Greece made good inroads in reclaiming her ancestral lands, gaining large sections of Epirus and Macedonia. Russia, Great Britain, Germany, Austria-Hungary and France intervened, and an uneasy peace was established. The Treaty of London was signed in May 1913. As a result, Turkey retained Constantinople but now had a mere foothold in eastern Thrace. The rest of the territory previously included in European Turkey was ceded to the Balkan allies. Greece also recovered Crete, which had achieved some autonomy after overthrowing Turkey in 1897 but was not officially awarded to Greece until 1913. The status of Albania and the Aegean islands was left undetermined, to be decided at a later conference of the great powers of the day (Great Britain, France, Russia, et al.).

The ink was barely dry on the Treaty of London when the victors began to quarrel over the spoils. This Second Balkan War was short-lived, and a peace treaty was signed in Bucharest on August 10, 1913. Greece retained her hold on Crete and secured more of southern Macedonia, including Salonica (Bulgaria had held some of this territory after the First Balkan War.). She also secured the eastern Aegean islands. As a result of the two Balkan wars, Greece had more than doubled her territory. Bulgaria obtained a strip of Macedonia and western Thrace but was obliged to return eastern Thrace to Turkey. Albania became an independent principality.

As a result of the Balkan Wars, relations between the Turks and the Greeks were considerably strained in 1913. Henry Morgenthau, who was U.S. ambassador to the Ottoman Empire in 1913, writes in *I Was Sent to Athens*, "[B]itter feelings were harbored by the Turks. They were being pushed out of one after another of their possessions and beginning to be fearful of being crowded into complete extinction as a nation. The instinct for self-preservation was aroused within them. They hated with a deadly hatred all Italians, Bulgarians, Serbs and Greeks. They yearned for an opportunity to strike back and take vengeance for their losses and humiliations."

Morgenthau writes that the Greeks were the only one of these hated races within striking distance. The Greeks alone had a considerable body of their population living within Turkish borders. They quickly became objects of petty persecution wherever they lived in Turkey.

"They [the Greeks] became objects of official suspicion on the part of the Turkish government," writes Morgenthau. "That government was concerned with more than just mere revenge. It was fighting for the life of Turkey as an independent nation. Recently deprived of its richest territories, Turkey was menaced with other losses at the hands of ambitious neighbors. Its capital, Constantinople (now within sight of enemy guns), had been coveted by Russia since the time of Peter the Great, and by Greece for many centuries before that."

The animosity between Turks and Greeks was exacerbated by changes within the Turkish government. The sultan had been steadily losing control of his nation. In 1908, just before the Balkan wars, revolutionaries formed the Committee of Union and Progress; it became better known as the Young Turks.[2] In 1913, the Young Turks forced the sultan to grant a constitution to the remnants of the Ottoman Empire; for all intents and purposes, they were now in control of the government. They deposed Sultan Abdul Hamid II and placed his brother, Mohammed (Mehmet V), a weaker leader, on the throne.

The Young Turks had just taken control when Henry Morgenthau arrived in Constantinople. He writes in *I Was Sent to Athens*, "Utterly incompetent and hopelessly weak, Mohammed was ruler merely in name. The real power was exercised by the Young Turks, whose outstanding conspirators were the Pashas Enver, Talaat, and Djemal. Their men set up the machinery of a sham constitutional government, including a parliament of two houses, a senate and an assembly. The Greek community had representatives in this body. It was of no advantage to them, however, as the parliament had no real authority."

The Turks of the Ottoman Empire had never assimilated the varied nationalities within their realm. In actuality, they didn't even control the economy, because commerce and industry were for the most part in the hands of the Greeks, Armenians, and Jews. When the Young Turks came into power (albeit behind the scenes), things took a downward turn. The minority peoples began to chafe under their harsher rule, with Greeks seeking to rejoin their lands with Greece and the Armenians and Kurds wanting separate states. This was doubly troubling to the Young Turks because these ethnic groups dominated large sections of Turkey. In western Asia Minor and Pontos, Greeks were in the majority; in eastern Asia Minor, Armenians held strong numbers; and in southeastern Asia Minor, Kurds were in the majority.

During this time, the Young Turks made overtures to Germany. Although they claimed to be a liberal, populist group, the Young Turks were in reality more militaristic. Their true goal was a Turkey strictly for Turks, a Muslim state with no Christians. They also wanted to reclaim the empire's might and power. According to Morgenthau, who was present at the time, one step toward that goal was Young Turk leaders forging friendships with the German ambassador at Constantinople. The Young Turks also established close relations with German officers who were brought in to train the Turkish army. Already the stage was being set for World War I, with Turkey's hatred of the Greeks tying in perfectly with Germany's plan for expansion into Asia Minor.

Morgenthau writes that Germany's strategy was to use Turkey and Bulgaria to separate Russia from her allies. After the war, Turkey and Bulgaria would become German states, opening a corridor for Germany's move into Mesopotamia and India. Germany was aware that there were large populations of proud Greeks and Armenians within Turkey who would put up a fight. In the confusion of war, they might organize independent armies that could threaten the Turkish-German lines of communication. With their knowledge of the country, they could act as spies against Germany. They would be especially dangerous along the coasts, both to the north, on the Black Sea, and to the west, on the Aegean. The Germans wanted to establish submarine bases in these locations, but the majority of the coastal inhabitants were Greeks. They would not easily give in to such bases to be built. Consequently, the Germans did all they could to incite violence among the Turks and the Greeks and Armenians. They fed a fire that had been smoldering for some time.

Meanwhile, the Young Turks saw the coming war as their chance to be rid of the Greeks. Before the war started, they began a systematic persecution of Greeks in coastal towns; their goal was to frighten them enough to make them flee. This reign of terror brought results: "Whenever we passed the Greek consulate we could see throngs of excited Greeks besieging its doors in an effort to get passports to leave the country," writes Morgenthau. "Our friends among the wealthy Greeks told me they were removing their valuables from the country; and repeated endless stories of the persecutions and hardships of their less fortunate brethren." Others attempted redress from the Turkish government but were met with no assistance, only rebuffs and insults. Things came to a head when fifty Greeks were murdered at Phocaea by Young Turks. War between Greece and Turkey was inevitable; war with the rest of the world was brewing as well.

During World War I, numerous pogroms were carried out against the Armenians and the Greeks. These were led by officers of the Young Turks, and most zealously by Talat Pasha, minister of the interior and a mastermind of the pogrom program. The Armenians were victims of outright genocide, as they had no outside state to rush to their aid. The Greeks suffered numerous massacres and mass numbers were driven from their lands. But with the world at war, the quiet genocide campaign was all but overlooked by other nations.

The Greco-Turkish conflict

Greece fought with the Allies during World War I; Turkey, of course, sided with Germany. The war ended in 1919 with the signing of the Treaty of Versailles, but there were numerous separate peace settlements among the nations involved. There was also the disposition of the lands of the conquered. The Treaty of Sèvres was intended to be the peace agreement between the Allied and Associated powers and Turkey (the Ottoman Empire). Under the Treaty of Sèvres, Greece was to be awarded much new territory, including eastern Thrace, Smyrna, and large adjacent districts in Asia Minor. Italy, Greece, and Turkey took issue with various parts of the treaty, and its ratification was delayed throughout much of 1919. This lack of ratification would ultimately prove disastrous for Greece.

Sultan Mehmed V, puppet ruler of the Turkish government at Constantinople, participated in the Sèvres talks and signed the treaty, but he was no longer in control. Outraged Turks, angered at the possible loss of more territory, revitalized the Nationalist movement. Fervent patriotism swept over much of the land. These Nationalists challenged the Allies' treaty and overthrew the peace settlement. What's more, despite treaty stipulations that they do so, the Turkish army never laid down their arms or disbanded. Unbeknownst to the Allies, they began using this period to build strength and incite nationalistic fervor. Every delay over the Treaty of Sèvres was only buying them time.

Meanwhile, Italy was making trouble in the Aegean. Angry over the disintegration of one of the earlier peace settlements, the Treaty of Saint-Jean-de-Maurienne, which would have given her control of Smyrna instead of Greece, Italy decided to take her spoils by force. By spring of 1919, she had begun occupying one point after another along the Adalia coast, heading north toward Smyrna. If she could maintain an Italian garrison at Smyrna, she could control the land she desired. The Italians needed to be prevented from achieving these aims, and in May it was agreed by the Allied powers that Greece would dispatch troops to Smyrna to maintain order. Greece had troops stationed at Macedonia, making them the closest Allied military force. In May 1919, Greek troops went ashore at Smyrna under the guns of Allied warships moored in the harbor. There were a few slight skirmishes and some Turkish soldiers were killed or taken prisoner, but on the whole, the landing was quiet.

Turkey had signed an armistice on October 30, 1918, and in the spring of 1919 also agreed to let Greek troops come ashore to deal with the Italian advance. After the Greeks took Smyrna with minimal fighting, they established themselves as administrators. For a while, all was calm. During that deceptive lull, the fateful decision was made to move Greek troops into the Turkish interior and try to reclaim ancestral Greek lands. In little over a year, the Greek army would begin its disastrous march into Turkey, again with the approval of the Allies. The Allies believed they had governmental control in Constantinople through their relationship with the sultan. Consequently, the Allied High Commissioner, Sir Horace Rumbold, directed Moustapha Kemal, a general in the Turkish army, to enter the interior for

TOP: *Two photos of renowned Greek statesman Eleftherios Venizelos.* BOTTOM: *Two photos of King Constantine of Greece.*

the purpose of disarming and demobilizing Turkish troops. Kemal was also supposed to ensure that all military supplies were destroyed.

The commissioner unwittingly played right into Kemal's hands. Unbeknownst to him, Kemal was part of the growing Nationalist movement. He had been plotting for a way to get into the interior, where there were troops and officers loyal to Nationalist ideals. Now this opportunity had fallen into his lap.

According to *Paris 1919*, by Margaret MacMillan, "Ataturk (as Kemal later called himself) managed to get himself appointed with sweeping powers for the whole of Anatolia. He felt, he would later say, 'as if a cage had been opened, and as if I were a bird ready to open my wings and fly through the sky.' The day after the Greeks landed in Smyrna, he left Constantinople with a visa from the British. Four days later, on May 19, he and his small party landed at the Black Sea port of Samsun. . . . Few people in Constantinople[3] had any idea of what he intended, and it was to be many months before the first hints of what was brewing in Anatolia reached Paris (where Treaty talks were still delayed). Lloyd George later claimed that 'no information had been received as to his activities in Asia Minor in reorganizing the shattered and depleted armies of Turkey. Our military intelligence has never been more thoroughly unintelligent.'"

Throughout that summer of 1919, Kemal moved incessantly across the Anatolian plateau, by car, train, and often horseback, building support for his cause. The Allies had inadvertently created the ideal environment in which Nationalism would flourish. The threat of more loss of Turkish lands, including areas around the straits and Constantinople, and the landing of Greek and Italian forces on Turkish shores bonded the Turks as nothing else could. Kemal's fiery rhetoric turned his soldiers into zealots, ready to drive all foreigners from Turkish soil. MacMillan quotes Kemal as saying, "If we have no weapons to fight with, we shall fight with our teeth and nails." In June, he announced the start of a national resistance, against the Greeks at Smyrna, the French in the south, and the Armenians in the east. He had also established a rival Turkish capital at Ankara.

By now, reports were filtering back to the Allies at Constantinople. They urged the sultan to recall Kemal, but when Kemal received the order on June 23, he simply resigned his commission and called a patriotic Turkish assembly, first at Erzeron and later at Sivas, on September 9, 1919. He broke the armistice and forged the New Turks, whose aim

TOP LEFT: *Moustapha Kemal, leader of the "new Turkey."* RIGHT: *Winston Churchill, Britain's Secretary of War at the time of the Smyrna crisis.* BOTTOM: *The "Big Four" at the Paris Peace Conference. Left to right, Vittorio Orlando, prime minister of Italy; British Prime Minister David Lloyd George; Georges Clemenceau, premier of France; and President Woodrow Wilson, of the United States.*

echoed that of the Young Turks. The sultan, doubtless under pressure by
the Allies, dissolved the Turkish parliament and denounced the Nationalists. By April 23, 1920, the National Grand Assembly had named Kemal as
head of the new government at Ankara.[4] The puppet sultan Mohammed V
was deposed. As a result of this change, by Kemal's reckoning all previous
agreements with the Allies were off. Kemal's actions violated the armistice of 1918. Not only did he break the peace treaty by reorganizing an
army he was supposed to disarm, but he also increased Turkish forces and
incited them to violence. By June 1920, the Turkish army was threatening
the British on the Ismid peninsula, the French in Cilicia, and the Greeks at
Smyrna. Although the parties involved did not yet realize it, the Treaty of
Sèvres was now rendered virtually irrelevant, as Kemal turned Turkey onto
a new, darker path. The countries of Asia Minor were about to undergo
drastic changes, but not those being debated in Paris.

The Allied powers had directed Greek troops to go ashore at Smyrna
to address the Italian problem, and this move was supported by American
President Woodrow Wilson, but for other reasons. Wilson believed that the
Christians of Asia Minor needed immediate protection from the Turks. He
thought the presence of Greek forces would protect the region's Greek citizens from any reprisal by the vanquished Turks until the territory's ultimate
disposition could be determined. Sending Greek troops seemed a fairly
safe move, as the Smyrna territory was largely Greek in population, and
therefore the troops would receive a mostly friendly reception. At the time
of the Greek army's landing, Wilson was also in the dark about Kemal's
treacherous behind-the-scenes maneuverings. He knew nothing about the
secret plans to build up a Turkish state. Wilson did not realize the presence
of Greek troops served only to inflame Turkish nationalism. Their arrival
fed into Kemal's plan to organize a fierce resistance and regroup the still
armed military.

Others, however, had strong misgivings about the presence of Greek
troops at Smyrna. Winston Churchill, then British Secretary of War, was
one. According to George Horton's report in *The Blight of Asia*, Churchill saw
the move as fraught with danger, not only for the Greek army but also for
the Greek civilians and the Christian population. Churchill noted that the
decision did not take into account the historic turbulence between Turkey
and Greece, and it added fuel to the religious fire, as it pitted Christian
Greek forces against Muslim Turkish forces on what the Turks considered

their territory. Churchill studied the problem from both the military and the political angles. He was convinced the Greek army would eventually meet with disaster in the rugged mountain terrain of interior Asia Minor. He was even more alarmed by the political ramifications. The defeated Turks were restless. Constantinople was strongly held by the Allies with their fleets in the Bosporus, but only a smattering of Allied soldiers were stationed elsewhere in Asia Minor. At the time, the Turks were in the majority in terms of armed soldiers. Churchill was convinced that having Greek troops set foot on Turkish soil at this time was inviting trouble. The Turks would retaliate. He knew it. He warned of this reaction, and of the threat of reprisal against Christian citizens in Turkey, but the British and French urged the Greek army ashore.

For nearly a year, things had been strangely quiet in and around Smyrna. It was now 1920, and the Allies were still gathered in Paris, hammering out the Treaty of Sèvres. In August, the document was finally signed, but its failure seemed inevitable. The Allied nations had no real idea how to deal with Turkey. Initially, they had thought to divide up the country, but it soon became clear that to do so was to pit Muslims against Christians throughout Asia Minor. (Since World War I, the Allies had hoped to divide up the Ottoman Empire, viewing it as one vast spoil of war. Russia, as always, sought the straits; France wanted coastal Syria and Adana; Great Britain wanted southern Mesopotamia [Iraq], and the ports of Haifa and Acre; Italy eyed the Dodecanese in the Aegean, plus an area in southwestern Asia Minor, including the coast from Adalia to Smyrna and inland to Konia. The infamous Treaty of Saint-Jean-de-Maurienne, which divided the Ottoman spoils among France, Britain, Russia, and Italy, was signed in 1917, before the war was even over, but was broken by 1919. The division of Turkish lands never took place due to the failure of the 1917 treaty, and the Bolshevik Revolution in Russia, which kept Russia from signing the treaty.) It was obvious that the original division scenario would create a long, bloody conflict. The Allies had also promised to help several smaller nations, Armenia and Kurdistan, find independence, but these promises were not fulfilled. The reasons are complex, but in a nutshell were based on the long financial commitments (and possible military aid) needed to ensure that these countries could stand on their own two feet. The Allied nations were tired of fighting (most had been involved in some conflict or another for decades), resources were drained, and the gains from supporting Armenia or Kurdistan were perceived as minimal. Thus, though they granted Armenia and Kurdistan their freedom on paper, they did not provide further support.

The Treaty of Sèvres promised an independent Armenia, incorporating part of Turkey. But in September 1920, less than a month after the treaty's signing, Ataturk's forces attacked Armenia from the south. The tiny nation fought back (its air force had only three planes), but was no match for the fierce and organized Turks. Armenia quickly fell, and in November signed an armistice with Turkey. By March 1921, Armenia was absorbed by the new Soviet republic, with the rising Joseph Stalin bringing the country to heel. The Armenian provinces of Kars and Ardahan were returned to Turkey. The border stands to this day.

The Kurds' dream of a free Kurdistan also vanished. With the Treaty of Sèvres disintegrating piece by piece throughout late 1920 and early 1921, the fate of Kurdistan was sealed. By March 1921, the Allies had distanced themselves from the treaty, according to Margaret MacMillan. In *Paris 1919*, she writes:

"By March 1921 the Allies had backed away from the vague promises of the Treaty of Sèvres. As far as Kurdistan was concerned, they were ready to modify the treaty in 'a sense of conformity with the existing facts of the situation.' The 'existing facts' were that Ataturk [Kemal] had denounced the whole treaty; he had successfully kept part of the Armenian territories within Turkey; and he was about to sign a treaty giving the rest to the Soviet Union. Kurdish nationalists might protest, but the Allies no longer had any interest in an independent Kurdish state."

The Kurds were somewhat of an enigma. A nomadic people, they were widely respected as tough fighters. MacMillan describes them thus in *Paris 1919:*

"They had little coherent history, merely conflicting myths about their origin. There had been no great Kurdish kingdoms and few Kurdish heroes except Saladin. Kurds were divided by tribes, by religion (most were Sunni Muslims, but there were Shias and Christians as well), by language, and by the fact that they were scattered among different nations. They had a reputation for being unruly."

The Kurds frequently fought each other, and because their culture was blurred with that of the Arabs, Persians, Turks, and even Armenians, it has been difficult to estimate their exact population. They lived in a "dangerous neighborhood," according to MacMillan, bordered on the north and east by Russia and Persia, to the west by the Turks, and to the south by the Arabs of Mesopotamia.

The Kurds had no powerful patrons at the Paris peace conference when the Treaty of Sèvres was drawn up. They also had no eloquent speakers from their own nation to represent them. Thus, when the paper promise failed, Kurdistan vanished.

On the Greek homefront, things were also in turmoil. Up until 1914, Greece had been ruled by King Constantine. At the start of World War I, Constantine's sympathies lay with Germany because the Kaiser was his brother-in-law. However, Prime Minister Venizelos, a brilliant Greek statesman, favored the cause of the Allies, and gradually, influenced the majority of Greek opinion in the Allies' favor. In 1917, King Constantine was forced to abdicate to his second son, Alexander. Greece then declared war and fought with the Allies. Venizelos was hailed as a hero as a result of the Allied victory and the spoils Greece was supposed to receive. Things might have stayed calm, but in a bizarre twist of fate, Alexander died of a monkey bite. Greece was thrown into upheaval, and in a stunning turnaround, Venizelos was defeated in the general election of 1920. Royalist supporters came back into power, reinstating King Constantine and causing concern among the Allies.

Constantine's return to power also caused shake-ups with the Greek military. In *The Blight of Asia*, George Horton writes:

"Reinstated in power, Constantine pursued his advantage by removing from command all officers of the Greek army who owed their positions to Venizelos. It so happened that these officers were by far the most experienced commanders amongst the Greeks. They were replaced by favorites of Constantine. The most grotesque example of this favoritism was his appointment of General Hadjanestes to the supreme command of the army of occupation in Ionia. This was the most important command in the army at the moment. The Greek troops in Ionia were operating in a most difficult country in the presence of a skillful and implacable enemy. General Hadjanestes, upon whom was placed the terrific responsibility of guiding his army in its precarious situation, was notoriously a nervous wreck at the time Constantine appointed him."

During 1920, the Greeks had pressed for Allied support to advance inland. Lloyd George, acting on behalf of the British, gave his endorsement, believing that such an advance might stem Turkish attacks against Constantinople. By August, Greek troops were not only providing reinforcement at Constantinople, but were also two hundred and fifty miles into the interior, having succeeded in occupying extensive regions of Anatolia, including the city of Broussa. Nonetheless, early in 1921, representatives of the British, French, and Italian governments met in London to reconsider revisions to the Treaty of Sèvres. A series of proposals were presented, but all were vehemently rejected by the Greeks and the Turks. According to George Horton, Constantine thought he had the opportunity to "eclipse the glory of Venizelos . . . and drive the Turks out of Asia Minor and assert Greek sovereignty over that entire country." As the year progressed, further military successes were achieved, and did bring the Greek armies within two hundred miles of Ankara, but their supreme attempt to capture the Turkish Nationalist capital failed. It was the turning of the tide of war for Greece.

About this time, a series of secret negotiations began to take place between France and Italy and the Turkish Nationalists. The Turks had astutely recognized that there were divisions among the Allies regarding disposal of lands and economic interests, and used these to their advantage. Soon, France decided to come to terms with Turkey, arguing that King Constantine's return to the throne nullified their obligation to Greece and called for revisions to the Treaty of Sèvres. As noted by F. Lee Bens in *Europe Since 1914*, France was influenced by several factors, ". . . the unwillingness of the war-weary French to continue to supply men and money for the difficult campaign against the Turkish Nationalists in Cilicia; jealousy of Great Britain whose [naval] preponderance made her the dominant force in the 'joint occupation' of Constantinople and the Straits; loss of sympathy for Greece after King Constantine's resumption of the throne in that country; and fear that Greece might become a mere satellite of her rival in the Near East."

France was also heavily influenced by economics. According to a lecture given by Monsieur Passereau, director of the French Commercial Bureau of Constantinople and published in the *Echo de France* in 1922, French private enterprises in Turkey were described thus:

"France has approximately 1,100,000,000 francs invested in private concerns in the Ottoman Empire. Her participation in the industrial activities of the Empire aggregates 53.5% of the total, as opposed to 13.6%

enjoyed by Great Britain and 32.77% by Germany. These organizations embracing activities in the form of banks, railways, ports, electric power plants, telephones, tramways, etc., extend over the entire domain of Turkey and surround the economic life of the Orient with a network of French interests. [*Author's note*: Such interests included the Imperial Ottoman and other banks, and the tobacco monopolies.] Railways: France has under construction and exploitation 2,077 kilometres, with an invested capital of 550,238,000 francs, as opposed to Germany's 2,565 kilometres and England's 610. France has 42,210,000 francs invested in mines in Turkey, besides about 80,000,000 in quays and ports." [*Author's note*: These investments were made in gold.]

On October 20, 1921, France signed a separate treaty, the Franklin-Bouillon Agreement, with the Turkish Nationalist government. As a result, French troops were withdrawn from Cilicia, and the northern frontier of Syria was modified to Turkey's advantage. In exchange, Turkey promised to look with favor upon certain economic concessions that France wanted. French capitalists, who precipitated the agreement, were eagerly seeking concessions from the Turks for railways and other commercial privileges.

"In exchange [for the Agreement], the French shamefully deserted their support of the Greeks, whom in 1919 they (along with Great Britain and the United States) had invited to take over the military occupation of Asia Minor," writes George Horton in *The Blight of Asia*. "Not only did the French withdraw their moral support from the Greeks and transfer their friendship to the Turks, but they 'abandoned' great quantities of ammunition in Asia Minor—practically making a present to the Turks of munitions of war with which to destroy their former allies, the Greeks."

Italy soon followed France's lead. While the Greeks were fighting the Turks from their base at Smyrna, the Italians were still at Adalia, on the southern coast of Asia Minor. Horton writes, "While this Greek campaign was in progress, it soon became notorious to military observers of all nations that the Turks were continually being supplied with ammunition 'bootlegged' to them from the Italian base at Adalia. Italy's ambitions regarding Asia Minor were stronger than her sense of duty to an ally. Italy already occupied the Dodocanese Islands off the coast of Asia Minor, and the peninsula itself has long been an object of Italy's scheme of colonial expansion. To have remained faithful to the Greek alliance would have been to help Greece eventually become the owner of Asia Minor. On the other hand, to have helped Turkey to repel the Greeks was to weaken both of Italy's rivals. The temptation was too strong for Italy to withstand it."

Now, Turkey had not only eliminated two enemies and won land concessions, but she had also received recognition as a nation from two major powers. She now had the upper hand in the conflict.

Meanwhile, Greek forces were strung out along a four-hundred-mile front, a situation they could not sustain. They knew it, and so did the Turks. Despite their appeals, Allied help was not coming. Time was running out.

Early in 1922, the great powers met again in Paris to attempt another revision of the Treaty of Sèvres, this one designed to conform to the demands of the Turkish Nationalists. Greece, which had received neither military aid nor money from the Allies, was now resigned to losing some territory in Asia Minor and having to negotiate a peace. But the Nationalists, sensing victory, demanded an immediate evacuation of Anatolia by the Greeks. The Greeks could not agree to this, and negotiations unraveled. Any attempts at a treaty were further broken when Italy revealed that she had signed a peace agreement with the Nationalists. This document "undertook to examine favorably Italian applications for railways, mines, and public works in Asia Minor," wrote Bens in *Europe Since 1914*.

During the conflict Greece, weakened by loss of support from France and Italy, was also not aided by Great Britain or the United States, as both nations remained carefully neutral. Each had warships in the harbor, and Great Britain protected the straits, but that was all. The United States was in a unique position because America had never declared war on Turkey during World War I, and therefore had never signed any other type of agreement with her, peace treaty or otherwise, and was not part of the Sèvres council. The United States essentially had no formal relations with the Turkish government. America was also the only nation not pursuing any land claims in Asia Minor. Her presence was that of moderator. To take sides would require a declaration of war, and most likely would generate open conflict as nations lined up once again to divide Asia Minor. The situation was both confusing and delicate.

Great Britain used King Constantine's reinstatement as a reason to distance herself from Greece and the Greek government's activities. Before Constantine's return, Great Britain's neutrality had been benevolent toward Greece, but at this critical moment, with military intervention essential to the Greek army's survival, she chose not to violate her neutrality and did not step in.

During 1922, the scenario that Winston Churchill and George Horton foretold became reality. The Turks followed a strategy that they had perfected through many years of battles and conquests. During the previous year, they retreated before the Greek advance, permitting the Greek army to capture mountain passes with only feeble resistance. The Greeks were lured farther and farther into the treacherous mountains just west of Angora. The Greek lines of communication were stretched so far that the army could barely maintain supplies from the coast. This perilous situation, combined with inexperienced commanders and war-weary troops (many Greek soldiers had been fighting for the past ten years, since the Balkan wars), made the Greeks easy targets.

On one fateful August day, the Turks struck with blistering impact. For three weeks, the battle raged along the Sakkaria River as the outmatched Greek army fought courageously to maintain its foothold. The power of the Turks was ultimately more than the Greeks could withstand, and they were pushed back westward along the Anatolia railroad, until they were four days' march from Smyrna. A general retreat by the Greeks soon fell into confusion, and the retreat became a rout. The Greek army fled through Smyrna in a desperate drive toward the coast. They knew what would befall them if they were captured by the Turks. Greek civilians immediately realized that hell was about to be unleashed. As Christians, they would be at the mercy of the enraged Muslim Turks, who were consumed by a zealous nationalism. The Turkish troops had only one aim: to reclaim Smyrna and surrounding towns for Turkey and drive out all Greeks.

Hundreds of thousands of refugees fled on the heels of the Greek army. On September 9, the Turkish Nationalist forces entered Smyrna. For the next twenty-one days, the catastrophe of Smyrna would play out as masses of Greek civilians huddled on the quay, praying for rescue.

After driving the Greeks out of Smyrna, the Nationalist forces, flushed with victory, were tempted to go after the British forces currently guarding the straits. They were deterred by Lloyd George's proclamation that Britain was "prepared to do her part in maintaining the freedom of the Straits and the existence of the Neutral Zones," and by the declaration of the British military commander in the Near East that "any attempt to violate the Neutral Zones will be resisted by all naval and military forces available."

The British at once fortified Chanak on the straits, and notified the Turks that if they came within fifteen miles of Chanak, they would be shelled. Turkish forces actually advanced to within twelve miles, within range of British guns, before Kemal reined them in. They then ended their planned assault on the straits, and abandoned ideas to invade Greece.

The Treaty of Lausanne

At the end of September, the Allied powers invited Greece and Turkey to a peace conference in Lausanne, Switzerland. Gathering in an old chateau, the great powers convened in a place of pristine beauty. Two assumptions were presented: that Turkish sovereignty would be restored in Thrace as far as the Maritza River and that until the peace treaty was signed, Turkish troops would stay out of the neutral zone and Thrace. An armistice convention was signed at Moudania on October 11, 1922. When the Allies invited the Turkish sultan to attend, Kemal called the Grand National Assembly at Angora, and on November 2 abolished the sultanship and declared Turkey a republic. Kemal did not attend the conference but instead sent his former general, Ismet Inonu. Inonu was intensely loyal to Kemal and would do all as instructed. He was in constant communication with Kemal, who cabled him from Ankara almost daily.

The conference was attended by delegates from Great Britain, France, Italy, Japan, the United States (as an observer, not a participant), Russia, Greece, Romania, Yugoslavia, and Turkey. The inclusion of Turkish delegates made this the only peace treaty that was negotiated, not dictated. Several treaties were proposed, but each time the Turks disagreed over certain economic or judicial concessions.

After endless haggling, a peace was worked out by July 1923. The Treaty of Lausanne was unlike that of Versailles, Trianon, Saint-Germain, Neuilly, or Sèvres, those products of the Paris Peace Conference. "Hitherto we have dictated our peace treaties," reflected Lord George Curzon, British assistant prime minister, according to *Paris 1919*. "Now we are negotiating with the enemy who has an army in being, while we have none, an unheard of position."

Kemal's behavior in breaking the armistice, organizing a rebellion, and attacking Greek troops who had Turkish permission (given by the sultan) to come ashore was ignored. The Turkish treatment of minorities and Christians was also not weighed. It was as if a war-weary world was simply eager to get some kind of treaty in place and put and end to conflict in Asia Minor.

This was probably true, but economic factors also played a role. Not only was there the issue of control of the Straits; there were also the much-desired oil fields of Mosul. In *American Accounts Documenting the Destruction of Smyrna by the Kemalist Turkish Forces September 1922*, editor Constantine G. Hatzidimitriou writes: "Yet even while the ruins of this ancient Christian city [Smyrna] were still smoldering, the despicable minions of commercial interest worked hand in hand with the Turkish government to minimize the tragedy and absolve the Kemalists of all responsibility. For, in 1922, Turkey controlled the oil-rich fields of Mosul, now part of Iraq, a rich prize which Kemal dangled before each of the western powers."

Edwin I. James, reporting in the *New York Times* of December 2, 1922, captured the situation this way: "A black page of modern history was written here today. Ismet Pasha stood before the statesmen of the civilized world and admitted that the banishment from Turkish territory of nearly a million Christian Greeks, who were two million only a few short years ago had been decreed. The Turkish Government graciously allows two more weeks for the great exodus.

"The statesmen of the civilized powers accepted the Turkish dictum and set about ways to get those thousands of Greeks out of harm's way before they should meet the fate of 800,000 Armenians who were murdered in Anatolia in 1910 and 1917.

"[H]ere, in the beauty of the winter sunshine of the Swiss Alps, diplomats have been for ten days talking political problems with the Turks, treating them as equals. Massacre and bloodshed seem very far away. But today, a change took place, and a new light was thrown on the situation. The facts are not new, the world knows the Turks' cruelty and massacres. But the way their crimes were presented this afternoon came like a clever stage effect.

"As an audience may change from smiles to tears, the diplomats here seem to have had their souls touched today as Lord Curzon unfolded the sinister story of the fate of the Greeks in Asia Minor; and today's events cannot but fail to have an important effect on the final settlement. In all probability no treaty will be written this session, and in two weeks the conference will be adjourned, it is believed, to meet again in a month or six weeks. In the meanwhile, the Turks will have time to think things over and become more reasonable or face consequences.

"Today's meeting was scheduled under the simple heading: 'Exchange of Prisoners.' The delegates rolled in luxurious automobiles to the old chateau. They left it two hours later with solemn faces. Within the ancient walls the shades of murdered thousands had poured in to have their say."

The talks were delayed for several weeks. When they reconvened, the emotions of December 1 seem to have been forgotten. Despite the impassioned pleas of several delegates, and a firestorm of letters to the editor (printed in the *New York Times* and other newspapers) calling for justice, the Turks largely had their way.

Very little remained of the Sèvres terms. According *to Paris 1919*, "There was no mention of an independent Armenia or Kurdistan and, although Curzon tried to add clauses to the new treaty giving protection to minorities, the Turks refused on the grounds of sovereignty. Turkey's borders now included virtually all the Turkish-speaking territories, from eastern Thrace down to Syria. The straits remained Turkish, but with an international agreement on their use. The old humiliating capitulation's were swept away. The Lausanne Treaty also provided for the compulsory transfer of populations, Muslims for Christians. Most Greeks had already left Turkey; now Muslim families from Crete to the borders of Albania were forcibly uprooted and dumped in Turkey, 'a thoroughly bad and vicious solution,' warned Curzon, 'for which the world will pay a heavy penalty for a hundred years to come.' The only exceptions to the transfer, by special agreement, were the Turks in western Thrace and the Greeks in Constantinople and on a couple of small islands. Communities have lingered on, harassed by a myriad of petty regulations and used as convenient scapegoats whenever relations have worsened between Greece and Turkey, as they did in the 1960s over Cyprus, and in the summer of 1999 over Kosovo."

Turkey's territory was increased over what she would have received under Sèvres. Mesopotamia, Arabia, Syria, and Palestine were recognized as independent of Turkey, but she advanced her European frontier to the line of the Maritza River, plus a small district to the west encompassing Karagach. In the Aegean, Turkey retained the Rabbit Islands, off the entrance to the Dardanelles, and the islands of Imbros and Tenedos. The Dodocanese, Rhodes and Castellorizo were ceded to Italy and all other Aegean islands to Greece. Turkey renounced her rights over Libya, Egypt, and Sudan and recognized Great Britain's annexation of Cyprus. (After World War II, the map of the world would change again.)

Under the Treaty of Lausanne, Turkey retained full military and naval forces, and was released from any claims by the Allied powers for reparations due to World War I. She was never punished or forced to acknowledge her part in the pogroms inflicted on Armenians, Greeks, and Kurds.

The lands of the Kurds were distributed to various powers. Some remained under Ataturk in Turkey; others fell under Reza Shah in Persia, and still others under Faysal in Iraq. None of these governments had any tolerance for Turkish autonomy. According to Margaret MacMillan in *Paris 1919*:

"[The] British for a time toyed with the idea for a separate administration for the Kurdish areas, recognizing that the Kurds did not like being under Arab rule. In the end, the British preferred to do nothing; Iraq became independent in 1932 without promising any special consideration to the Kurds. In Turkey, Ataturk and the nationalists dropped their earlier emphasis on all Muslims together and moved to establish a secular and Turkish state, to the dismay of many Kurds. The language of education and government was to be Turkish; indeed, between 1923 and 1991 Kurdish was at first discouraged then outlawed. In 1927, the Turkish foreign minister assured the British ambassador that the Kurds were bound to disappear like what he described as 'Red Hindus;' if the Kurds showed any disposition to turn nationalist, Turkey would expel them, just as it had done with the Armenians and Greeks."

MacMillan notes that the Kurds have "never accepted their fate quietly," and Kurdish nationalism did grow stronger with each passing year. The promises made at the Treaty of Sèvres were not forgotten, and a free Kurdish state remained both a dream and a hope, a desire that would continue to burn well into the twentieth century.

Inonu returned home from the treaty talks to a hero's welcome. The former sultan was spirited into exile, where he died alone some years later. In the autumn of 1923, the last foreign troops left Constaninople. Turkey once again belonged to the Turks. Kemal would rule Turkey until his death in 1938, at which time Inonu would take control.

One of the great debates behind the Treaty of Lausanne was, of course, over the Straits. It can be argued that Turkey's historic control of the

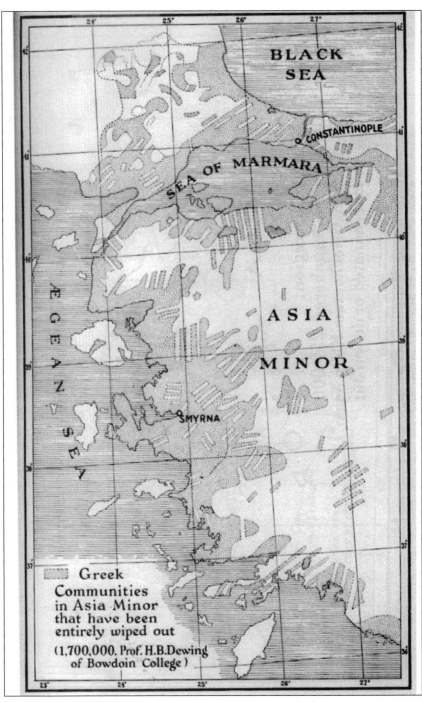

Map illustrating the Greek communities in Asia Minor that were wiped out.

straits greatly influenced the Treaty of Lausanne and the favorable treatment of Turkey. In the early stages of negotiations, Turkey played her hand
well, accepting the principle of freedom of passage. Great Britain, which
had previously opposed opening the straits to warships, now was an advo-
cate. Russia, which under the czars had coveted control of the straits and
access to the Mediterranean for decades, was now under Communist rule.
Because of the new regime, she reversed her position and now sought to
close the straits altogether.

The reason for the change of position was based on the role of the
straits in World War I. Turkey controlled and closed them during the Great
War, seriously handicapping the Allies. As a result, Great Britain saw that
in future conflicts, having the straits open to warships, and under international control, could be beneficial in maintaining a close watch on Russia.
For exactly that reason, Russia was opposed. She did not care to have a
strong British navy on her doorstep, nor did she like the nations around her
having access and growing stronger. Surprisingly, Turkey remained aloof
from the conflict, not siding with Russia as might have been supposed, as
Russia aided her during the recent war with the Greeks. According to *Turkey
at the Straits*, Turkey no longer needed Russia's assistance, as she now had
regained Constantinople and won nearly every concession she sought at
Lausanne. Remembering Russia's previous ambitions regarding the straits,
she decided not to align too closely with this onetime ally.

Many statesmen, including Henry Morgenthau, George Horton,
and Lord George Curzon, had warned about giving Turkey control of the
straits. Why let a nation with such an unruly nature become a power once
again? They argued that the straits should be under international control,
and that Turkey be kept in a more subordinate position. The Dardanelles
should be converted into an international waterway, and Constantinople
should be protected under the League of Nations.

The result of the Lausanne treaty was the International Straits
Commission, which operated under the League of Nations. The commission
hammered out an agreement that allowed freedom of passage for warships
and international control, with some concessions made to the Turks as to
the form and extent of this control. Provisions were made as to number of
ships, size of fleet, tonnage, merchant vessels, day and nighttime operation,
and various war-time scenarios, including those situations in which Turkey
was neutral and when she was not. Passage of aircraft and submarines was

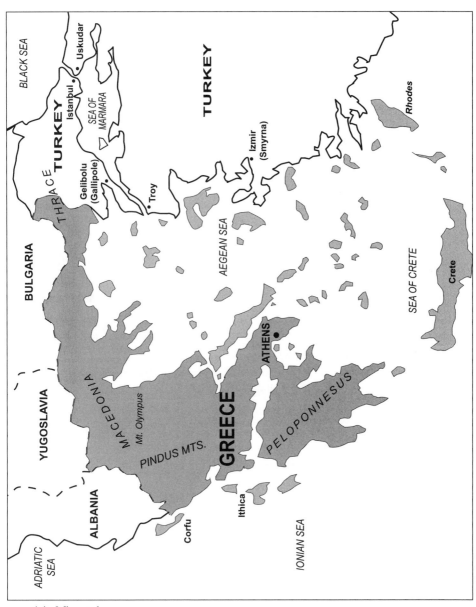

Asia Minor today.

also debated and recorded. A demilitarized zone was established along the shores of the Dardanelles and the Bosporus. For a time, the great debate over the straits was over.

There are those, such as Henry Morgenthau and George Horton, who believed that the League of Nations might have handled the Treaty of Lausanne differently. The league, which was in its infancy, having just formed in 1920, was charged with the daunting task of brokering the treaties that ended World War I. In fact, the covenant for the league was written into these treaties. Morgenthau and Horton also believed that if the United States had been a member, the discussions might have evolved along another path. But though President Wilson was committed to the league, the Congress was not. If the United States had been a member, it might have pushed for sterner measures against Turkey due to her breaking the armistice and persecuting minorities. President Wilson was concerned over the treatment of the minorities under Ottoman rule. Because the United States was the only one of the Allies without land claims in Asia Minor, she might have added a voice of reason. Even though the United States created the league, thanks to the vision of President Wilson, Congress, not happy with certain conditions of the Treaty of Versailles, refused to support the venture. As it turned out, too many of the other member nations had their own goals regarding the division of the Ottoman Empire and those aims influenced decisions and delayed ratification. Italy and France had already committed treachery against the Greeks by signing a separate peace with Turkey (thus voiding the Treaty of Sèvres), and Great Britain's stance remained carefully neutral, which, while understandable, wound up working in Turkey's favor.

Adding to the problem were the many complex issues the league had to face. When it convened to discuss the Treaty of Versailles, the spirit of the meeting was to create covenants that would help prevent wars. In fact, the initial purpose of the league was to act as mediator between nations so that armed conflicts could be avoided and peace maintained. Having to deal with the many peace settlements of World War I, the league became embroiled in much more complex issues, and had to execute various provisions of the treaties, settle disputes arising from postwar readjustments, and heal a variety of other national ills created by the war. The league successfully intervened in postwar conflicts between Finland and Sweden, and between Poland and Lithuania, but did not intervene until too late in the Greco-Turkish conflict. The reasons for this are not clear, as Turkey broke the armistice, but most likely are due in part to the league being a fledgling organization and to the conflicting motives of its members. By the time Greece and Turkey were called to a peace conference, the Greeks and other minorities had been driven from Turkey, and a huge refugee issue was looming. The league brokered the Treaty of Lausanne and stepped in to aid Greece with the refugee problem, but these measures were a bit late.

Given Turkey's history of turbulent relationships with those at her borders, many statesmen, including Henry Morgenthau, believed the league should have taken a stronger stand during the conference on the Treaty of Lausanne. Morgenthau writes in *I Was Sent to Athens*, "If the European countries have control of Constantinople, they can eventually influence the Turks and keep them in check, because possession or non-possession of Constantinople determines the status of Turkey. If she obtains Constantinople, she becomes a world power again. If she does not, she becomes a succession state." Morgenthau argued that no one at that time wanted to see Turkey as a world power, capable of "making international mischief." He also pointed out that, Constantinople was the sixth largest and most important city in the world (at that time). To leave it in the hands of the Turks "would be the most terrible blunder of the age, because it would give them a chance to re-establish themselves."

Morgenthau's outrage was the result partly of Turkey's harsh treatment of minorities and Christians. He writes, "The Chauvinism of the Turks is so well-known and so extreme that, unless restrained, they will not permit the minorities to exist. They will find some new device or resort to some of the old devices for exterminating the non-Moslem populations." As we know, Morgenthau's recommendations did not come to pass regarding Constantinople, and the issues of Muslim versus Christian and the treatment of minorities remain critical in Asia Minor.

The issue of the oil fields of Mosul nearly broke up the conference. After tantalizing the Allies with this prize, the Turks tried to keep the territory north of Iraq. In mounting their claim, the delegation said the Kurds present within the territory were really Turks, citing the *Encyclopedia Britannica* as a source for this statement. Accordingly, they stated, the land should remain Turkey's. Curzon, who was not going to relinquish Great Britain's claim, said scornfully, "It was reserved for the Turkish delegation to discover for the first time in history that the Kurds were Turks. Nobody has ever found it out before." Sensing a stalemate, the conference agreed to refer the oilfield issue to the League of Nations, which awarded them to Iraq in 1925.

The Greco-Turkish conflict's fallout extended far beyond Greece. It also caused casualties among world leaders. It had toppled Venizelos, and shortly before work began on the Treaty of Lausanne, Lloyd George fell from grace. A few years after its signing, Curzon would die, in 1925, worn out from years of work and debate. The debates, alliances, and upheavals that swirled about the world's governments during the period carried within them the seeds of World War II. Stalin and Communism were on the rise in Russia. A young Mussolini was present at the Treaty of Lausanne, and already a young Adolf Hitler was making a name for himself in Germany with talk of a new and powerful Fatherland. Within little more than a decade, World War II would erupt in Europe. When the conflagration swept across nation after nation, the catastrophe of Smyrna and the ill-fated Greek advance began to fade from history. The tragic exodus, the brutalities, the heroes, and the plight of the refugees were forgotten as the world rocked with bloody conflict on numerous fronts. As time passed, only the dispossessed remembered.

End Notes

1. The Greek War of Independence raged for nine years, from 1821-1829

2. The Young Turks was a progressive, partisan movement established by military students in 1889. When the Committee of Union and Progress was formed in 1906, the Young Turks joined this party. They brought about a second constitutional era by revolting against Sultan Abdul Hamid II. They were the force behind the Armenian genocide and other pogroms.

3. The Allies were meeting in Constantinople, which was temporarily controlled by the British during the "limbo" period between the Treaty of Sèvres and the Treaty of Lausanne. Settlement talks were under way in Paris regarding the much discussed Treaty of Sèvres.

4. Ankara was originally called Angora. It remains the capital of Turkey.

CHAPTER 9

A Hero Is Honored

I want to laugh with the common man,
Wherever he chance to be,
I want to aid him when I can,
Whenever there's need of me.
　　　　　—Silas H. Perkins, "The Common Road"

*W*HEN ASA JENNINGS DISEMBARKED IN LONDON after the Smyrna rescue, he had no idea he had become a hero. A short man with spectacles and a shy smile, Jennings seemed overwhelmed by the media attention. He was not comfortable in a hero's role, yet a hero he was. Stashed in his luggage were the highest civilian and military awards bestowed by the Greek government, testaments of thanks from a grateful nation.

In December 1922, the Greek government awarded Asa Jennings two honors, one civil, one military, for his work during the Smyrna catastrophe. He received the Distinguished Cross of Our Savior and Greece's highest war honor, the Medal for Military Merit, first class. This was the first time in Greek history that both decorations had been awarded simultaneously to the same person. Along with the medals was a citation:

> *Honorable Mr. Asa K. Jennings*
> *The Common Committee of the Non-liberated Hellens, recog-*
> *nizing with gratitude your majestic and valuble service in*
> *saving 300 thousand refugees exposed to the danger of being*

*slaughtered by the blood-thirsy Kemal, and the many dangers
and labor to which you were submitted during their transportation and safe-conduct in Greek territory, Herald You, the
real altruist, for this humanitarian action, Its benefactor and
declare you Its Honorary Member.*

The President　　　　　*Gen. Scty*　　　*The Members*

Jennings was invited to an audience with the king of Greece, and was also received by the ecumenical patriarch of the Greek Orthodox Church. According to the Greek newspaper *Eleftheron Vima*, the patriarch thanked Jennings for his actions at Smyrna, and invited him to convey the gratitude of the patriarchate to the Near East Relief Association for the enormous efforts it exerted on behalf of all Christians. The patriarch sent back the following telegram with Jennings, which was reprinted in the American press:

"The celebration of Christmas is a greater blessing for the Greek people, as they congratulate the great American nation whose philanthropy saved hundreds of thousands of Christians from a certain death. Your sympathy and philanthropy are unequaled examples and an inspiration for the whole world.

"Helping Greece in her hour of greatest hardship, you saved millions of souls who sought refuge within her borders. Greece will never forget you. To you, philanthropic citizens of America, we publicly declare our eternal gratitude. I pray to God Almighty and bid them inform the pious masses of this at all the Liturgies of the Church. I pray that All-Holy God bestows His blessings upon the president, the government, and the people of your great democracy."

There is no question that Jennings was weary after the feverish days at Smyrna. Most likely he would have enjoyed some time to rest and relax with his family—his wife, two sons, and a daughter. They had all been through a stressful period and undoubtedly were eager to return home to the States. But there was still work to be done, and Jennings knew he could help. As it turned out, he would become a significant player at the Lausanne conference. The United States was not officially involved in the Treaty of Lausanne, but had sent three observers to the conference. One of them was Admiral Mark Bristol, who had worked with Jennings at Smyrna. Bristol recommended that Jennings be part of the International Commission on

DOUBLY HONORED BY GREECE

Two Decorations for A.K. Jennings of Utica for Services in Asia Minor.

Copyright, 1923, by The Chicago Tribune

ATHENS. Sec. 27 – The Greek Government has awarded its highest civilian honor, the Golden Cross of Saint Xavier and the highest war honor, the Medal of Military Merit, to Asa K. Jennings of Utica, N.Y., for his work with the Near East Relief in directing the evacuation of 500,000 refugees from Asia Minor.

This was the first time in history that both medals were awarded to the same person simultaneously.

The Greek Government also has asked the United States to permit it to award the Medal of Military Merit to the commanding officers of the twelve American destroyers which assisted in the evacuation of the Greek refugees.

December 28, 1922, New York Times

Newspapers around the world noted Jennings's receipt of high honors from Greece. Here is an article from the Chicago Tribune.

Ἐντιμώτατον Κύριον

ASA K. GENNINGS

Ἡ Κοινὴ τῶν Ἀλυτρώτων Ἑλλήνων
Ἐπιτροπεία ἀναγνωρίζουσα μετ᾽ εὐγνω-
μοσύνης τας μεγίστας καὶ πολυτίμους
ὑπηρεσίας Σας ὑπὲρ τῆς διασώσεως 300
χιλ. προσφύγων, ἐκτεθειμένων εἰς τὸν
κίνδυνον νὰ σφαγῶσιν ὑπὸ τοῦ αἱμοβό-
ρου Κεμὰλ, καὶ τοὺς πολλαπλοὺς κό-
πους καὶ κινδύνους, εἰς οὓς ὑπεβλήθητε
διὰ τὴν μεταφορὰν καὶ διάσωσιν αὐτῶν
εἰς τὴν Ἑλληνικὴν γῆν διακηρύττει
Ὑμᾶς τὸν ὄντως ἀλτρουϊστὴν διὰ τὸ
ἀνθρωπιστικὸν αὐτὸ ἔργον ὡς εὐεργέτην
της καὶ σᾶς ἀναγορεύει ἐπίτιμον μέ-
λος αὐτῆς.

Ο ΠΡΟΕΔΡΟΣ   Ο ΓΕΝ. ΓΡΑΜΜΑΤΕΥΣ

TA ΜΕΛΗ

English Translation

Hon. Mr. ASA K. JENNINGS

The Common Committee of the Non-liberated
Hellens, recognizing with gratitude your majestic
and valuable services in saving 300 thousand
refugees exposed to the danger of being slaughtered
by the blood-thirsty Kemal, and the many dangers
and labor to which you were submitted during their
transportation and safe-conduct in Greek territory.
Herald You, the real altruist, for this humanitarian
Action. Its benefactor and declare you Its Honorary
Member.

The President   Gen. Scty

The Members

Shown is actual Greek citation, and on the right, the English translation of the Greek
commendations.

exchanging Greek and Turkish prisoners of war, and Jennings agreed to the task. He would also act as an unofficial representative of the minorities.

The situation was delicate. Emotions were running strong and there was lingering antipathy between the Turks and the Greeks. The Turks held many more Greek and Armenian prisoners than the Greeks held Turks, as the Turks prevented all males ages seventeen to forty-five from leaving Turkey. Initially, the Turks said they would allow one Greek and one Armenian to leave for each Turk returned by Greece. Under this arrangement, all Turks would soon be returned but many Greeks and Armenians would remain trapped. However, although the initial terms were followed at first, the agreement was later amended, and within three weeks of the official signing of the peace treaty, all Greek and other prisoners of war were repatriated. Additionally, amnesty was granted to all prisoners of war.

Even with such an agreement in writing, the prisoner exchange was still fraught with possible pitfalls. It would take a special individual to negotiate his way around the conflicts and debates that were sure to arise, and Jennings seemed to be that man. He was respected by Turkey's leader, Ataturk (Kemal), and the Greeks knew that. They realized he would be more effective in dealing with the Turkish government than any Greek diplomat, so the Greeks allowed Jennings to act on their behalf. For their part, the Turks were willing to deal with Jennings because they knew he was the "Admiral" and hero of Greece. He could easily gain access to Greek officials at any time of day or night, whereas a Turkish diplomat would never be given that kind of entrée. Thus, Turkey appointed Jennings as its representative. Jennings tried not to take sides in the proceedings; his aim was to end the conflicts the war created and begin the work of rebuilding.

William T. Ellis, a reporter for the *Saturday Evening Post*, writes, "Logically, Jennings should have gone to Greece to bask in the sunshine of Greek gratitude. [Instead] he did become a member of the prisoner-of-war exchange commission. There he seemed not to hate the Turks enough to please the Greeks, and he was once roundly rated in the Greek Parliament. Such is gratitude. Now he is back in Smyrna in charge of a new Turkish-American social service work for young people. He might be on a lecture platform in America—that deadfall for more than one great doer—but instead is quietly carrying on by helping to meet human needs; still 'Jennings of Smyrna.'"

Tagmata Aristeias kai Stratiotika Metallia tis Ellados [Orders of Distinction and Military Medals of Greece]
By George John Beldecos
Hellenic War Museum
Athens, 1991

Greek Cross of Military Merit (p94)

Established in the year 1917 through decree (legislative? royal?) on 31 October 1917. Awarded to regimental colors and to individual servicemen and civilians for outstanding deeds on the battlefield or for keeping the legitimate order and security of the State.

The medal, a work by French sculptor Andre Rivaud, made of white medal or silver, has the shape of a vertical sword that sets within a circular laurel wreath. On a horizontal, elongated field there is a saying inscribed (or embossed) "Η ΤΑΝ Η ΕΠΙ ΤΑΣ." On the reverse side there appears written "ΕΛΛΑΣ 1916-1917." Customary dimensions of the medal are 43 x 48 mm.

The Cross of Military Merit has 3 orders which are indicated by the addition to a plain ribbon of the lowest order a bronze laurel branch for the first order or a bronze star for the second order. The ribbon, with a width of 38 mm, is black in color with turquoise stripes along the edges.

For each mention in the order of the day, the honorees affix silver-gilded stars, just as with its model, the French Croix de Guerre.

In accordance with the Order of the Provisional Government of Thessaloniki, those awarded the Cross of Military Merit, First Class, had the legal right to obtain a free tract of land.

The Distinguished Cross of Our Savior, Second Issue (pp24-5)

With the enthronement of King George I, certain changes to the insignia of the Order of Our Savior were implemented. In accordance with the vote by the Second National Assembly on 27 July 1863 and by (royal?) decree 21 November 1869, the bust of King Otto was replaced by the crosses of the originally planned (?) Icon of Christ, which is encircled with the inscription "Η ΔΕΞΙΑ ΣΟΥ ΧΕΙΡ ΚΥΡΙΕ ΔΕΔΟΞΑΣΣΤΑΙ ΕΝ ΙΣΧΥΙ," while the Bavarian coat-of-arms was removed from the reverse side and the inscription changed to "Η ΕΝ ΑΡΓΕΙ Δ' ΕΘΝΙΚΗ ΤΩΝ ΕΛΛΗΝΩΝ ΣΥΝΕΛΕΥΣΙΣ ΑΩΚΘ". Changes were also made to the stars, which replaced the sign of the Order with the Icon of Christ.

Likewise, the size of the crosses of the three orders were adjusted to be the same. After that, it was decided (?) that in the case of a promotion from the rank of Commander to that of Supreme Commander, to the awardees would be given the corresponding star in a separate case. This practice was followed only in certain cases—like when there was testimony for a rescue—but nevertheless, it didn't spread.

After the period of the Balkan Wars and WWI, there were many awards to the Officers of the Land Army and of the Royal Navy. After the establishment of the Order of George the First, in 1915, awards of the insignia of the Order of Our Savior were very rare.

In accordance with the Articles 9, 10, and 11 of the decree (royal?) of 20 May 1833, the highest permitted order of distinction to the Officers and Public Officials was defined accordingly with the degrees to which they possessed the following [criteria]:

Silver Cross (after 14 years' of service) to Captains (or equivalent rank) and Secretariats of the First Rank.

Gold Cross to Lieutenant-Colonels or Directors of Second Rank.

Archangel to Majors-General or equivalent rank with the Deputy Chief Justice of the Supreme Court of Appeal.

Supreme Archangel to Majors-General who complete a six-year period holding that rank or to Lieutenants-General after the passing of a three-year period.

TOP LEFT: *The Greek Medal of Military Merit (also called the Greek Cross of Military Merit).* BOTTOM: *The Distinguished Cross of Our Savior.* TOP RIGHT: *An explanation of what the decorations mean is included.*

Dr. George Sherwood Eddy, of the Foreign Division of the International Committee of the YMCA, made a similar observation: "But what was more significant, he [Jennings] not only gained the gratitude of the Greeks, he won the love and confidence of the Turks themselves. At the Lausanne conference he helped, as an unofficial member, to arrange for the exchange of some 40,000 prisoners between the Greeks and the Turks. His friends who aided him in saving Greeks were now called to the parliament of the new Turkish republic as members of the cabinet, and his best friend became minister of education."

Jennings also made news when he sprang to the defense of the U.S. Navy regarding Smyrna. Edward Hale Bierstadt of the State Department, wrote a book after the Smyrna crisis, *The Great Betrayal*. In it, Bierstadt charged that the U.S. economic policy (neutrality) that forced U.S. ships to refrain from military involvement contributed to the Smyrna disaster. The book set off a firestorm of outraged letters from both the public and those present at Smyrna, who thought the account diminished the huge rescue and aid efforts provided by the U.S. Navy. Asa Jennings felt called to bear witness and wrote to the State Department, outlining Bristol's quick response to aid the refugees and provide "swift succor." His letter had an impact, and was enclosed with all official responses regarding activities at Smyrna.

After the great rescue, Jennings had continued working for the YMCA as international secretary, but in 1923 Turkish officials and Admiral Bristol urged him to return to Smyrna to assist them in developing welfare work for the youth of the country. Jennings agreed, and this first effort took the form of the Smyrna Community Welfare Council, which operated in cooperation with several other Turkish groups. In 1928, the work was reorganized as the American Friends of Turkey, which was incorporated in the United States in 1930, although the headquarters remained in Ankara. Jennings served as executive vice president, and during his tenure contributed invaluable expertise on social and educational issues to various Turkish government departments, organizations, and institutions.

There were those in Greece who decried the fact that Jennings assisted the Turkish youth, but for Jennings it was never about Greek or Turk but rather about filling a need. He had been asked to help the children, and he did so. His one guiding principle was to go where he was needed. Smyrna was where he was initially assigned; the people still needed help, so he aided them, regardless of nationality.

For the rest of his days in the Near East, Jennings was affectionately known as "the Admiral" because of his role in directing the rescue ships of Smyrna. He was a familiar figure walking up and down the streets, brimming with ideas and committed to bettering the region for the sake of the children. One wonders if he did not stop from time to time and gaze at the quay, remembering those dark days when the waterfront was filled with tormented souls seeking escape.

The hectic pace of his work eventually took its toll. Jennings had never had a strong physical constitution, as he had been weakened by tuberculosis when he was younger. He had pursued his globe-trotting career by sheer force of will. But before long, the stress of travel and long hours caught up with him. On January 17, 1933, Jennings was in Washington, D.C., to confer with attachés from the Turkish Embassy. That evening, he had dinner with his old friend and Smyrna colleague Rear Admiral Mark Bristol. Bristol was now president of the American Friends of Turkey and continued to be an admirer of Jennings's efforts to foster goodwill in the Near East. While walking back to his quarters, Jennings was stricken with chest pains; he hailed a cab, but died of a heart attack en route to the hospital.

News of his death traveled around the world. In the short span of fifty-six years, Jennings left an indelible mark on the events of his time. His brave actions at Smyrna saved thousands of lives. What makes Jennings so remarkable is that he was always real—a true "everyman." Jennings was not imposing physically, but he had indomitable courage. In the direst of circumstances, he took a stand and exhausted every avenue in order to rescue the desperate citizens of Smyrna. Jennings was neither general nor statesman; he was an ordinary man caught in extraordinary circumstances. He could easily have fled, turning his back on the panicked refugees as someone else's problem. Yet he not only stayed, but he risked his life as well to save an entire population from almost certain death. Without Jennings's quick actions and unflinching commitment to save the refugees, they surely would have perished.

Equally enduring were Jennings's quieter exploits. He had a deep commitment to aiding the world's youth, and believed that education is vital. To the end of his days, he worked toward the goal of education for the youth of Turkey.

The *New York Times* hailed him as a philanthropist and wrote the following tribute on January 29, 1933:

"A 'Y' Man

"Asa Jennings was one of those indispensable 'Y' men. He had done 'Y' war work in France. He had assisted in post-war 'Y' work in Czechoslovakia. Then he was sent to Smyrna. He had been there but a few weeks when the Smyrna disaster came. His heroic part in getting the ships of the Aegean to carry to the coasts of Greece the 300,000 Greeks and Armenians, left homeless in the streets and on the quays between the Turks and the sea, won for him the sobriquet 'Admiral' and the grateful memory of those who he had befriended in that crucial moment. Greece gave him double honors, civilian and military. And some day, no doubt, there will be erected on the Island of Mytilene a memorial of his extraordinary service. But he did not stop with what he had done for the Greeks and Armenians. Later he went to Angora with a group of his own gathering to work as friends with and for Turkey in the training of her children and her youth. In devotion to that cause he literally gave his life."

Another obituary read, in part, "He possessed a keen mind, executive ability, a wonderful memory for facts, names and faces, deep love for his fellow men and a genial, optimistic disposition. He was courageous, untiring and modest, and deeply loved and respected by his associates."

Jennings left behind his wife, Amy, and three children, Asa, Wilbur, and Bertha.

Jennings's grandson Roger Jennings saluted him with these words: "My closing comment in the light of the facts and impressions that I received from the various sources is that Asa K. Jennings, a man I never met, was just a Y.M.C.A. man trained to serve others as best he could. He rose to the occasion when it was demanded of him, and he accomplished the impossible because he loved humanity first."

Asa Kent Jennings, hero of Smyrna, is buried in Cleveland, New York, just north of Syracuse.

THE NEW YORK TIMES, JANUARY 29, 1933

A "Y" MAN

ASA JENNINGS was one of those indispensable "Y" men. He had done "Y" war work in France. He had assisted in post-war "Y" work in Czechoslovakia. Then he was sent to Smyrna. He had been there but a few weeks when the Smyrna disaster came. His heroic part in getting the ships of the Aegean to carry to the coasts of Greece the 300,000 Greeks and Armenians, left homeless in the streets and on the quays between the Turks and the sea, won for him the sobriquet "Admiral" and the grateful memory of those whom he had befriended in that crucial moment. Greece gave him double honors, civic and military. And some day, no doubt, there will be erected on the Island of Mytilene a memorial of his extraordinary service. But he did not stop with what he had done for Greeks and Armenians. Later he went to Angora with a group of his own gathering to work as friends with and for Turkey in the training of her children and youth. In devotion to that cause he literally gave his life.

The New York Times *story of Jennings's passing.*

ASA K. JENNINGS DIES IN CAPITAL

Florida Philanthropist Stricken on Street While on Visit to Turkish Envoy.

SAVED 300,000 in SMYRNA

As Y.M.C.A. Secretary There When Turks Captured City, He Rescued Greeks From Foes.

Special to The New York Times.

WASHINGTON, Jan. 27 – Less than twelve hours after his arrival here to confer with attaches of the Turkish Embassy, Asa K. Jennings, widely known philanthropist and organizer in Near East relief work, was stricken with a sudden illness while walking near the White House and died early tonight on the way to a hospital in a taxicab. Mr. Jennings had left the home of Rear Admiral Bristol just before he became ill. Physicians indicated death was from natural causes, but at a late hour no certificate had been issued.

Mr. Jennings arrived here early yesterday from his home in Winter Park, Fla. Admiral Bristol, at whose home he was staying, said a conference with the Turkish Ambassador was the object of his visit.

Widely known as a philanthropist, Mr. Jennings was active in welfare work and only recently returned from a trip to Turkey. He had been the only American member of a Turkish child welfare commission. He was executive president of the American Friends of Turkey and spent much of his time in relief work there.

After the Word War Mr. Jennings went to the Near East to conduct welfare work with the Y.M.C.A. It was during this period that he organized the American Friends of Turkey. Admiral Bristol, former American High Commission in Turkey is president of the organization, and a great admirer of the work of Mr. Jennings in fostering good-will between Turkey and the United States. Mr. Jennings leaves a son, Asa W. Jennings of New York, and a daughter in Florida.

Educated At Syracuse

Special to The New York Times
UTICA, N.Y., Jan. 27 – Asa K. Jennings was about 55 years old. His parents lived in Cleveland, N.Y. He was educated at Syracuse University and was admitted to the Northern New York Conference of the Methodist Episcopal Church in 1908. He was ordained an elder in 1912. He had served in several posts until he went to France as a Y.M.C.A. secretary.

Headed Relief Works in Smyrna.
At the time Smyrna was captured by the Turks in September, 1922, Mr. Jennings immediately began relief work for 300,000 persons. Only a month in the city in the capacity of a Y.M.C.A. secretary in charge of work among boys, he suddenly found himself confronted with one of the great disasters of modern times and roused himself to perform miracles of relief. He first established a hospital for women and children and housed others in buildings along the waterfront. Then he set out to obtain a fleet of vessels to carry the refugees to safety, and it was necessary to evacuate more than a quarter of a million persons within ten days. He persuaded the captain of an Italian vessel to carry 2,000 to the adjacent island of Mitylene, where Mr. Jennings found several Greek merchant vessels.

Executing a rapid-fire of communication with the American warships in the vicinity and with the Greek Government, he succeeded in having these ships placed under his orders, and sailed into the harbor of Smyrna on board one of them with a small American flag at the masthead. Hence his popular title in those regions of "Admiral of the Fleet."

Praised by Naval Commander
Fifty ships in all, large and small, two of them transatlantic liners, took part in the evacuation, which went on day and night throughout the week ending Sept. 30, the last day of the period allowed by the Turkish authorities. Commander Powell, senior United States naval officer at Smyrna said: "The ships were brought into the harbor under the command of Mr. Jennings of the Y.M.C.A., and were escorted and loaded by officers and men of the American destroyers. It was only through the energy and zeal and stubborn

insistence of Mr. Jennings that these ships were obtained."
Originally a clergyman and a resident of Utica, N.Y., Mr. Jennings served in France with the Y.M.C.A. in the World War, and then in Czechoslovakia before going to Smyrna. Subsequent to the Turkish capture of the city he was head of the Community Welfare Council there. Greece awarded the Golden Cross of St. Saviour and the highest war honor, the Medal for Military Merit, to him.

January 28, 1933
New York Times

An excerpt from a New York Times *editorial which ran at the time of Jennings's death.*

Other Heroes

Jennings wasn't the only American honored for work at Smyrna. The Greek government also bestowed the Medal of Military Merit upon the commanders of the twelve American destroyers that assisted in the evacuation.

Among those honored were: Halsey Powell, of the destroyer *Edsall*; Byron McCandless, of the *Parrott*; Herbert Ellis, of the *MacLeish*; Samuel

OBITUARY
"ADMIRAL" ASA K. JENNINGS

While in Washington Friday, January 27, 1933, "Admiral" Asa K. Jennings, as a result of a heart attack, passed to his reward. Since September 1901, when the "Admiral" entered Association work, he held a number of important positions, and his record as a secretary was broken only by six years of service as a pastor. No better statement could be offered than that which appeared in an editorial in the New York Times on Sunday, January 29:

> His heroic part in getting the ships of the Aegean to carry to the coasts of Greece the 300,000 Greeks and Armenians, left homeless in the streets and on the quays between the Turks and the sea, won for him the sobriquet 'Admiral' and the grateful memory of those whom he had befriended in that crucial moment. Greece gave him double honors, civic and military. and some day, no doubt, there will be erected on the island of Mitylene a memorial of his extraordinary service. But he did not stop with what he had done for Greeks and Armenians. Later he went to Angora with a group of his own gathering to work as friends with and for Turkey in the training of her children and youth. In devotion to that cause he literally gave his life.

In "Admiral" Jennings' departure the Young Men's Christian Association suffers a tremendous loss in that we shall see his face no more, but his spirit of love, of devotion, of inspiring effort and of vision will continue with us to inspire through the years to come.

He is survived by his wife, two sons, Asa Will and Wilbur, and a daughter Bertha. Mrs. Jennings may be reached at 9 Hammond Street, Mohawk, New York.

Photo of Roger Jennings, Asa Jennings's grandson, along with a copy of Asa Jennings's obituary.

Bryant, of the *McCormick*; Harrison Knauss, of the *Simpson*; Alfred Atkins, of the *Bulmer*; Edwin Walleson, of the *Lawrence*; John Rhodes, of the *Litchfield*; Charles Blackburn, of the *Hatfield*; Rufus Zogbaum, of the *Gelmer*; Howard Welbrook, of the *Fox*; John Barleon, of the *Kane*; Walter Edwards, of the *Bainbridge*; Rufus Mathewson, of the *Hopkins*; Harry Pence, of the *McFarlane*; D. Bruce Ware, of the *Overton*; Carlos Bailey, of the *Sturtevant*; Richard Field, of the *Goff*; Leslie Jordan, of the *Barry*; and Henry Fuller, of the *King*.

The request also applied to Captain A. J. Hepburn, chief of staff at Constantinople, who was in command of Smyrna forces from September 9 through the sixteenth, aboard the USS *Scorpion*. Later, Captain Halsey Powell assumed command of the *Scorpion* and Hepburn began his tenure in Constantinople. The Greeks did not forget the captains and crews who worked so tirelessly to rescue the imperiled families crowded on the quay.

At home, the U.S. Navy was also recognized for its heroic efforts abroad. Mayor John F. Hylan, of New York City proclaimed October 27, 1922, "Navy Day" in the city, calling for all businesses and citizens to

CITY TO PAY TRIBUTE TO THE NAVY TODAY
New York Times (1857-Current file); Oct 27, 1922; ProQuest Historical Newspapers The New York Times (1851 - 200;
pg. 10

CITY TO PAY TRIBUTE TO THE NAVY TODAY

Birthday of Theodore Roosevelt Also to Be Observed by Patriotic Societies.

ALL SHIPS TO BE DECORATED

Mayor Issues Proclamation — Praise for Destroyers' Work at Smyrna.

Mayor Hylan issued a proclamation yesterday suggesting appropriate observance today of "Navy Day" and calling attention to the fact that it is also the birthday of Theodore Roosevelt. The proclamation follows:

"To the People of New York: The Navy Department, co-operating with the Navy League and other patriotic societies, has set aside Friday, Oct. 27, the natal day of Theodore Roosevelt, as 'Navy Day,' on which to pay tribute to the past and present services of the navy. A nation-wide celebration is planned, with the fleets of the navy and merchant marine specially decorated on that occasion.

"The observance of Navy Day deserves the co-operation of every inhabitant of the City of New York. Throughout our history an effective navy has stood guard as the first line of defense at our sea gates. In prestige, power and commerce New York has steadily advanced, conscious of protection from aggression afforded by the ships of the navy and the loyal, sturdy boys that manned them.

"Great, prosperous and independent have we become, firm in the security of a great defensive weapon ready to challenge a hostile fleet. Whether in the paths of peace or the waters of war, the reliance which we have placed on our strong and wonderful navy and able and heroic seamen has aided in our triumphant forward march.

"At the request of the sponsors of Navy Day, I hereby call upon all patriotic societies and organizations, business houses and citizens to aid in a fitting observance of Navy Day by the display of the national colors and appropriate exercises. All vessels in the municipal service will be appropriately decorated for the occasion, and the owners of all other vessels in the port are urged to do likewise in appreciation of the splendid record of our Navy in the promotion of national greatness.

"In witness whereof, I have hereunto set my hand and caused the seal of the City of New York to be affixed, this 26th day of October, in the year of our Lord, 1922.   "JOHN F. HYLAN, "Mayor of the City of New York."

Tribute to the navy for its rescue work and relief of famine in Smyrna, Asia Minor and other parts of the Near East was paid by Charles V. Vickrey, General Secretary of the Near East Relief, who, after reviewing a number of earlier events, said that incidents innumerable of the Navy as a life-saving and a purely humanitarian organization could be cited, but that the one that brings it closest to the hearts of the world today is the part it played in the tragedy recently enacted at Smyrna, when United States destroyers made it possible to get food and supplies to 400,000 people starving in a panic-stricken, burning city.

This newspaper clipping from the New York Times *describes Navy Day.*

display national colors, as well as all ships in the harbor. The proclamation was issued in tribute to the work of American destroyers at Smyrna.

Commenting on the tribute was Charles Vickrey, general secretary of the Near East Relief; Vickrey was quoted in the *New York Times* as saying: "[A]fter reviewing a number of earlier events . . . incidents innumerable of the Navy as a life-saving and a purely humanitarian organization could be cited, but . . . the one that brings it closest to the hearts of the world today is the part it played in the tragedy recently enacted at Smyrna, when United States destroyers made it possible to get food and supplies to 400,000 people starving in a panic-stricken, burning city."

Eleftherios Venizelos, former premier of Greece, sent this Christmas message to the American Red Cross on December 26, 1922. It was reprinted in the *New York Times* on December 27 of that year.

"Ex-Premier Venizelos of Greece in a Christmas message to the American Red Cross expressed the gratitude of the Greek people for America's generosity in succoring millions of refugees.

"'Through the American Red Cross and other organizations,' the message said, 'you came to the rescue[—]your flour feeding them, your blankets, arriving to rob the Winter of its terrors, and your doctors saving the sick.

"'We face the future with courage, but we are conscious of its perils. Only by the continuance of your help can misery be permanently removed.

"'Praying to the same God and celebrating the nativity of the same Christ, we express our thanks.'"

The United States did not forget Greece, and aid continued well into the next year. According to the *New York Times*, by June 24, 1923, the United States had spent more than $18,000,000 for relief work in the Near East, more than half of that going to Greece. America's contribution was eight times that of other nations. Not only was money sent, but also goods, which helped avoid the depletion of Near East markets, because at that time demand greatly exceeded supply. Workers from the American Red Cross, Near East Relief, the YMCA, the American Women's Hospitals, and other agencies continued to be stationed in Greece and the Near East for years after the Smyrna catastrophe, aiding the refugees and children orphaned by the crisis as they struggled to reclaim a normal life.

The U.S. Navy maintained a fleet of from six to twenty destroyers in Smyrna waters for more than a year. At the end of October 1923, six remained, quietly assisting wherever they were needed.

CHAPTER 10

Lost History Rediscovered

*H*OW DID THE STORY OF ASA JENNINGS'S BRAVE RESCUE
fade from history? Here was a man who practically single-handedly rescued
hundreds of thousands of people, yet few today know his name. He received
the highest honors from the Greek government, yet no modern Greek would
name an American as hero of the catastrophe.

There are no answers as to why Asa Jennings's feat has faded into the
mists of time; we can only speculate. A number of factors seem to come
into play.

Asa Jennings was always an unassuming man. Although fame found
him for a time during the years immediately following Smyrna, Jennings
was never comfortable with the attention. He spent limited time on the
lecture circuit, and, in fact, according to reporter William Ellis, downplayed
his efforts when asked about them. After Smyrna, Jennings was eager to get
back to doing what he loved—working with youth in impoverished areas
to improve their lot. He was passionate about helping the people of Asia
Minor, and continued working on a range of fronts to develop programs
that would enhance their quality of life.

Jennings could have penned a best-selling autobiography, but that was
not his way. Consequently, all that remained after his death were faded
newspaper reports and a short story of his role in the rescue featured in the
book, *Spirit of the Game*, by R. W. Abernethy. There were also accounts from
friends and colleagues noted in newspapers and other publications, and
these were widely read at the time. However, as the years passed, these tales
became merely dusty archives, largely forgotten.

In 1922-1923, there was heavy media coverage of the Smyrna crisis and of Jennings's role in the rescue. If history had not intervened, most likely the world would have followed the aftershocks in this region. But this was not to be. As fate would have it, the tragedy of Smyrna was soon diminished by events that shook the world. By the 1930s, barely a decade after the catastrophe, Hitler had come to power in Germany. Within the next few years, the Nazi juggernaut rolled across Europe and nation after nation became part of Hitler's regime. By 1941, the world was at war—in Europe and in the Pacific. The pogroms, evictions, and atrocities of the Greco-Turkish conflict were all but forgotten. Four years of fierce fighting, the horrors of the Holocaust, and the earth-shattering arrival of the atomic bomb consumed the attention of the world.

The years of World War II were a historical epoch, wreaking vast political, cultural, and social changes. The war and its aftermath were so all-consuming that much of what went on before was simply swallowed up. The earlier events belonged to the past. No one looked back—the world was swept forward on an incredible wave of change, changes in the balance of power, in technology, in society, and on the homefront.

World War II spawned many heroes, and they were larger than life— stalwart generals, brave soldiers, fierce resistance fighters, dogged survivors, intrepid spies. The heroes of Smyrna vanished.

If Jennings had lived, his story might have survived longer, but he died young, at age fifty-six in 1933. His early death undoubtedly contributed to the fading of his deeds. He was no longer in the public eye, no longer present as a reminder of those dark days and his dramatic role. If Jennings had been alive during World War II, most likely he would have gotten involved. He was known in international circles, and his experience could have aided efforts in the Near East or in Europe. Jennings commanded respect, and his quiet, diplomatic manner, combined with a strong resolve, would have made him influential. Given his altruistic history, it is certain that he would not have sat on the sidelines. But Jennings did die, and in the postwar whirlwind of change his name gradually faded from public consciousness.

But what of the Greeks? How could they forget? Again, this question has no precise answer. Thousands of Greeks thanked him during the rescue. Later, their government awarded Jennings its highest military and civilian accolades. Never before had anyone, Greek or otherwise, received both honors simultaneously. Yet try finding a trace of recognition of Asa Jennings in Greece today. There is ancient history for all to enjoy, but detailed information on the rescue, on Jennings? That does not exist.

The Greek government's medals and citations exist—this is fact. They were located not in Greece, however, but at the home of Asa Jennings's grandson Roger Jennings. Numerous media accounts of the day reported on their award, as well as Jennings's audience with the king and with the ecumenical patriarch of the Greek Orthodox Church. Yet no museum in Greece has any exhibit, account, or document recording Asa Jennings's heroic efforts. Even more mystifying, there is no official mention of the great rescue itself. It is as if a dark period of history was erased.

In the course of researching this book, it was also almost impossible to find information on the evacuations in Greece. An extensive search was conducted but yielded nothing. Among the places I visited are Estia Nea Smyrnis, an Onassis foundation in Athens; the Ministry of National Defense Hellenic War Museum in Athens; the Hellenic Maritime Museum in Piraeus; the National Historical Museum of Athens; the Centre for Asia Minor Studies in Athens; Enosis Mikrasiaton Kallonis in Lesvos; newspaper and Aegean University archives in Mytilene and Lesvos; the World Cultural Foundation of Hellenism in the Diaspora in Athens; and the Ecumenical Patriarchate in Constantinople (now Istanbul), Turkey. While in Athens, every issue from September 1922 of *Ta Nea*, the largest and most prominent Greek newspaper, was reviewed. Though *Ta Nea* covered the war, its politics, and the arrival of the refugees, it made no mention of Jennings nor of the rescue effort.

The stories of the catastrophe have lived on primarily through tales told from generation to generation. A few interviews were videotaped, but this was done relatively recently, in the late twentieth century. Dig around, and you can find testimonials handed down through families; these describe what it was like fleeing the Turks, and capture those traumatic days on the quay. Indeed, many of these accounts were featured in books of the day, and in more-recent stories (many of which are referenced in this book). But such accounts are not found in museums, archives, or official repositories.

Also strange is that the more-modern books make no references to American ships, and sometimes have not a word of Asa Jennings. It is as if they never existed. For that information, extensive research was done, and documentation was found, from sources all over the world. But if you talk with the elders in Greece, the remaining few who were there, who survived the quay, they know the truth. They will tell you of the American ships, and of the Americans who helped. Why the story of this epic event disappeared from public record in Greece remains a mystery.

Again, one can only theorize, but the reason may be based in part on the climactic changes that wracked the nation both before and after Smyrna. At the time of World War II, Greece had been in conflict for a very long time. Her young men had fought and died in two Balkan wars, World War I, the Greco-Turkish conflict, and World War II. During World War II, Greece was occupied by the Nazis, and many of her citizenry suffered under that regime. Between these wars, she underwent several changes in government, and was plunged into poverty after absorbing the thousands of Smyrna refugees. It is possible that many Greeks who were present at Smyrna did not survive the war. It is possible that during these decades of upheaval, history was simply not officially recorded. With the country in such turmoil, survival was the priority, not historical archives. It is also possible that if such records existed, they were lost during World War II, or during the Greek civil war and conflict with Albania, which ravaged Greece right after the Second World War.

Old wounds also led people to choose to forget this period. The conflict between those who supported the king and those who supported Venizelos in the 1920s left wounds that ran incredibly deep. Neighbors and families were split by this political division, and even Greeks in America were caught up in the turmoil. The animosity lasted for decades. Healing is relatively recent, so it is understandable that few would risk reviving the conflict by revisiting this chapter in history.

By the time the dust from these conflicts had settled and some semblance of peace lay upon Greece, the events of Smyrna would have seemed far removed. Like the rest of the world, she turned her face forward, not back. In time, only the elders would remember the rescue ships and the man who led them.

The story of Asa Jennings's brave resolve needed to be told once again, so that current and future generations would remember. It is important to know that one person can make a difference, even in the most extreme circumstances. Asa Jennings didn't just believe this; he lived it. We can aspire to do the same.

The story of the captains of the American ships and their crews also needed to be shared. Despite being hamstrung by the politics of the day, these officers risked lives and careers to get involved. Prevented from direct military intervention by government order, they walked the finest of lines—and occasionally stepped over them—to keep order and protect the refugees. They pushed for rescue efforts and, once that was achieved, worked ceaselessly on numerous fronts to get everyone out. They provided transport, food, medical care, and supplies, and continued to aid the refugees once they were relocated.

It is also important to note the commitment of other countries in the Smyrna tragedy; captains and ships from Great Britain, France, and Italy worked with American personnel to coordinate rescue efforts, despite the political conflicts.

Last but not least, the courage of the relief workers from Near East Relief, the YMCA/YWCA, American Red Cross, and the American Women's Hospitals must be recognized. These brave souls stood by the refugees in the face of the rampaging Turks. They provided escape and shelter to those they could directly aid, and some lost their lives trying to prevent Turkish assaults. On the quay, they worked tirelessly, supplying food, medical care, and support to the wretched thousands until the rescue was complete. They rescued thousands of Greek and Armenian orphans from Turkey, saving them from almost certain death. These workers then remained at the refugee camps, tending to the orphans and to any others who needed their care. This was one of the largest relief efforts in history, and the commitment of these American workers should not be forgotten.

The politics of Smyrna may long be debated, but the bravery and resolve of Asa Jennings and the others involved in the rescue cannot be disputed. His role, and theirs, should not remain lost to history any longer.

ROYAUME DE BELGIQUE

Ministère des Affaires étrangères
du Commerce extérieur et de
la Coopération Internationale

Avec les compliments
de la DIRECTION DES ARCHIVES

The Library of Congress

The Library of Congress
June 21, 2006

KAUTZ FAMILY
YMCA ARCHIVES

ANDERSEN LIBRARY, SUITE 318
UNIVERSITY OF MINNESOTA
MINNEAPOLIS, MINNESOTA 55455

Logos of the U.S. Library of Congress and the Kautz Family YMCA Archives at the University of Minnesota. Both were invaluable sources. Also shown, correspondence from Belgium's Diplomatic Archives of Foreign Affairs.

EMBASSY OF ITALY
WASHINGTON D.C.
———
OFFICE OF THE NAVAL ATTACHE

CABLE ADDRESS
DIFEITALIA WASHINGTON
PHONE. : (202) 612-4530
FAX.:   (202) 518-2344

ADDRESS
3000 WHITEHAVEN ST. N.W.
WASHINGTON, D.C. 20008

21 June 2001

Our Ref.: 2228 /COM6.0.0.

Mr. Chris PAPOUTSY
P.O. Box 322
Rye Beach, NH 03871

Dear Mr. PAPOUTSY:

Enclosed is additional documentation on Admiral Gaetano B. PEPE which we just received from the Italian Navy's Office of Historical Archives. This information confirms that during the period 27 October 1921 – 23 September 1922, Admiral PEPE was on board the yacht, *GALILEO,* and would thus appear to render support to the information in your book.

With kind regards, I am

Sincerely,

for **Giovanni BORTOLATO**
Rear Admiral, Italian Navy
Naval Attaché

Bruno CONCINA
Capt., Italian Navy
Assistant Naval Attache'

Letter from the embassy of Italy.

MINISTRY OF DEFENCE
ADMIRALTY LIBRARY, 3-5 Great Scotland Yard, London SW1A 2HW

Telephone	(Direct dial)	020 7218 5446
	(Switchboard)	020 7218 9000
	(Fax)	020 7218 8210

C. & M.Papoutsy
P.O.Box 322
Rye Beach
NH 03871
U.S.A.

Your Reference
#

Our Reference D/NHB/22/1

Please quote ADL/00/071

Date
24 March, 2000

Dear Chris and Mary Papoutsy,

Thank you for your letter.

I regret I have not been able to trace a comprehensive list of all the ships, whether naval or mercantile, which at one time or another were involved in the evacuations from Smyrna in 1922. However, there are a few partial listings available from newspaper accounts and in particluar from a rather long and discursive series of articles entitled 'Smyrna and After' in **The Naval Review** 1923 – no author is given, and they are too long to photocopy, I'm afraid. Warships mentioned by name are :

British: IRON DUKE, KING GEORGE V, AJAX, BENBOW, CARDIFF, CURACOA, TRIBUNE,SENATOR, SPARROWHAWK, hospital ship MAINE. Reinforcements available at the Dardanelles: REVENGE, RAMILLIES, 2nd Light Cruiser Squadron, 1st, 2nd & 3rd Destroyer Flotillas, 2nd Submarine Flotilla, ARGUS, ARK ROYAL. The logs of the various ships will note other ships in company day-by-day.

Greek: KILTIS, LEMNOS, HELLE (+ Torpedo Boats), GEORGIOS AVEROFF

French: WALDECK ROUSSEAU, ERNEST RENAN, EDGAR QUINNET

Italian: VENEZIA

United States: destroyers

Merchant ships named: BAVARIA, ANTIOCH, MAGIRA

Logs and reports of proceedings of the British warships and formations are held in Admiralty Records at the Public Record Office, Ruskin Ave., Kew, Richmond, Surrey, where you or your agent will have to carry out your research in person: the P.R.O. can provide a list of professional research agents who can undertake this work on your behalf. The on-line catalogue of Admiralty records can be accessed via http://catalogue.pro.gov.uk

It may be possible to compile a list of merchant ships at Smyrna from entries in contemporary editions of **Lloyd's List**: if these are not available through local reference libraries, the Guildhall Library, Aldermanbury, London EC2P 2EJ will be able to help.

For information about the warships of other nations, please contact:

Naval Historical Center, Department of the Navy Library, Bldg.44, Washington Navy Yard,

DC 20374

Bibliothèque du Service Historique de la Marine, Château de Vincennes, BP2, 00300 Armées, France

National Library, Odos Venizelou 32, 1056 79 Athens, Greece

Ufficio Storico della Marine Militare, Via Romeo Romei 5, 00136 Roma., Italy

You may also find some material of interest in the collections of Centre for Asia Minor Studies, Kydathineon 11, 105 58 Athens, Greece.

Photographs of the British ships involved will be available through the Imperial War Museum, Lambeth Road, London SE1 and the National Maritime Museum, Romney Road, Greenwich, London SE10.

Yours sincerely

Iain MacKenzie
Curatorial E

Letter from the Ministry of Defense, Admiralty Library, London.

Embassy
of the Federal Republic of Germany

- Naval Attaché -

February 24th, 2000
4645 Reservoir Road, N. W.
Washington, D. C. 20007 - 1998
Phone: (202) 298-4292
Fax.: (202) 298-4321

Mr. and Mrs.
Chris and Mary Papoutsy
PO Box 322
Rye Beach, NH 03871

Dear Sir, Dear Madam,

I am writing you on behalf of Captain Richard Himstedt, Naval Attaché to the Embassy
of the Federal Republic of Germany.
I would like to inform you about two mail addresses, where you can receive the information that you want.
Please feel free to contact following addresses for your further questions.

a) Militärgeschichtliches Forschungsamt
　(Military Historical Research Center)
　Villa Ingenheim
　Zeppelinstraße 127/128
　14471 Potsdam
　Germany

b) Bundesarchiv / Militärarchiv
　(Federal Archives / Military Division)
　- Abteilung IV -
　Wiesentalstraße 10
　79115 Freiburg im Breisgau
　Germany

I hope, that I could help you in this matter. If you need any further information, please feel free to call me.
My phone number is (202) 298-4293.

By order of the Naval Attaché

Sincerely,

Marco Worm
Senior Chief Petty Officer

Letter from the embassy of the Federal Republic of Germany.

Militärgeschichtliches Forschungsamt
Abt. Ausbildung, Information und Fachstudien

Zeppelinstraße 127/128
D-14471 POTSDAM
Tel.: 0331 / 9714-564
Fax.: 0331 / 9714-507
AllgFspBw: 85329 – 88
mgfa-potsdam@t-online.de

05.04.2000

Chris und Mary Papoutsy
PO Box 322
Rye Beach, NH 03871
USA

TgbNr.: 00-0381   Si
(Please quote in correspondence)

Subject: Evacuation from Smyrna, September 1922
Reference: Your letter dated 15.02.00
Enclosures: -

Dear Sir, Dear Madam,

thank you very much for your request. Unfortunately we cannot answer it, because we do not
have any archives but only a library. So we don't have any records.
But I would like to inform you about two addresses from archives in Germany, where you can
receive perhaps further information that you want.

For civil records and governmental reports: For military records:

Bundesarchiv   Bundesarchiv / Militärarchiv
                                                - Abteilung IV -
56064 Koblenz   Wiesentalstr. 10
                                                79115 Freiburg im Breisgau
Germany   Germany

They may have the material you need.
However I can make you no great hope to find records in German archives because it had been
a conflict between Turkey and Greece. Therefore you will find further documents in Turkish
and Greek archives.

With kind regards
On order

Sieg M.A.
Kapitänleutnant

Letter from the embassy of the Federal Republic of Germany.

OFFICE OF THE ARMED FORCES ATTACHES

EMBASSY OF SWEDEN
WASHINGTON, D.C.

Page: 1 (1)

TELEFAX

Tv. M. Papoutzy
Fax: (603) 436-9855
Ref:

From: Anita Lindbohm
Ref:
Subject:

Dear Mr Papoutzy,

Colonel Boijsen has asked me to contact you regarding the request that you sent to the Swedish Navy Museum. Since they have not responded we suggest that you contact the American Embassy in Stockholm, Captain Michael Anderson, who is the Naval Attache.

His e mail address is

DAO@USEMB.SE

He can also be reached by phone at +46 8 783 53 36 or by fax at + 46 8 662 80 46

Sincerely,

Anita Lindbohm

Embassy of Sweden
1501 M street, N.W.
Washington, D.C. 20005-1702

phone: (202) 467-2663
(202) 467-2600 (op)
E-mail anita.lindbohm@foreign.ministry.se

fax: (202) 467-2659

Letter from the Naval Attache, the Embassy of Sweden.

VINCENNES, LE **0 9 AOUT 2000**

MARINE NATIONALE

SERVICE HISTORIQUE

N° **2425** SH/Mar/DAB/RH/NP

Monsieur Christos PAPOUTSY
P.O. Box 322
Rye Beach, NH 03871
ETATS-UNIS

O B J E T : Recherche historique.
REFERENCES : 1/ Votre lettre du 20 juillet 2000,
2/ Lettre N° 670 SH/Mar/DAB/RH/NP du 8 mars 2000.
P. JOINTES : Quatre. *NB all correspondence numbered*

Monsieur,

Comme suite à votre demande, j'ai l'honneur de vous faire parvenir ci-joint, à titre exceptionnel et gracieux, copie des rapports suivants, relatifs à l'évacuation des réfugiés de Smyrne en septembre 1922, susceptibles d'intéresser votre étude :

- rapport mensuel du contre-amiral Dumesnil, commandant la division navale du Levant, en date du 30 septembre 1922 (cote 1 BB⁴ 19),

- transmission du commandant de la division navale du Levant au Haut Commissaire de la République Française en Orient, N° 573 DNL/2. du 9 septembre 1922, du compte-rendu de mission à Smyrne, n° 572 DNL/2, du 8 au 9 septembre 1922 (cote 1 BB⁷ 249),

French vessels
HOVA
- rapport de mission du torpilleur d'escadre HOVA, N° 27 du 13 octobre 1922, annexes P et C (cote 1 BB⁷ 249),

SOMALI
- rapport d'ensemble sur la mission du SOMALI à Moudania (6 au 13 septembre 1922), en date du 21 septembre 1922 (cote 1 BB⁷ 249).

COPIES : DAB/RH - Archives (2)

Correspondance à adresser :
Service historique de la Marine — Château de Vincennes — Boîte postale n° 2 — 00300 Armées
Téléphone 01 43 28 81 50 — Télécopieur 01 43 28 31 60

pour Paris - archival repository

Je vous invite à nouveau à venir à Vincennes, ou à déléguer tout correspondant de votre choix, pour y consulter les archives de ces opérations, classées dans les sous-séries 1 BB⁴ et 1 BB⁷, et sélectionner les documents dont vous souhaiteriez obtenir une reproduction.

La salle de lecture est ouverte du lundi au vendredi de 09H00 à 17H00 ; toutefois les communications sont suspendues entre 12H00 et 14H00. La fermeture estivale annuelle est fixée pour l'été 2000 du lundi 7 août au vendredi 18 août inclus.

French transport vessel
TOURVILLE
Je vous suggère également de prendre contact avec le Service historique de la marine à Toulon (passage de la Corderie BP 45 83800 Toulon), qui conserve les journaux de bord du transport TOURVILLE pour la période 1909-1926.

Naval History Archives
Veuillez agréer, Monsieur, l'expression de ma considération distinguée.

Le conservateur en chef Agnès MASSON
directeur des archives et bibliothèques de la marine,

Letter from the French Marine Nationale.

Col.M.Fahir ALTAN
Turkish General Staff
Press, Public Relations and Information Department
6100-Bakanlıklar/Ankara

Chris and Mary Papoutsy
P.O.Box 322
Rye Beach, NH 03871

16.06.2000

Dear Chris and Mary PAPOUTSY

Classification process of the documents that you have requested to be used in your book that is about the people who emigrated from Izmir in September 1922, is still continuing. On the other hand there is no any published work by the Military History and Strategic Studies Department of the Turkish General Staff on that subject.

Hoping that the book list given below would be beneficial in your research, wish you success in your studies.

1. Konstantin T. RANTİS; 01 KASIM 1921'den sonra
Yunanistan'ın Dış meselelerinin Durumu, Atina 1922.
2. Dr. Kemal ARI; Büyük Mübadele (Türkiye'ye Zorunlu
Göç 1923-1925), Tarih Vakfı Yurt Yayınları, İstanbul 1995
3. Alexander Anastasius PALLİS (Çev.: Orhan AZİZOĞLU);
Yunanlıların Anadolu Macerası, Yapı Kredi Yayınları, İstanbul 1997
4. Engin BERBER; Sancılı Yıllar (İzmir 1918-1922 Mütareke ve
Yunan İşgali Döneminde İzmir Sancağı), Ayraç Yayınevi, Ankara 1997

Letter from the Turkish general staff of Colonel M. Fahir Altan in Ankara, which calls the forced deportation an "emigration."

Bibliography

Abernethy, R. W. "The Great Rescue." In *The Spirit of the Game: A Quest by Basil Mathews, and Some Short Stories by A. E. Southon and R. W. Abernethy*, by Basil Mathews. The Camp Fire Library, vol. 1. New York: George H. Doran Company, ca. 1926.

Allen, Harold B. *Come Over into Macedonia: The Story of a Ten-Year Adventure in Uplifting a War-Torn People*. New Brunswick, NJ: Rutgers University Press, 1943.

Allied and Associated Powers (1914-1920). *The Treaties of Peace 1919-1923*. vol. 1. New York: Carnegie Endowment for International Peace, 1924.

Andrews, Jasmine P. *Demetrios the Survivor.* [Philadelphia?]: Xlibris Corporation, 2000.

Archigenes, Demetris I. *Martyries apo ti mikrasiatiki katastrofi* [Witnesses of the Asia Minor Catastrophe]. Athens: Estia Nea Smyrnis, 1973.

Associated Press. "Athens Regime Is Formed: How the Revolt Started." Mytilene, September 28, 1922. *New York Times*, September 29, 1922.

———. "Christian Exodus Put at 1,250,000: Greek Patriarch in Appeal Says That $125,000,000 Will Be Needed for Winter Relief; Praise for United States; A. K. Jennings Said to Have Been Chiefly Responsible for Saving 300,000 at Smyrna." Constantinople, October 18, 1922. *New York Times*, October 14, 1922.

———. "Turks to Give Smyrna Refugees More Time: So London Hears, but Evacuation from That Port Was Reported Stopped Monday." London, October 3, 1922. Smyrna, October 2, 1922. *New York Times*, October 4, 1922, 3.

Austin, Walter F., ed. *The Great Events of the Great War*. Vol. 7 of *The Great Events by Famous Historians*, edited by Charles F. Horne. N.p.: The National Alumni, 1920.

Avery, Margaret A. *Asa Jennings*. Copenhagen: Altekst, 1987.

Barton, James L. *Story of Near East Relief (1915-1930): An Interpretation*. New York: The Macmillan Company, 1930.

Beldecos, George J. *Hellenic Orders, Decorations and Medals*. Athens: Hellenic War Museum, 1991.

Benns, F. Lee. *Europe Since 1914*. New York: F. S. Crofts & Co., 1930.

British Navy. Records of the Naval Forces, 1799-1979. Records of HM Ships, 1669-1977. [HMS *Iron Duke*, HMS *King George* V, HMS *Ajax*, HMS *Benbow*, HMS *Cardiff*, HMS *Curacao*, HMS *Tribune*, HMS *Senator*, HMS *Sparrowhawk*, etc.] n.p.: 1922. The National Archives, Kew, UK.

Bristol, Mark D. [see U.S. Navy].

Bryson, Thomas A. *American Diplomatic Relations with the Middle East, 1784-1975: A Survey*. Metuchen, NJ: The Scarecrow Press, Inc., 1977.

Buzanski, Peter Michael. *Admiral Mark L. Bristol and Turkish-American Relations, 1919-1922*. Ph.D. diss., University of California, Berkeley, 1960.

Centre for Asia Minor Studies. *Smyrna: Metropolis of the Asia Minor Greeks*. Athens: Ephesus Publishing, n.d. ca. 1995.

Chapuisat, Édouard. "Smyrna, the City of Smyrna Before the Destruction." Foreword in *Report on Turkey*, by George Horton. Athens, Greece: Nea Synori, A. A. Livani, 1991.

Chaïdemenou, Filio. [See Haïdemenou, Filio]

Chicago Tribune. "Doubly Honored by Greece: Two Decorations for A. K. Jennings of Utica for Services in Asia Minor." December 28, 1922. Dobkin, Marjorie Housepian. *Smyrna 1922: The Destruction of a City*. New York: New Mark Press, 1998.

Dounis, Christos E. *Ta navagia stis ellinikes thalasses 1900-1950*. vol. 1. Athens: Finatec-Multimedia A. E., 2000.

Dragatsis, Christos. "The Dragatsis Family 1745-2001, an American Experience." (Genealogical history of family privately held by author.) Joliet, IL: privately printed, 2001.

Eddy, Sherwood. "Can Jennings Work Another Miracle?" *Christian Century Journal* (June 18, 1925): 796-8.

Ellis, William T. "Jennings of Smyrna." *Scribner's* (August 1928): 230-5.

Ellis, William T. "The Hate Sowers." *Saturday Evening Post* 196, no. 17 (October 27, 1923): 40, 158.

French Navy. Naval Division of the Levant. Records Series 1BB^4 and 1BB^7 [September 1922]. Service historique de la Marine, Chateau de Vincennes, France. [Material includes ship log entries, telegrams, correspondence, and official reports.]

Gage, Nicholas. *Greek Fire*. New York: Alfred A. Knopf, 2000.

Genikon epiteleion stratou [General Staff of the Hellenic Army]. *To telos tis ekstrateias 1922* [The End of the Campaign in 1922]. Tomos evdomos, *I ekstrateia eis tin mikran asian (1919-1922)* [Vol. 7, *The Campaign in Asia Minor (1919-1922)*]. Athens: Ekdosis diefthynseos istorias stratou [Publication Office of Army History], 1962. Reprinted 1989. References are to 1989 edition.

Gilbert, Martin J. *The First World War: A Complete History*. New York: Henry Holt and Company, 1994.

Grabill, Joseph L. *Protestant Diplomacy and the Near East: Missionary Influence on American Policy, 1810-1927*. Minneapolis: University of Minnesota Press, 1971.

Grose, Howard B. "Splendid Work of a 'Y' Secretary for Christian Cause in Turkey." *Journal* (Chattanooga, Tenn.), July 1925. Reprinted in the *New York Times*, July 8, 1923.
Haïdemenou, Filio. *Treis aiones, mia zoi*. Athens: Ekdotikos Organismos Livani, 2005.

Hatzidimitriou, Constantine G., ed. *American Accounts Documenting of the Destruction of Smyrna by the Kemalist Forces, September 1922*. New York: Aristide Caratzas, Melissa International, 2005.

Hellenic Communication Service. "Smyrna, September 1922: Searching for the Truth about the Evacuations." Survey, October 10, 2003, www.helleniccomserve.com/smyrnasurvey.html.

Hemingway, Ernest. *In Our Time*. New York: Charles Scribner's Sons, 1923.

Horton, George. *The Blight of Asia*. New York: The Bobbs-Merrill Company, 1926. Reprint, Chicago: Hellenic American National Council, n.d. (ca. 2004). References are to 2004 edition.

————. *Recollections Grave and Gay: The Story of a Mediterranean Consul*. Indianapolis: The Bobbs-Merrill Company, 1927.

————. *Report on Turkey: U.S. Consular Documents*. Athens: The Journalists' Union of the Athens Daily Newspapers, 1985.

Housepian, Marjorie [see Dobkin, Marjorie Housepian].

Kalfoglous, Ioannis I. *Historical Geography of Asia Minor*. Translated and edited by Stavros T. Anestides. Athens: Centre for Asia Minor Studies, 2002.

Kapetanopoulos, Pavlos. "1915-1922, the Greek Holocaust: The Modern Day Genocide of the Greeks of the Pontos and Micra Asia." VHS. (Massachusetts?): Omogenia Hellenic Productions, n.d. ca. 1998.

Kapsi, Gianni P. *1922: I mavri vivlos: Oi martyrikes katatheseis ton thymaton, pou den dimosiefthikan pote*. Athens: Ekdotikos Organismos Livani, 1992.

Karagianis, Lydia Kouroyen. *Smoldering Smyrna*. New York: Carlton Press Corps, 1995.

Kartsaklides, Basil G. *Justice to the Greek Cause*. New York: Cosmos Greek-American Printing Co., 1950.

Kautz Family YMCA Archives, compiler. *YMCA Biographical Files: Asa Kent Jennings Papers, 1922-1962*. Collection No. Y.USA.12. Box 101. Kautz Family YMCA Archives: University of Minnesota Libraries.
Keegan, John. *The First World War*. New York: Alfred A. Knopf, 1999.

Kennan, George F. *The Fateful Alliance: France, Russia, and the Coming of the First World War*. New York: Pantheon Books, 1984.

Latant, John H., ed. *Development of the League of Nations Idea, Documents and Correspondence of Theodore Marburg*, vols. 1 and 2. New York: The MacMillan Company, 1932.

Lenczowski, George, ed. *United States Interests in the Middle East*. Washington, D.C.: American Enterprise Institute for Public Policy Research, 1968.

MacMillan, Margaret. *Paris 1919: Six Months That Changed the World*. Foreword by Richard Holbrooke. New York: Random House, 2001.

Marder, Brenda L. *Stewards of the Land: The American Farm School and Greece in the Twentieth Century*. Macon, GA: Mercer University Press, 2004.

Megalokonomos, Manolis. *I Smyrni: Apo to archeio enos fotoreporter*. Athens: Ermis, 1992.

Mertes, Cara, Constantine Limperis, and John Moraetis. "Smyrna's Shadow: The Catastrophe of 1922." VHS. New York: Cara Mertes & Constantine Limperis, 1988.

Miller, Geoffrey. *Straits: British Policy Towards the Ottoman Empire and the Origins of the Dardanelles Campaign*. Hull, England: The University of Hull Press, 1997.

———. *The Millstone: British Naval Policy in the Mediterranean, 1900-1914, the Commitment to France and British Intervention in the War*. Hull, England: The University of Hull Press, 1999.

Morgenthau, Henry. *All in a Life-Time*. In collaboration with French Strother. Garden City, NY: Doubleday, Page & Company, 1922.

———. *Ambassador Morgenthau's Story*. Garden City, NY: Doubleday, Page & Co., 1918.

———. *I Was Sent to Athens*. In collaboration with French Strother. Garden City, NY: Doubleday, Doran & Company, Inc., 1929.

Murat, John. *Anatomia stin aitia kai stin aformi gia ti mikrasiatiki katastrofi tou 1922*. Miami: M.P. Academus; International Press, 1993. (Same volume also titled in English as *Anatomy of a Disaster: the Great Betrayal, Chicanery, Treachery.*)

Naval Society. "Smyrna and After." *The Naval Review* 11, no. 3. (August 1923): 538-749.

New York Times. "Boys Clubs in Turkey Are Outgrowth of Refugee Aid: Asa K. Jennings of the Y.M.C.A., Who Led in Removal of Greeks from Smyrna, Is Responsible for New Organizations in Six Turkish Cities." August 9, 1925.

———. "Greece Honors Jennings: Confers Two Decorations Upon American for Aid at Smyrna." December 27, 1922.

Paozi-Paradeli, Konstantinos. *Ta ploia tou polemikou naftikou 1829-1999*. 2nd ed. Athens: Ekdoseis Astraia, 1999.

Reinhardt, Richard. *The Ashes of Smyrna*. New York: Harper & Row, 1971.

Shotwell, James T., and Francis Deak. *Turkey at the Straits: A Short History*. New York: The Macmillan Company, 1940.

Smith, Michael Llewellyn. *Ionian Vision: Greece in Asia Minor 1919-1922*. London: Allen Lane, 1973.

U.S. Navy. "Report of Operations" [for the weeks of July 1922]. In *War Diary. Confidential. Commander [Mark L. Bristol], U.S. Naval Detachment in Turkish Waters (United States High Commissioner). July 1, 1922 to July 31, 1922, inclusive. Vol. 42*. Washington, D.C.: n.p., 1922. Naval Records Collection of the Office of Naval Records and Library. Record Group 45. Entry 520. Navy Subject Files, 1911-27. Box No. 836. National Archives Building, Washington, D.C. (National Archives Microfilm Publication T829C, roll 418).

U.S. Navy, "Report of Operations" [for the weeks of August 1922]. In War *Diary. Confidential. Commander [Mark L. Bristol], U.S. Naval Detachment in Turkish Waters (United States High Commissioner) August 1, 1922 to August 31, 1922, inclusive. Vol. 43.* Washington, D.C.: n.p., 1922. Naval Records Collection of the Office of Naval Records and Library. Record Group 45. Entry 520. Navy Subject Files, 1911-27. Box No. 836. National Archives Building, Washington, D.C. (National Archives Microfilm Publication T829C, roll 419).

U.S. Navy," Report of Operations" [for the weeks of September 1922]. In *War Diary. Confidential. Commander [Mark L. Bristol], U.S. Naval Detachment in Turkish Waters (United States High Commissioner) September 1, 1922 to September 30, 1922, inclusive. Vol. 44.* Washington, D.C.: n.p., 1922. In Naval Records Collection of the Office of Naval Records and Library, Record Group 45. Entry 520. Navy Subject Files, 1911-1927. Box No. 836. National Archives Building, Washington, D.C. (Miscellaneous Records of the Office of Naval Records and Library. Records Group 45. National Archives Microfilm Publication T829C, roll 419).

U.S. Navy. *War Diary. Confidential. Commander [Mark L. Bristol], U.S. Naval Detachment in Turkish Waters (United States High Commissioner), July 1, 1922 to July 31, 1922, inclusive. Vol. 42.* Washington, D.C.: n.p., 1922. In Naval Records Collection of the Office of Naval Records and Library. Record Group 45, Entry 520. Navy Subject Files, 1911-27. Box No. 836. National Archives Building, Washington, D.C. (Miscellaneous Records of the Office of Naval Records and Library. Records Group 45. National Archives Microfilm Publication T829C, roll 418).

U.S. Navy. *War Diary, Confidential. Commander [Mark L. Bristol], U.S. Naval Detachment in Turkish Waters (United States High Commissioner). August 1, 1922 to August 31, 1922, inclusive. Vol. 43.* Washington, D.C.: n.p., 1922. In Naval Records Collection of the Office of Naval Records and Library. Record Group 45. Entry 520. Navy Subject Files, 1911-27. Box No. 836. National Archives Building, Washington, D.C. (Miscellaneous Records of the Office of Naval Records and Library. Records Group 45. National Archives Microfilm Publication T829C, roll 419).

U.S. Navy. *War Diary. Confidential. Commander [Mark L. Bristol], U.S. Naval Detachment in Turkish Waters (United States High Commissioner). September 1922. Vol. 44.* Washington, D.C.: n.p., 1922. In Naval Records Collection of the Office of Naval Records and Library. Record Group 45. Entry 520. Navy Subject Files, 1911-27. Box No. 836. National Archives Building, Washington, D.C. (Miscellaneous Records of the Office of Naval Records and Library.

Records Group 45. National Archives Microfilm Publication T829C, roll 420).

U.S. Navy. "Report of Smyrna Disaster, September 1922." In *War Diary. Confidential. Commander [Mark L. Bristol], U.S. Naval Detachment in Turkish Waters (United States High Commissioner). March 1, 1924 to March 31, 1924, inclusive.* Washington, D.C.: n.p., 1924. In Mark Lambert Bristol Collection, Manuscript Division of the Library of Congress, Washington, D.C.

Yiannakopoulos, Georgios A., ed. *Refugee Greece: Photographs from the Archive of the Centre for Asia Minor Studies.* Athens: A. G. Leventis Foundation and Centre for Asia Minor Studies, 1992.

Research Sources

Diplomatic Archives of the Ministry of Foreign Affairs in Brussels, Brussels, Belgium

"Enas Aiwvas, Tuo Patpioges," George Katpamodotzos

Estia Neas Smyrnis, Athens, Greece

French Marine Nationale, Naval History Archives, Boite Postale, France

Holocaust Memorial Observance Committee of Asia Minor, Basilios Theodosakis, chair

Japanese Information and Culture Center, Mr. Yamashiao, Washington, DC

Kautz Family YMCA Archives, University of Minnesota, Minneapolis, MN

Kingdom of Belgium, Ministry of Foreign Affairs of External Commerce and International Cooperation, "Navy" Archival Department

Military History Department, National Institute for Pearce Studies, Tokyo, Japan

National Archives and Records Administration, Washington, DC

National Archives of the U.S. Department of State, Washington, DC

National Archives of the U.S. Naval Records Collection, Washington, DC

Ministry of Defense, Admiralty Library, London, England

Superior Naval Command of the Dodecanese, Ministries of the Naval Italian Archives

The British Library at St. Paneras, London

Videorecordings

Kapetanopoulos, Pavlos, "1915-1922 The Greek Holocaust, The modern day genocide of the Greeks of Pontos and Micra Asia," produced and directed by Pavlos Kapetanopoulos, 107 min., Omogenia Hellenic Productions, 1998, videocassette.

Unpublished Interviews by Authors

Haidemenou, Filio, Mikrasiatiki Katastrofi survivor, interview by authors, September 8, 2005, Athens. Hand-written notes, collection of the authors, Rye Beach, NH.

Unpublished Materials

Jennings, Asa K., "Report for Mrs. Emmons Blaine of Work Accomplished in Smyrna, Turkey, February 29, March 1, 1928," Unpublished report. Private collection of Roger C. Jennings, grandson of Asa, New York.

Index